RESEARCH IN TECHNICAL COMMUNICATION

RESEARCH IN TECHNICAL COMMUNICATION

Edited by
Laura J. Gurak and Mary M. Lay

Contemporary Studies in Technical Communication
Bill Karis and Stephen Doheny-Farina, Series Advisers

Westport, Connecticut
London

Library of Congress Cataloging-in-Publication Data

Research in technical communication / edited by Laura J. Gurak and Mary M. Lay.
     p. cm.—(Contemporary studies in technical communication)
    Includes bibliographical references and index.
    ISBN 1–56750–665–8 (alk. paper)
    1. Communication of technical information—Research. I. Gurak, Laura J. II. Lay,
Mary M. III. Series
T10.5 .R46 2002
601′.4—dc21   2002025553

British Library Cataloguing in Publication Data is available.

Library of Congress Catalog Card Number: 2002025553
ISBN: 1–56750–665–8

First published in 2002

Praeger Publishers, 88 Post Road West, Westport, CT 06881
An imprint of Greenwood Publishing Group, Inc.
www.praeger.com

Printed in the United States of America

The paper used in this book complies with the
Permanent Paper Standard issued by the National
Information Standards Organization (Z39.48-1984).

P

In order to keep this title in print and available to the academic community, this edition
was produced using digital reprint technology in a relatively short print run. This would
not have been attainable using traditional methods. Although the cover has been changed
from its original appearance, the text remains the same and all materials and methods
used still conform to the highest book-making standards.

Contents

Introduction

Technical communication research spans many areas, in terms of both content and methodology. Such research is exciting, because it provides rich analyses rooted in a range of disciplines and perspectives. Yet for the beginning as well as the seasoned researcher, this richness can sometimes be confusing, requiring at once a clear sense of focus and a broad sense of possibilities. Unlike a more narrowly defined field of study, research in technical communication covers events as diverse as organizational issues, Internet and online communication, technical writing, gender and political studies, and so on. A quick scan of the tables of contents for the major journals in the field illustrates this diversity. What the field has in common, however, is an interest in the relationship between applied areas—in particular, sciences and technologies—and the ways in which language is used to convey, construct, and communicate these areas.

Our contribution to this effort is this book, a collection of essays on the range of methods and perspectives one can bring to the study of technical communication. Essays in this collection fall into two major categories. The first six chapters focus on foundational research methods and issues, including ethics, ethnography, textual analysis, historical research, survey and questionnaire research, and experimental work. The second six chapters provide perspectives on applying and contextualizing one's research, covering audience considerations, usability, feminist analysis, cultural studies, science and technology studies, and research in cyberspace. These essays are meant to raise key concepts and provide additional resources. This book is not meant as a "how-to" but rather as an overview of the possible methodological choices and perspectives one can bring to the field. Therefore, the essays present the principles of data collection and interpretation or the methodological distinctions of a particular method that is appropriate to technical communication research. Also, the essays reflect upon the process of importing into and employing these methodologies in the research field of technical communication or on how technical communication research has contributed to the development and application of these methodologies. The majority of the essays also offer a case study to illustrate the research approach either from the authors' own research studies or from published studies by others. As such, we hope this book is useful for graduate seminars in technical communication research, for working professionals embarking on a work-related research project, or for faculty who advise graduate research projects.

The book begins with a chapter by Lee-Ann Kastman Breuch, Andrea M. Olson, and Andrea Breemer Frantz that addresses the ethical issues one must face when conducting research. Their focus on researcher responsibility is important in an age where all human subjects research is under an increasingly tight spotlight. As they note, such a perspective has been lacking in technical communication studies, and their chapter offers a good starting place for this book.

Chapter 2 provides a thoughtful discussion by Susan M. Katz about ethnographic research. Her personal perspective and her use of a single-case example (ethnographies performed in two organizations) to illustrate her points work well to provide readers with a sense of the important features of ethnographic research for technical communication studies. Noting that ethnography came to technical communication research by way of composition studies, Katz describes the uses of ethnography, as well as the decisions researchers will need to make along the way.

In Chapter 3, Carol A. Berkenkotter explores textual analysis; specifically, she focuses on three approaches: rhetorical analysis, discourse analysis, and genre analysis. As she notes, even though each approach is unique, all three share the common characteristic of being tools for helping us understand the relationship between texts and their contexts. Her essay explores the methodological assumptions involved in textual analysis and provides practical advice on how to develop research questions and analyze texts.

Chapter 4, by Teresa Kynell and Bruce Seely, describes historical research methods for use in technical communication research. The authors provide a broad overview of historical research, covering topics such as interpreting the past and gathering information. Their case study is useful—

they describe how one of the authors went about writing a history of technical communication. This case illustrates the power and also the difficulty of performing historical research and touches on such relevant areas as primary source material, archival work, and the challenge of contextualizing one's work.

The next two chapters switch from what is often considered more qualitative work (ethnography, textual analysis, historical studies) to more empirical, quantitative work. In Chapter 5, Daniel J. Murphy discusses the use of surveys and questionnaires. He notes that these methods are among the most popular in social science research because they are efficient and versatile, and they can often be generalized. Beginning with an overview about the role of theory, the essay covers important issues about informed consent, echoing some of the comments made in Chapter 1. Murphy ties his comments to his own study of communication media use among aerospace engineers and scientists.

Chapter 6, by Davida Charney, describes experimental and quasi-experimental research, beginning with a discussion of the various roles for experimental research in technical communication. This essay offers a solid overview of such research, including examinations of experiments as causal inquiry and principles for experimental research. Topics such as validity, randomization, and design are also addressed, and, like the chapter before it, Charney's chapter also echoes the Breuch, Olson, and Frantz opening chapter on issues of informed consent and ethics.

The next six chapters discuss applying and contextualizing one's research within certain critical perspectives, beginning with Chapter 7 by Jo Allen and Sherry Southard on identifying and accommodating audiences. Their purpose is to address what they perceive as a major flaw in published research in technical communication, that is, an omission by researchers of the implications of their work for audiences—not readers of the articles, but actual people, the end-users of our research. They make their case by starting with a section arguing that considerations of audience, as they define it, have by and large been omitted from technical communication studies, replaced instead by more general considerations of ethics. They suggest ways to broaden the discussion by considering the implications of our research on a range of audiences.

In Chapter 8, Roger A. Grice provides a description of the means and uses of usability research in technical communication. The essay begins with two personal anecdotes about using the computer, anecdotes that will resonate with anyone but in particular with technical communication professionals. Focusing on what he calls the "complete user experience," Grice outlines six dimensions of usability and goes on to explain how each is useful in understanding the user experience. He reminds us that usability testing can be based on a number of disciplinary perspectives, from cognitive psychology to market research, and ends with a section on how to make a wide-ranging assessment to evaluate the user experience.

Chapter 9, by Mary M. Lay, provides an overview of feminist research and connects this method (or perspective, as Lay notes) to technical communication research. She points out that feminist research is not one thing only and that the varied perspectives on women, men, gender, and sex all make for competing and varied views on what constitutes feminist criticism. Still, she provides a clear list of common features of such research and connects this method/perspective with studies in technical communication research, including studies of workplace issues, rhetorical studies of science, and gender-power relationships. Her essay ends with a case analysis, Beverly Sauer's use of feminist criticism to study mine safety issues.

In Chapter 10, Charlotte Thralls and Nancy Blyler discuss how the perspectives offered by cultural studies can inform research in technical and professional communication. They note that this perspective allows researchers to pay attention to the political settings in which technical communication takes place. Noting cultural studies' connections to both feminist and poststructuralist theory, they describe how a cultural studies lens can help illuminate the frameworks in which meaning is not only produced but also represented and circulated. They connect this review with work in technical and professional communication by noting that researchers must note their own positions in relation to the subjects they are studying. They cite recent research, including an ethnographic study at a software company, to illustrate their claims.

Chapter 11, by John Monberg, describes how research methods from science and technology studies (STS) can provide a framework for those who study technical writing. Opening with a quote from Carolyn Miller's classic essay "What's Practical about Technical Writing?" Monberg argues that STS offers an important perspective, because it looks beyond the practical applications of technology toward the social, philosophical, and historical points of view. Like feminist analysis, STS scholars employ a range of perspectives but are usually united in their desire to critique, not just explain. Monberg notes that technical writing creates representations of things, and that these representations are not neutral. The essay goes on to critique the notion of rationality in science and technology and offers alternative models for technical communication research.

Finally, Chapter 12, by Laura J. Gurak and Christine M. Silker, looks at how three traditional modes of technical communication research—

ethnography, rhetorical (textual) analysis, and survey research—are changed and complicated when conducted over the Internet. Each of these three sections of the essay contrasts such research "IRL" (in real life) versus the same type of research when conducted over the Internet. The chapter also addresses the growing world of research that takes Web pages as its primary artifact of analysis and concludes with a case example of a study that used Internet postings as its primary data source.

We hope this collection of essays will help the new researcher in technical communication get a feel for the playing field and also help the seasoned researcher conduct his or her own research as well as teach and advise graduate students. It is an exciting time to be doing technical communication research, and we look forward to watching and learning as the field continues to grow and change.

Finally, we wish to thank those who have contributed to this collection. Originally, Patricia Goubil-Gambrell presented the idea for such a collection to Jimmie Killingsworth, who was then the editor for the Association of Teachers of Technical Writing (ATTW) book series. Before she left Texas Tech University for an industrial position, Patricia had gathered the first versions of at least half of the essays published here, and Jimmie had encouraged this collection in the beginning stages. We then took over the effort at the same time that Bill Karis and Steve Doheny-Farina took over for Jimmie. In addition, we wish to thank Lenna Constantinidies for her editorial and other assistance. Finally, the authors represented in this collection added their patience, expertise, and goodwill as we brought this collection to publication.

CHAPTER 1

Considering Ethical Issues in Technical Communication Research

Lee-Ann Kastman Breuch,
Andrea M. Olson,
and Andrea Breemer Frantz

In the "Code of Ethics" written by the Association of Teachers of Technical Writing (ATTW), core principles are discussed that guide technical communicators' behavior as instructors, practitioners, and researchers. These core principles (which are discussed in detail later in the code) include the following:

> To act honestly, fairly, responsibly, and professionally in our relationships with students, colleagues, employers, and research subjects. To provide clear, accurate, appropriate, and effective technical communications. To recognize the power of language to shape thoughts, values, and actions and to accept responsibility for the likely consequences of our language. To accept our responsibilities to the public for our technical communications. (http://www .rhetoric.umn.edu/resources)

As these core principles demonstrate, in terms of ethics, technical communicators must be aware of their responsibilities in any number of roles: as teachers, workplace professionals, and researchers. Literature about technical communication and ethics reflects these multiple concerns. For example, ethics have been discussed in terms of classroom instruction (Hawthorne, 2001; Jacobi, 1990; Kienzler, 2001; Russell, 1993), behavior of business or technical communicators (Faber, 2001; Lewis & Speck, 1990), and ethical dilemmas (Katz, 1992; Winsor, 1988).

Even though the term "ethics" can be understood in a number of contexts in technical communication, the field has avoided probing some important issues and concerns in our approach to research. As Allen and

Southard point out in this collection, one issue that has been neglected is the responsibility of researchers to identify and accommodate *audience* in their research, that is, to investigate concerns that technical communicators would find worthwhile and important. We agree that audience identification and accommodation is an important concern in technical communication research; however, this concern does not negate the importance of also looking at the ways in which we conduct research and the ethical choices we make as researchers. We contend that, in fact, without a reflexive attitude that encourages self-criticism of research conduct, the integrity of our research—indeed, our relationships with participants, data, audiences, and colleagues—may be compromised. Thus, although we underscore the importance of audience (as seen in our parting questions about audience concerns in Table 1.1), we turn our focus toward ethics in conducting research, which we deem as a crucial responsibility of researchers.

In considering ethics in this discussion, we specifically address researcher responsibilities and ethical issues that arise when conducting research. As Paul V. Anderson (1998) points out, a focus on research and ethics in these regards has been somewhat neglected by fields such as composition and writing studies, and perhaps even by technical communication. "As we've adopted research methods from [various] disciplines, we've gained a great deal of knowledge about how to employ the methods.... However, we haven't simultaneously developed our understanding of the measures we must take when using these methods to assure that we treat our research participants ethically" (p. 65). Anderson asserts that further discussion about research ethics is necessary among scholars in our field. In answer to this call, some technical communication organizations have produced statements that address research specifically (see the Society for Technical Communication Ethical Principles for Technical Communicators at http://www.stc-va.org/fofficer.htm; ATTW Code of Ethics at http://www.rhetoric.umn.edu/resources). For example, the following statement from the ATTW Code of Ethics clearly suggests that technical communicators have the responsibility:

> To protect the security, confidentiality, and privacy of the information we are entrusted with; to adhere to standard principles of research with human subjects by obtaining informed consent and maintaining the privacy and confidentiality of research results.

This statement is a helpful beginning, and in this chapter we hope to build on this statement by fleshing out more specifically the ways in which technical communication researchers can and should act ethically. Our hope

Table 1.1.
Questions about Ethical Issues

Issue/category of issues	Question for researcher
Consent	Does the consent form contain the information a research participant needs to make a "well-informed" decision whether to participate or not?
	Is the consent form written in a manner that is comprehensible to potential participants?
	Is consent from potential participants given voluntarily and without coercion?
	Does the consent form contain the information required by the IRB, including the risks and benefits?
	Has the consent form been approved by the university IRB and all other relevant entities (e.g., business organization)?
Confidentiality	Who will have access to the data collected in your research project?
	How will data be secured and stored? (in locked files, etc.)
	How will data be used? How may they be used?
	What would prevent data from being kept confidential? Under what conditions would you break confidentiality?
	What can you do prior to the study to ensure confidentiality for participants?

(Continued)

is that this chapter will continue, as Anderson advocates, a necessary discussion of ethical practice, as well as provide helpful guidelines for beginning and experienced researchers in technical communication. Specifically, we suggest that technical communication researchers do the following to address ethics in research: (1) acknowledge the importance of ethics in research; (2) become familiar with literature about ethics; (3) identify ethical issues that may arise; (4) comply with Institutional Review Boards; and (5) actively reflect on ethics while conducting research.

Manipulation of Data	How will research participants be recruited and selected?
	Is the sample of human participants representative of the population to which you want to generalize results?
	Are data recorded accurately?
	How and when are you writing the research hypotheses or expectations?
	Are analyses appropriate for the data and your research questions?
	How will you ensure that data are reported correctly?
	What will you do if results turn out differently than you expected or hoped?
Relationship with Audience(s)	How many different ways may the prospective audience for this research be defined?
	What knowledge need does the research seek to fill for the audience(s)?
	How has the researcher initiated a relationship with the audience? (through dialogue, review, etc . . . ?)
	How has the researcher responded to audience criticism, questions, suggestions?
Validity and Reliability	What steps has the researcher used to ensure that the data reflect honest and careful attention to the research process, the well-being of participants, and responsibility to readers?
	Can the results be replicated? If not, *should* they be?
	What method(s) of triangulation has the researcher employed?
	What theory (theories) has the researcher used to guide her inquiry?
	Has she treated the theories fairly and completely?
	Can the researcher employ mentors, readers, or collaborators that triangulate analysis?

(*Continued*)

Role of the Researcher	How does the researcher define her role in the field (participant? observer? Some combination?)
	What is the importance of "distance" and some "objectivity" to this field and how does the researcher plan to achieve it?
	How does the researcher define her relationships with participants?
	What steps can the researcher take to ensure continued *awareness* of researcher responsibility/role issues?
	What strategies does the researcher have to acknowledge and deal with potential role conflicts?
	How does the researcher define her responsibilities to her audience as she writes about her data and interpretations?

ACKNOWLEDGING "ETHICS"

Our application of the concept of "ethics" is much the same as the statement about research advocated in the ATTW Code of Ethics. That is, research ethics refer to the responsibility of the researcher to demonstrate accuracy and integrity in research activities such as conducting research, communicating with participants, and reporting research results. As we further break down this understanding of ethics in technical communication research, we acknowledge that research ethics in technical communication could encompass many issues; however, in this chapter we highlight five issues that we believe are especially important for ethically conducting research in technical communication. They are consent of participants, confidentiality, avoiding manipulation of data, reliability and validity of research methods, and the role of the researcher. In explaining these issues, we borrow from fields such as psychology, sociology, and anthropology—fields that have established guidelines for ethics—to further our discussion.

In our address of ethics in technical communication research, we have also discovered that another issue is inherently connected to ethical research issues, and this issue is legality. Ethics and legality are connected because certain ethical or unethical behaviors could result in legal consequences. The connection between ethics and legality is also present in the creation of certain laws that are designed to protect research participants and to attempt to guide ethical conduct in research; many of these laws have important history. For example, standards such as informed consent, risks/benefits identification of research, and freedom from coercion were established in the Nuremberg Code that was developed for the Nuremberg Military Tribunal and that provides guidelines for conducting research with human participants (Landrum, 1999; OHRP). In addition, the National Institutes of Health (NIH) established policies for protecting human subjects in 1966, and these policies gained regulatory support in the 1974 National Research Act. The Institutional Review Board (IRB) was established by those subsequent regulations as a way to implement and enforce mandates of the U.S. federal government Office for Protection from Research Risk (OPRR). In this chapter, we focus mostly on Institutional Review Boards (the IRB)—and we explain how IRB guidelines can help researchers address ethical issues.

In the next section, we highlight specific themes and key concerns relevant to a comprehensive discussion of research ethics in the fields of technical communication. Because research strategies in technical communication are so varied, we intentionally draw on issues that pertain to both quantitative and qualitative methods to provide a broad-based examination. In addition to reviewing work in technical communication and composition studies, we have included information from fields such as psychology, sociology, and anthropology to further generate research guidelines for technical communication researchers.

BECOMING FAMILIAR WITH ETHICAL RESEARCH

Becoming familiar with ethical research in technical communication requires interdisciplinary study. Because technical communication has borrowed from fields such as psychology, anthropology, and composition studies in developing its own guidelines for ethical research, in this section we review how technical communication and these other fields have discussed and in some cases regulated ethical guidelines.

In "Simple Gifts: Ethical Issues in the Conduct of Person-Based Composition Research," Paul V. Anderson (1998) suggests that although we have sound practices in text-based research, our research involving human participants is still in need of attention (p. 64). In November 2000, College Composition and Communication responded to this call by creating a set of recommendations on the ethics of conducting research on students in writing courses (see "Recommendation of the CCC Ad Hoc Committee on the Ethical Use of Students and Student Writing in Composition Studies"). In addition, recent contributions such as *Ethics and Representation in Qualitative Studies of Literacy* by Gesa Kirsch and Peter Mortenson

(1996) have brought more attention to research ethics in the arena of composition studies.

However, in the field of technical communication, we have fewer explicit sources about ethical research. One such explicit source is found in Lynnette Porter and William Coggin's *Research Strategies in Technical Communication* (1995)—a handbook that reviews methodological approaches. This handbook includes one helpful chapter devoted to ethics in technical communication research. Citing the Society for Technical Communicators Code of Ethics, these authors promote that researchers create their *own* code of ethics by first getting approval for research methodology, accurately conducting research, opening the research to other experts, and giving credit where appropriate (p. 75). Another explicit source is the article "Ethics of Engagement: User-Centered Design and Rhetorical Methodology," in which Michael Salvo (2001) discusses the ethics of research in user-centered design. Salvo proposes a dialogic ethics that can guide user-centered design methods involving technology and humans (p. 273).

Many other sources on research issues in technical communication seem not to be focused on ethics, but on research methodologies in composition or technical communication research. For example, Gesa Kirsch and Patricia A. Sullivan's (1992) edited collection *Methods and Methodology in Composition Research* includes helpful discussions of "Research Problems and Issues" such as methodological pluralism (Kirsch, 1992), validity and reliability in coding (Grant-Davie, 1992), and collaborative scholarship (Roen & Mittan, 1992). Although these discussions do not focus exclusively on ethics, the authors of these chapters bring up what we would consider to be ethical issues: the consideration of methods for research and ways to achieve validity and reliability in research. Similarly, issues about researcher roles have been discussed, but not necessarily as an ethical issue. In "Evaluating Qualitative Inquiry in Technical and Scientific Communication," Ann Blakeslee, Caroline Cole, and Theresa Conefrey (1996) discuss at length the implications of considering participant input in qualitative studies. In describing the tension between researcher and participant roles in terms of interpreting data from the study, these authors encourage researchers to "solicit and use our participants' perspectives and authority—even when they may differ from our own" (p. 125). Suggesting that qualitative research benefits from interaction with participants about their contributions to the research, they assert that research is more thorough when it considers alternative perspectives by including input from research participants (p. 135).

More direct references to ethics are found in the work of researchers who have explored technical communication from a sociological angle, particularly in ethnographic studies. In "Research as Rhetoric: Confronting the

Methodological and Ethical Problems of Research on Writing in Non-academic Settings," Stephen Doheny-Farina (1993) suggests that "[t]he more we expose the arguments that guide our research actions, the more ethical our research can be. It is this ethical stance that will be our primary source of authority" (p. 254). Doheny-Farina argues that ethnography is more ethical when the researcher confronts his or her role in the process, acknowledging that the researcher's close involvement in an ethnography influences the research findings.

It is important to note that research in technical communication in the past two decades has included ethnographies and other sociological research that address workplace cultures (e.g., Doheny-Farina, 1986; Martin, Feldman, Hatch, & Sitkin, 1983; Mumby, 1988). For guidance on ethnographies and qualitative research methods, technical communication researchers have turned to leading scholars in anthropology such as Clifford Geertz and Edward M. Bruner. Geertz's (1983) notion of "interpretive explanation," which serves as an important guide for anthropologists—and more recently the rest of the social sciences—who seek to weave narratives together through "thick description" as a means by which cultures may be understood (p. 22, *Local Knowledge*). Similarly, anthropologist Edward M. Bruner (1986) notes that "an implicit narrative structure" guides ethnographic methods (p. 139). As Geertz and Bruner illustrate, interpretive explanation and thick description are important to accessing, understanding, and constructing the data we collect and create as we engage cultures in the field. However, such inquiry requires the researcher—as the key instrument of evaluation—to understand and constantly reflect on his or her role and responsibilities (Denzin, 1985; Ellis, 1991; Ronai, 1992; Rosaldo, 1989). Ethnographies and other sociological research may give rise to other ethical issues. Some of those issues include how we communicate/write about our investigations (Atkinson, 1992; Geertz, 1988; Kleinman, 1993; Richardson, 1995; Van Maanen, 1995), feminist methodologies and their relationship to interpretive methods (Collins, 1986; Clegg, 1975; Kirsch & Mortenson, 1999; Smith, 1986), and participatory action and social intervention in research (Gaventa, 1993; Park, Brydon-Miller, Hall, & Jackson, 1993; Simonson & Bushaw, 1993). If technical communication continues to use ethnographic and other sociological research methods, we should be aware of these complications.

Whereas the field of technical communication has addressed ethical issues sometimes implicitly, and more often in terms of qualitative methods, research ethics in the field of psychology are more explicit and are more thoroughly stated. This is not to say that the field of psychology has the prototype for ethical research standards, or that the research standards and principles are detailed enough to cover all the very specific and complicated situations students and researchers encounter. To the extent, however, that the fields of technical communication and psychology both conduct research with human participants, are often subject to the same IRB approval process and requirements, and are presumably subject to the same laws, there is reason to believe that research ethics in technical communication could be expanded and made more explicit by making use of the work already done in psychology.

The first American Psychological Association (APA) code of ethical standards was published in 1953, followed by eight published revisions during the next forty years, the most recent in 1992, which is the "Ethical Principles of Psychologists and Code of Conduct" (aka the Ethics Code). The Ethics Code describes six general principles and eight ethical standards with multiple subparts (APA, 1992). (This document may be viewed at the APA Web site http://www.apa.org.) The general principles are competence, integrity, professional and scientific responsibility, respect for people's rights and dignity, concern for others' welfare, and social responsibility (APA, 1992). There is also a separate document published by APA, titled "APA Ethical Principle 9: Research with Human Participants," which outlines ten principles (APA, 1982). Unlike the ethical principles and standards of other disciplines, the APA Ethics Code was developed empirically by collecting descriptions of ethical dilemmas that APA members actually experienced (Pope & Vetter, 1999). This method was used to more closely represent the issues that members encountered.

A helpful discussion of general principles of ethics in research can be found in the Belmont Report, a report that is a written summary of work done by the National Commission for the Protection of Human Subjects of Biomedical and Behavioral Research. This report describes three ethical principles: respect for persons, beneficence, and justice (Gillespie, 1999; National Commission for the Protection of Human Subjects of Biomedical and Behavioral Research, 1979; OHRP). Respect for persons is based on respecting people's autonomy and protecting those with limited autonomy. In research, respect for persons is operationalized via informed consent, which includes sharing information with research participants and doing so in a manner and context that ensures their comprehension. Consent is valid only if it is given voluntarily and given without coercion. Respect for persons is also demonstrated by protecting the confidentiality and privacy of research participants. Beneficence is promoting people's well-being by doing no harm, maximizing possible benefits, and minimizing possible harm. In research, beneficence is operationalized via assessment of risks and benefits of the research, analyzing the research design, and conveying risk/benefit information in research and informed consent documents. Also, those responsible for conducting the research should continuously monitor data. Justice is based on the question, Who ought to receive the benefits of research and bear its burdens? Justice in research manifests itself in the fair selection and treatment of research participants. Additionally, the Belmont Report describes the consideration researchers should make about the distributive fairness of research. Are social, racial, sexual, and cultural biases in society leading to an unfair distribution of research benefits and/or burdens? In response to the reports, the Department of Health and Human Services established regulations, most recently revised in 1991. These regulations are titled the Code of Federal Regulations, Title 45, Public Welfare, Department of Health and Human Services, National Institutes of Health, Office for Human Research Protections, Part 46 Protection of Human Subjects (http://ohrp.osophs.dhhs.gov/human subjects/guidance/45crf46.htm).

As this brief overview demonstrates, we can enrich our understanding of ethics in research by studying not only technical communication but also how fields such as psychology, anthropology, and composition studies have discussed and in some cases regulated ethical guidelines.

IDENTIFYING ETHICAL ISSUES

This discussion about ethics provides a helpful introduction to ethical issues we believe are important to address in technical communication research: informed consent, confidentiality, manipulation of data, reliability and validity, and role of the researcher. In the following sections, we describe each of these issues and offer suggestions for addressing them in technical communication research.

Informed Consent

Consent is a research participant's agreement to participate in a research study. Informed consent is based on sharing sufficient information with a potential participant in a manner that is comprehensible. Valid consent is given by the potential participant voluntarily and without coercion or undue pressure (APA, 1992; Gillespie, 1999; National Commission for the Protection of Human Subjects of Biomedical and Behavioral Research, 1979). Ethically, informed consent demonstrates respect for persons, especially respect for autonomy (Gillespie, 1999). Also, assessing risks and benefits demonstrates the ethical principle of beneficence (Gillespie, 1999).

By clearly stating the purpose(s), risks, benefits, and right to voluntarily participate, which also means the right to quit at any time, the potential participant will be made aware of the facts he/she needs to be "informed." Although it may be frustrating to have research participants drop out of a study, it is paramount that their freedom to do so is upheld. Legally, obtaining informed consent from a participant or participant's legal representative is a frequent requirement of research studies conducted at federally funded institutions and sometimes other organizations/institutions. Practically, informed consent conveys information to a potential research participant about the study and does so in a consistent manner across participants. The basic parts of informed consent include purpose of the study, duration of expected participation, procedures, foreseeable risks, reasonably expected benefits, alternative procedures/treatments, extent confidentiality will be maintained, conditions if there is more than minimal risk, whom to contact with questions, and a statement that participation is voluntary and the participant may quit the study at any time without penalty. (The Code of Federal Regulations, 1991, Title 45, Part 46, Section 46.116 describes the general requirements of informed consent.) In most studies, the consent form must be a written document and signed by the participant once that participant has read the form, understood it, asked questions about it, and voluntarily agreed to it. Also a copy of the form should be given to the participant to retain.

"The most common questions or requests for clarification that an IRB will ask deal with the matter of informed consent" (Gillespie, 1999). It is not uncommon for investigators to be asked to make changes to the initial consent form they send to an IRB. In some studies, there is an element of deception. Talking with those at an IRB should help clarify if the deception is necessary, what risks it may impose, and what the implications are for informed consent.

Confidentiality

Recalling the Belmont Report, which describes three ethical principles, confidentiality demonstrates the ethical principle of respect for persons. Confidentiality is not the same as anonymity, although both may serve to protect the privacy of the participant. In its strictest form, if a researcher promises anonymity to a participant, not even the researcher would know who contributed what data (APA, 1982). Confidentiality means protecting data or information gathered from and about participants. Confidentiality also means not sharing that information unless the participant provides written consent or unless it was stipulated up front and the participant agreed to how the data would be used and with whom it may be shared (or there was other authorization, such as legal) (APA, 1992). Depending on the study and type of research design, it may be important for an investigator to be able to link data back to the specific participants. In such cases, the agreement to do so should be made upfront, stipulated in the consent form.

Considering that investigators may have a certain amount of social and situational power when conducting a research study, and considering that participants act according to assumptions they may have about how their data will be treated, what should the default about confidentiality be? We find it helpful to refer to a stated APA standard in this case. APA, Principle 9, Standard J states, "Information obtained about a research participant during the course of an investigation is confidential unless otherwise agreed upon in advance" (p. 7, APA, 1982). Consider the fact that many research participants may be naive to what should occur in a research experience. Participants may have the implicit assumption that the investigator will act in a way that does not harm them or infringe on their freedoms of autonomy and privacy.

It is important to note that promising confidentiality to a research participant does not ensure that data are guaranteed to remain as such. "The law does not safeguard the confidentiality of all research data. Under a wide range of conditions, an investigator can be legally required to supply information about individuals to the police and the courts, even when the information is collected in the course of research in which confidentiality has been promised to the respondent" (p. 72, APA Ethical Principle 9, 1982). This guideline may be more relevant for studies that investigate illegal behaviors of people; however, it may be something to address in the informed consent and in how the data are recorded and stored. Whether your research is about illegal behavior or not, this is an important point to keep in mind.

Dealing with anonymity and confidentiality may be more prevalent than you realize. For example, imagine you are conducting a research study at a local company. The study is designed to learn more about how employees use technical writing support services at the company. Suppose you distribute surveys to collect ratings from several departments and you informed the participants that you would report data back to the Technical Writing Center, broken out by department. Now, suppose you received a survey back from only one person in a given department. Do you report that data? Suppose the leader of another department wants to see the data for her department employees, yet that was not part of the agreement made upfront. Would you share that information with her?

Manipulation of Data

What does it mean to manipulate data? The perspective taken here is a very broad one. Manipulation of data includes the acts of falsifying, changing, dropping, or selectively using information you gather during research. Manipulation of data may take a variety of forms, some more obvious than others. For example, it should be obvious that false changes made to data would be a form of manipulation to be avoided. In other words, one should not falsify raw data, such as transcripts, observation notes, or survey responses. Avoiding manipulation of data also suggests that you not fabricate data, or that you change your hypotheses to fit your data results after the study has been conducted. At the beginning of a study, the way participants are recruited and selected may be a form of manipulation if done in a systematic fashion with the expectation that certain samples will yield certain data. For example, suppose you wanted to assess how effective a technical communication class has been for college students. You decide to use senior thesis grades as indicators of effectiveness. Suppose you sample only those students from the "honors" class. This is an obvious example of a nonrepresentative sample, but it shows that manipulation may take place at many different stages of research. (Recruitment and selection of participants relates to the ethical principle of justice, especially if people of vulnerable or disadvantaged populations are asked to participate.)

Many ethical issues in conducting research are not clear-cut. Dealing with data is no exception. For example, consider what it means, ethically, to remove data from analyses because they are outliers. Some may argue to avoid this type of data manipulation, whereas others might respond that leaving outliers in a data set would skew the results, misrepresent the data, and should be avoided.

Reliability and Validity

Reliability refers to the consistency with which research is approached (Grant-Davie, 1992, p. 281), and validity concerns the ability of a research system (i.e., coding, statistical analysis, synthesis of qualitative data) to "measure whatever it is intended to assess" (Lauer & Asher, 1988, p. 140). Said in other words, reliability and validity have to do with the extent to which measurements and results are consistent and accurate. Researchers must attempt to collect data with fairness and accuracy; they must be aware of biases and treat research participants fairly.

The questions of reliability and validity are perhaps no more vexing than in recent discussions about qualitative research methods. In an arena where the researcher's voice and presence are undeniable, where one's influence is acknowledged and "objectivity" questioned, and where participants' perspectives are sometimes unreliable, inconsistent, or in direct conflict with the theory that grounds the investigation, the greatest challenge is to create something readers have *faith* in, something that rings true to both the researcher and those who read the account.

How does a researcher convince readers that his or her investigation and interpretations are both believable and useful to the discipline? In *Qualitative Evaluation and Research Methods*, Patton (1990) answers this question with three issues researchers must be prepared to address in detail throughout the research process.

1. What techniques and methods were used to ensure the integrity, validity, and accuracy of the findings?
2. What does the researcher bring to the study in terms of qualification, experience, and perspective?
3. What paradigm orientation and assumptions undergird the study? (p. 461)

Using these three areas—methods, researcher *ethos*, and paradigm orientation—a researcher may create checkpoints in the process that examine how the argument addresses potential reader concern. Although all three checkpoints are important to consider, for the sake of time and space, we highlight the first suggestion made by Patton—techniques and methods.

One means of potentially increasing validity and reliability is to pursue methods that triangulate. In *Local Knowledge*, Geertz (1983) notes that ethnographers rely on "convergent data" from triangulation approaches to verify conclusions (pp. 156–157). Triangulation may occur when a researcher employs multiple methods (e.g., survey methods alongside participant observation and in-depth interviews) to approach the same questions; multiple sources (using a variety of participants, a wide cross-section of opinion, or a variety of sources such as print, visual, and interpersonal); multiple researchers (using mentors, collaborators, user testing, participant evaluation, or some combination of all); or multiple theories to inform the inquiry and evaluation of the data. The key to triangulation is that from a variety of angles, the data ultimately come to the same—or close to the same—conclusions. Readers may question the validity or reliability of data that comes from one source or one perspective, but if twenty people from three different perspectives generally offer similar corroborating insights, the text takes on new authority.

In addition to triangulation, researchers should openly acknowledge their roles and the impact of their presence on a given study. Although doing so undoubtedly raises questions of subjectivity, acknowledging one's role in research reinforces the authenticity and honesty of a researcher's work. And, as Patton suggests, researchers can also strengthen their work by consciously drawing from the body of research relevant to the inquiry they conduct. Validity and reliability are issues that resolve themselves only with the careful and honest attention of the researcher to the measurement, methods, and processes used, both as the research is conducted and when it is written for public scrutiny.

Negotiating the Complex Role of the Researcher

"Enter into the world. Observe and wonder. Experience and reflect. To understand a world you must become part of that world while at the same time remaining separate, a part of and apart from" (Patton, 1990, p. 199). Halcolm's charge to his research students here underscores one of the most difficult issues for researchers—how to negotiate the complex demands of the researcher's role in the field. Defining the role of the researcher is extremely difficult because a researcher's role is often very individualized in each research endeavor. Although the role of the researcher is always changing, it is the *process of defining* one's role that we are most concerned with here.

Because we study people—their behaviors, their communication practices, their interpersonal relationships, and their responses to organizational structures and perceptions of power, to name but a few recent inquiry lines in the field—as researchers, we are all challenged to carefully evaluate ourselves as well as our participants and the dynamic, highly charged interpersonal space between us. How can we feasibly immerse ourselves within a given field and somehow still manage to distance ourselves enough to maintain the integrity of the data we gather? How do we establish relationships with participants that foster trustworthiness and ensure access to the information we seek and still maintain the estrangement we need to avoid accusations of undue influence? What do we do when our responsibilities as a researcher come into conflict with our responsibilities as humans and community members? What are our responsibilities—to our participants, to our audiences, to ourselves—as chroniclers of what we observe?

These questions raise important issues about what roles we assume, what claims we make, and what practices we adopt as researchers in the field and teachers of future researchers. When connected to ethics, the researcher's role reflects the ethical principle of beneficence. Researchers have the responsibility to assess the research design, as well as risks and benefits to participants. The role of the researcher is crucial to both qualitative and quantitative research. What makes this issue so challenging is that the researcher serves as the primary "instrument" or tool throughout the processes of discovery, interpretation, and communication of the data. The choices researchers make in the field—for example, whom to interact with, what to observe, how to record, and which audience to write for—must be to be conscientious and self-aware.

Although we have no definitive answers to questions about researcher role, we advocate considering a researcher's role through constant reflection. Drawing from Rosaldo's (1989) notion of "positioned subjects," we offer three vantages from which the researcher may examine the necessary responsibilities and goals in an effort to purposefully explore his or her role in the field. A strategy commonly used in ethnographic research to reflect on such positioning involves keeping a reflective journal. Such a journal is often separate from other notes, and its purpose is to continually analyze the researcher's motivations for action, reactions to specific data, and feelings about the research process. We recommend keeping a journal that examines three key vantages concerned with ethics and researcher responsibilities—positioning the researcher's role, positioning relationships with participants, and positioning research goals. In reflecting on the researcher's role, a researcher might consider how he or she aims to study—as a participant within the field, or as an outside observer? Journal entries about positioning relationships with participants might address concerns such as the types of interactions between participants and researcher, duration of contact, previous histories, and potential for harm. Reflecting on research goals would require the researcher to evaluate why the research is necessary, how the research will advance disciplinary knowledge and awareness, who benefits from the researcher and why, and why and how to ensure that data reflect care and avoid misrepresentation.

Positioning one's researcher role is an ongoing process of observation, analysis, and negotiation. Thus, reflection on these issues is dynamic throughout the processes of discovery, analysis, and writing. In addition, reflection on these issues provides a mechanism through which the researcher can examine, from an ethical standpoint, the ways in which his or her role affects participants and ultimately the research goals.

COMPLYING WITH INSTITUTIONAL REVIEW BOARDS OR HUMAN SUBJECTS COMMITTEES

As our discussion of ethical issues has demonstrated, dealing with ethics requires that researchers ask many questions of themselves and the studies they design. Another necessary step for researchers is to comply with Institutional Review Boards, also known as Human Subjects Committees, in order to ensure institutions that some ethical issues have at least been considered by the researcher. In this section, we discuss this very important step and offer practical suggestions for completing IRB forms.

The main purpose of IRBs is to protect the welfare of research participants (Gillespie, 1999). To that primary end, IRBs use an established set of criteria, based upon the principles of the Belmont Report, for evaluating research proposals. Included is the consideration of the methods by which informed consent is secured and the balance of risks and benefits. Students or faculty who want to conduct research must obtain IRB approval prior to recruiting research participants and collecting data. All research universities should have an IRB, even though undergraduate colleges and community colleges may or may not have one.

The first step in working with an IRB is to gather information. Contact the university IRB chairperson or office and request written instructions about the procedures you are supposed to follow and forms that need to be completed. In addition, ask for examples or samples of completed documents, such as consent forms, descriptions of risks/benefits, descriptions of research methodology, and participant selection procedures.

There are three types of reviews that may be conducted for research that involves human participants. The first is an administrative review to determine whether research is exempt, which is deemed to be of minimal or no risk (research that involves classroom instruction often falls into this category). The second type is an expedited review for which there is only minimal risk. The third type is full committee review, which is for research that has more than a minimal risk. Each of the three types will take progressively more time. For example, an exempt review may be completed within a week, whereas a full committee review may take a month or more. Because the different types of reviews may require different paperwork, consult with an IRB member or staff person to help select the type of review that matches your research.

An application for the use of human participants in research will contain a variety of questions and items. Although some forms may differ slightly, the following information is usually gathered: project title; principal investigator and co-investigator's names and contact information; inclusive dates of the research; funding agency information; advisor if applicable; where the study will be conducted; a summary of your research question, purpose, methods, and tasks; the research participant population characteristics; how research participants will be identified, recruited, and contacted; risks and benefits to participation; how confidentiality of data will be treated; informed consent processes; and a copy of the consent form and copies of any instruments/surveys that you propose to use.

Although providing this information is required for IRB approval, we suggest that completing an IRB form also can serve a very functional purpose in thinking about ethics. That is, in detailing information about one's study, a researcher has the opportunity to reflect on ethical issues that may arise. For example, the IRB form requires that researchers create a consent form for research participants. Researchers can use this opportunity to think carefully about the requirements for consent they outline for participants, in addition to how the participants will be treated in the study, how confidentiality will be agreed upon, and how participants will be kept informed of the study. Similarly, as researchers outline methods, they can reflect on issues such as reliability and validity, as well as their role in conducting the research. Considering IRB forms in this way may make the process less painful and more applicable to the researcher. And even though thinking of IRB forms in this way may be a healthy exercise, of course completing the form does not guarantee that additional ethical issues won't arise in the process of a research project. Ethical issues do arise, but IRB forms at least provide some helpful guidelines for both researchers and participants.

ACTIVELY REFLECTING ON ETHICS

We have asserted throughout this chapter that technical communication researchers have certain responsibilities concerning ethics: (1) acknowledging the importance of ethics; (2) becoming familiar with literature about ethics; (3) identifying ethical issues in research; and (4) complying with Institutional Review Boards when conducting research. Considering ethics in this thoughtful way means asking important questions of ourselves and our studies.

To conclude this chapter, we offer the suggestion that technical communication researchers should take regular opportunities to actively reflect on ethical decisions made in their research studies. Although the ATTW Code of Ethics provides a starting place, as our chapter has suggested, the subtleties and individual adjustments that researchers need to make are quite complex. Therefore, borrowing from Rosaldo's notion of "positioning," our parting advice is to encourage researchers to keep a journal in which they can reflect on ethical principles and issues that arise in research. Table 1 suggests possible questions for reflection in such a journal, and we have also indicated the ethical issue to which the questions refer. We hope that addressing these questions will lead to thoughtful reflection and discussion. Actively reflecting on ethics is one way that researchers in technical communications can be responsible researchers.

REFERENCES

American Psychological Association. (1982). APA Ethical Principle 9: Research with human participants. Washington, DC: American Psychological Association.

American Psychological Association. (1992). Ethical principles of psychologists and code of conduct. *American Psychologist, 47*, 1597–1611.

Anderson, P.V. (1998). Simple gifts: Ethical issues in the conduct of person-based composition research. *College Composition and Communication, 49, 1*, 63–89.

Atkinson, P. (1992). *Understanding ethnographic texts.* Newbury Park, CA: Sage.

ATTW Code of Ethics. (1999). *Technical Communication Quarterly, 8, 3*, 268.

Blakeslee, A.M., Cole, C., & Conefrey, T. (1996). Evaluating qualitative inquiry in technical and scientific communication: Toward a practical and dialogic validity. *Technical Communication Quarterly, 5, 2*, 125–149.

Bruner, E.M. (1986). Ethnography as narrative. In V.W. Turner & E.M. Bruner (Eds.), *The anthropology of experience* (pp. 139—155). Urbana: University of Illinois.

Clegg, S. (1975). Feminist methodology—fact or fiction? *Quality and Quantity, 19*, 83–97.

Code of Federal Regulations. (1991). Protection of human subjects. Department of Health and Human Services, National Institutes of Health, Office for Protection from Research Risk (45 C.F.R. 46). Available FTP: http://ohrp.osophs.dhhs.gov/human subjects/guidance/45cfr46.htm.

Collins, P.H. (1986). Learning from the outsider within: The sociological significance of black feminist thought. *Social Problems, 33, 6*, S14–32.

Cross, G.A. (1994). Ethnographic research in business and technical writing: Between extremes and margins. *Journal of Business and Technical Communication, 8, 1*, 118–134.

Denzin, N. (1985). Emotion as lived experience. *Symbolic Interaction, 8, 2*, 223–240.

Doheny-Farina, S. (1986). Writing in an emerging organization: An ethnographic study. *Written Communication, 3, 2*, 158–185.

Doheny-Farina, S. (1993). Research as rhetoric: Confronting the methodological and ethical problems of research on writing in nonacademic settings. In R. Spilka (Ed.),

Writing in the workplace: New research perspectives (pp. 253–267). Carbondale: Southern Illinois University Press.

Faber, B.D. (2001). Gen/Ethics? Organizational ethics and student and instructor conflicts in workplace training. *Technical Communication Quarterly, 10, 3,* 291–318.

Gaventa, J. (1993). The powerful, the powerless, and the experts: Knowledge struggles in an information age. In P. Park et al. (Eds.), *Voices of change: Participatory research in the United States and Canada.* Westport, CT: Bergin & Garvey.

Geertz, C. (1988). *Works and lives: The anthropologist as author.* Stanford, CA: Stanford University Press.

Geertz, C. (1983). *Local knowledge: Further essays in interpretive anthropology.* New York: Basic Books.

Gillespie, J.F. (1999). The why, what, how, and when of effective faculty use of institutional review boards. In G. Chastain & R.E. Landrum (Eds.), *Protecting human subjects* (pp. 157–177). Washington, DC: American Psychological Association.

Grant-Davie, K. (1992). Coding data: Issues of validity, reliability, and interpretation. In G. Kirsch & P.A. Sullivan (Eds.), *Methods and methodology in composition research* (pp. 270—286). Carbondale: Southern Illinois University Press.

Hawthorne, M.D. (2001). Learning by doing: Teaching decision making through building a code of ethics. *Technical Communication Quarterly, 10, 3,* 341–356.

Jacobi, M.J. (1990). Using the enthymeme to emphasize ethics in professional writing courses. *Journal of Business Communication, 27, 3,* 273–291.

Katz, S.B. (1992). The ethic of expediency: Classical rhetoric, technology, and the Holocaust. *College English, 54, 3* 255–275.

Kienzler, D. (2001). Ethics, critical thinking, and professional communication pedagogy. *Technical Communication Quarterly, 10, 3,* 319–340.

Kirsch, G. (1992). Methodological pluralism: Epistemological issues. In G. Kirsch & P.A. Sullivan (Eds.), *Methods and methodology in composition research* (pp. 247–269). Carbondale: Southern Illinois University Press.

Kirsch, G., & Mortenson, P. (Eds.) (1996). *Ethics and representation in qualitative studies of literacy.* Urbana, IL: NCTE.

Kirsch, G., & Mortenson, P. (1999). Toward an ethics of research. In G. Kirsch (Ed.), *Ethical dilemmas in feminist research* (pp. 87—104). Albany: State University of New York Press.

Kirsch, G., & Sullivan, P.A. (Eds.). (1992). *Methods and methodology in composition research.* Carbondale: Southern Illinois University Press.

Kleinman, S. (1993). The textual turn. *Contemporary Sociology, 22, 1,* 11–13.

Landrum, R.E. (1999). Introduction. In G. Chastain & R.E. Landrum (Eds.), *Protecting human subjects* (pp. 3–19). Washington, DC: American Psychological Association.

Lauer, J.M., & Asher, J.W. (1988). *Composition research: Empirical designs.* New York: Oxford University Press.

Lewis, P.V., & Speck III, H.E. (1990). Ethical orientations for understanding business ethics. *Journal of Business Communication, 27, 3,* 213–232.

Lincoln, Y.S. & Guba, E.G. (1985). *Establishing trustworthiness. Naturalistic inquiry* (pp. 289–331). Beverly Hills, CA: Sage Publications.

Martin, J., Feldman, M.S., Hatch, M.J., & Sitkin, S.B. (1983). The uniqueness paradox in organizational stories. *Administrative Science Quarterly, 28, 3,* 438–453.

Mumby, D.K. (1988). *Communication and power in organizations: Discourse, ideology and domination.* Norwood, NJ: Ablex.

National Commission for the Protection of Human Subjects of Biomedical and Behavioral Research (1979). *The Belmont report: Ethical principles and guidelines for the protection of human subjects of research*. Washington, DC: National Institutes of Health. Available FTP: http://ohsr.od.nih.gov/mpa/belmont.php3.

National Institutes of Health (1995). *Guidelines for the conduct of research involving human subjects at the National Institutes of Health*. Available FTP: http://ohsr.od.nih.gov /guidelines.php3.

Office for Human Resource Protections (OHRP) *Institutional Review Board guidebook*. Washington, DC: National Institutes of Health. Available FTP: http://ohrp.osophs.dhhs .gov/irb/irb_guidebook.htm.

Park, P., Brydon-Miller, M., Hall, B., & Jackson, T. (1993). *Voices of change: Participatory research in the United States and Canada*. Westport, CT: Bergin & Garvey.

Patton, M.Q. (1990). *Qualitative evaluation and research methods*. 2d ed. Newbury Park, CA: Sage Publications.

Pope, K.S., & Vetter, V.A. (1999). Ethical dilemmas encountered by members of the American Psychological Association: A national survey. In D.N. Bersoff (Ed.), *Ethical Conflicts in Psychology* (2d ed.). Washington, DC: American Psychological Association. (Reprinted from 1992 *American Psychologist, 47,* 397–411.)

Porter, L., & Coggin, W. (1995). *Research strategies in technical communication*. New York: John Wiley & Sons, Inc.

Recommendation of the CCC Ad Hoc Committee on the Ethical Use of Students and Student Writing in Composition Studies. CCC Ad Hoc Committee on the Ethical Use of Students and Student Writing in Composition Studies. November 1, 2000.

Richardson, L. (1995). Narrative and sociology. In J. Van Maanen (Ed.), *Representation in ethnography* (pp. 198–221). Thousand Oaks, CA: Sage Publications.

Roen, D.H. & Mittan, R.K. (1992). Collaborative scholarship in composition: Some issues. In G. Kirsch & P. A. Sullivan (Eds.), *Methods and methodology in composition research*, pp. 287–313. Carbondale: Southern Illinois University Press.

Ronai, C.R. (1992). The reflexive self through narrative: A night in the life of an erotic dancer/researcher. In C. Ellis & M.G. Flaherty (Eds.), *Investigating subjectivity: Research on lived experience* (pp. 102–124). Newbury Park, CA: Sage.

Rosaldo, R. (1989). Introduction: Grief and the headhunter's rage. *Culture and truth: The remaking of social analysis* (pp. 1–21). Boston: Beacon.

Russell, D.R. (1993). The ethics of teaching ethics in professional communication: The case of engineering publicity at MIT in the 1920s. *Journal of Business and Technical Communication, 7.1,* 84–111.

Salvo, M.J. (2001). Ethics of engagement: User-centered design and rhetorical methodology. *Technical Communication Quarterly, 10, 3,* 273–290.

Simonson, L.J., & Bushaw, V.A. (1993). Participatory action research: Easier said than done. *American Sociologist 24.1,* pp. 27–37.

Smith, D.E. (1986). Institutional ethnography: A feminist method. *Resources for Feminist Research, 15, 1,* 6–13.

Snow, D.A., & Morrill, C. (1993). Reflections on anthropology's ethnographic crisis of faith. *Contemporary Sociology, 22, 1,* 11–13.

Stoecker, R., & Bonacich, E. (1992). Why participatory research? *American Sociologist, 2, 1,* 5–14.

Van Maanen, J. (1995). An end to innocence: The ethnography of ethnography. In J. Van
    Maanen (Ed.), *Representation in ethnography* (pp. 198–221). Thousand Oaks, CA:
    Sage Publications.
Winsor, D.A. (1988). Communication failures contributing to the Challenger accident:
    An example for technical communicators. *IEEE Transactions on Professional Com-
    munication, 31, 3,* 101–107.

CHAPTER 2

Ethnographic Research

Susan M. Katz

Ethnographic research is both rewarding and demanding. It is rewarding (and valuable) because it provides a window into the lives and work of people within specific organizations or cultures with a level of detail that is not otherwise available. However, it is demanding because it requires that the researcher have a great deal of time (hundreds of hours of observation), a great deal of patience (to analyze hundreds of pages of data), and a great deal of faith (that order will arise out of the chaos).

In this essay, I describe how I worked within the demands of this methodology for a study of newcomers learning to write in two diverse organizations.[1] Because my approach to ethnography was somewhat unstructured, researchers who are considering ethnography but uncomfortable with this approach should be aware that a more systematic method than that described here is possible (see, e.g., Cross, 1994a). Throughout this chapter I refer to books and articles that provide more detailed information for those who wish to pursue ethnographic research.

A BIT OF HISTORY

Today we can easily "know about" many other people, cultures, or settings through a variety of resources (e.g., books, magazines, newspapers, movies, the Internet), but it is much more difficult to "know" others. Lofland (1971) tells us that we can only "know" others "through our own direct, face-to-face association with them, extending over some significant period of time" (p. 1). This desire to "know" others led anthropologists to develop ethnographic research methods. Anthropologists recognized that to understand the way of life of an unknown group of people, they would have to live with those people long enough to see things, to some extent, as insiders. Before they could begin to understand these people, anthropologists would first have to gain access, establish rapport, and develop trusting relationships. They would have to observe (and participate in) everyday activities and through these activities move from "knowing about" these people to "knowing" them (Lofland, 1971).

Although those of us who do research in technical communication are not likely to study the type of alien cultures studied by anthropologists, we are interested in "knowing" the people who work in various organizational settings. Many of us have found that a good way to accomplish this knowing is by borrowing methods from anthropologists such as Clifford Geertz. Geertz (1973) tells us that ethnography is not a matter of methods—it's not the techniques used to gather data—it's what results from the use of those methods. "What defines [ethnography] is the kind of intellectual effort it is: an elaborate venture in ... 'thick description'" (p. 6). A thick description provides a detailed picture of the culture: of the people and how they look, how they sound, where they live, what they value, what they eat, what they do for fun, and so on. The creation of a thick description is what the researcher does primarily for him- or herself—it's the researcher's "knowing" made explicit. This thick description becomes the structure that allows the researcher to interpret the data (the notes, transcripts, texts, photographs, etc.) and create some type of account of the culture (a book, an article, a film) that honestly represents what that culture is like and allows his or her readers to "know about" the culture.

The account itself cannot include the entire "thick description" as the ethnographer understands it, but it will include enough of that description to illustrate and support the findings the researcher chooses to report. As I write this sentence, I realize how problematic this sounds—especially the implicit suggestion that the researcher is reporting selectively. However, if we think about research of any kind, it always comes down to what questions the researcher is trying to answer, what data the researcher can provide, what results make the most interesting, appropriate, yet faithful, account. No one reports everything that he or she sees, does, learns. Even researchers in the hard sciences make decisions—both conscious and unconscious—about what to include and exclude when they write the formal reports of their work. (For a particularly explicit discussion of this point, see Gilbert and Mulkay, 1984, pp. 39–111.)

Ethnography came into research in technical communication by way of composition research. One of the earliest ethnographic studies in composition, if not the earliest, is Shirley Brice Heath's (1983) *Ways with Words*, the report of a nine-year study of children's acquisition of literacy skills. Arguably one of the most influential books in the field of composition, Heath's work brought the techniques of ethnographic research to the attention of writing scholars and is a model for the serious student of ethnography.

The influence of *Ways with Words* and other ethnographic studies in composition on research in technical communication can be traced with a surprising degree of specificity. As Geoffrey Cross (1994b) reports, "the first rigorous ethnographic studies in business and technical communication were published in 1985 by people associated with Rensselaer Polytechnic Institute" (p. 118), and he cites the work of Anne Herrington, Stephen Doheny-Farina, Denise Murray, and Lee Odell as the first such instances. There are some obvious connections here: Lee Odell was the dissertation advisor for the ethnographic dissertations of Rensselaer doctoral students Herrington and Doheny-Farina, and (with Dixie Goswami) the editor of the book that published Murray's report. (Lee was also my dissertation advisor at Rensselaer, and thus his influence will be felt throughout this piece as I refer to my own research.)

In the years since 1985, we have seen use of these methods gain in popularity, as evidenced by articles both reporting ethnographic studies and about ethnographic methods in collections such as Bazerman and Paradis (1991), Spilka (1993), and Duin and Hansen (1996); in journal articles such as Sullivan and Spilka (1992) and Segal, Brent, and Vipend (1998); and books such as those of Cross (1994a) and Dautermann (1997). Thus we can say with some confidence that researchers in our field find these anthropological methods of use in answering and asking questions about how people write in the world of work.

USES FOR ETHNOGRAPHIC METHODS

With any research project, the first steps must be about research design. To create a research design, the researcher has to figure out what it is that he or she is interested in investigating and decide what methods are most appropriate for conducting the investigation. (See Maxwell, 1996, for an excellent model of qualitative research design and a thoughtful discussion of how to use the model.) Ethnographic methods are useful for many types of studies relevant to technical communication. For example, Doheny-Farina and Odell (1985) tell us that ethnographic methods can be used to identify patterns of behavior that are important within a particular group, build theory about the role of written communication in a particular organization, or test theories or claims from prior research (p. 531). MacNealy (1999) suggests that ethnographic studies can help identify problems, propose hypotheses, describe working conditions, and develop theory about effective document design (p. 216). A more extensive list can be found in Cross (1994b), who suggests that ethnographic research can

- Provide historical accounts
- Explain and refine theory
- Reinforce our conceptual structures of composing
- Expand and complicate our structures of composing
- Provide teachers with knowledge closer to experience
- Disprove categorical theories
- Provide grounded hypotheses and questions to investigate (pp. 130–131)

(See also Sullivan and Spilka, 1992, for an excellent discussion of "when and how qualitative research is helpful to technical communicators.")

Ethnographic methods were appropriate for my study because I was interested in finding out how new employees in organizations learned to write according to the conventions of that organization. This phenomenon was related to theory in two different areas, both of which aided me in formulating research questions. Concepts of the *discourse community* as an entity that constrains and enables writers were important for identifying and understanding organizational or group conventions that affected the writing of employees within a group. Theories of *organizational socialization* attempt to explain how newcomers learn to behave/act/perform appropriately in workplace settings, and I hoped to see if those theories could also explain how newcomers learned a specific behavior—writing—within that setting. In a very real sense I was doing an empirical study to determine the validity of what were predominantly theoretical concepts. If I could identify discourse conventions specific to a particular setting, I could support the concept of the discourse community. If I saw newcomers and their coworkers enacting strategies suggested by organizational socialization theories, I could strengthen the validity of those theories and show their relevance for the field of technical and professional communication.

IMPORTANT DECISIONS

Once a researcher decides that ethnographic methods can help achieve his or her purpose(s), there are two major tasks that must be undertaken before the study can begin: Finding a site for the study and figuring out what the researcher's role will be within that site.

Finding an Ethnographic Site

Gaining access to an organization for the purpose of research is never easy. Gaining access for the amount of time necessary for an ethnographic study is a truly daunting task. First, the researcher has to think of an appropriate site—a site where he or she can observe the kinds of behaviors relevant to the research questions—and then the researcher has to convince the organization to grant permission for the study. The most important assistance I received with this problem came from a "Doing Research" column in *The Bulletin of the Association for Business Communication* which described how four researchers gained access to organizational sites for their own research purposes (Rogers, 1993).

After reading the article, I made a list of everyone I knew—family, friends, neighbors, colleagues—who worked in an organization that might be appropriate for investigating the questions I had about how newcomers learn to write.[2] I contacted all of these people, explained what I hoped to do, and asked for an introduction to someone in their organization with the authority to grant permission. I was able to make appointments with three government auditing agencies, two private engineering firms, a technical documentation firm, and a banking firm.

When I met with these individuals, I not only described my study and what I was asking of them, but I also tried to address some specific concerns that the organization was likely to have. Although the level of concern will vary from organization to organization, researchers need to be prepared to discuss how they will (1) protect the privacy of individual participants, (2) protect the privacy of the organization, and (3) avoid disclosure of the organization's proprietary information. (For additional information about "informed consent" and "confidentiality," see Breuch, Olson, and Frantz, this volume.)

For research sponsored by an accredited college or university, the research design will need to be approved by an Institutional Review Board (IRB). (See Breuch, Olson, and Frantz, this volume, for a discussion of the history and purpose of IRBs.) The members of these review boards are often unfamiliar with qualitative research and will need specific, detailed descriptions of how the researcher will ensure confidentiality and avoid coercion of participants. They may also ask about how and where you will store your data, how long you plan to use that data, and how you will dispose of the data once you are finished. In my own case, the review board rejected my proposal twice before finally approving it. Dealing with these issues at such an early stage may give the researcher an opportunity to clarify the goals of the study and provide valuable ideas for describing the study to prospective participants.

The proposal that I wrote for the Rensselaer IRB provided the basis for a proposal that I could show to the site managers who had agreed to meet with me. In addition to explaining how I would protect the confidentiality of the participants and the organization, the site proposal outlined exactly why I was conducting the research, what I would be doing at their site (including information such as how often I would visit, how many people I would want to observe/interview, how much of their employees' time I would take up, how many hours/days/weeks/months I planned to be there), and what I would give them in return.

In my case, I offered to write a report based on my observations of newcomers. The report would describe what kinds of information newcomers needed to learn about writing and how they learned it. Because writing was valued within all of these organizations, I hoped that information that might help their new employees learn organizational conventions quickly would be useful to them. After presenting my proposal to gatekeepers at the seven organizations described above, I was given permission to conduct my research at all three government auditing agencies and one engineering firm. However, only one of the government agencies had new employees for me to observe. This left me with a choice between two very different organizations, and I decided to use both of them to see whether the findings from one site were comparable to findings from the other.

Planning the Researcher's Role

Although many books and articles have been written that discuss and describe how researchers can and should conduct themselves while gathering data (see, for example, Cross, 1994b; Glesne, 1999; Lindlof, 1995; MacNealy, 1999; Segal et al., 1998), the most useful discussion can still be found in the 1985 Doheny-Farina and Odell article (pp. 512–517). This article specifically focuses on writing ethnographers, describes four different roles (complete observer, participant-as-observer, complete participant, and observer-as-participant) that researchers can adopt, and explains the advantages and disadvantages of each role.

Regardless of the role of the researcher, one of the biggest concerns with this type of study is what Goetz and LeCompte (1984) call "observer effect"—the tendency of participants to respond (during interviews) and act (while being observed) as they think the observer wants. This behavior may be deliberate or inadvertent, but it is always a concern. Researchers need to protect the integrity of their data by walking a fine line between letting the participants know what is being studied (researchers have an ethical responsibility to inform participants of the nature of the study) and giving away so much information that the participants can determine desired outcomes. Again, Doheny-Farina and Odell (1985) give advice on dealing with observer effect—advice such as "remaining on site for an extended period of time, talking with a variety of participants in a variety of situations, and confirming conclusions by drawing on multiple sources of data" (p. 515). (See also Doheny-Farina, 1993.)

GATHERING DATA

Ethnographers use a wide variety of methods to gather data, but I only talk here about the most common methods: observation, interviews, and textual analysis. Because one of the crucial aspects of this type of research is methodological triangulation (Doheny-Farina & Odell, 1985, p. 509), prospective ethnographers should investigate other methods (e.g., surveys, tests, focus groups) in addition to these before producing a research design. (See MacNealy, 1999, for an excellent discussion of a variety of methods that can be used to enhance an ethnography.)

Observation

Although I have said that ethnographers use a variety of methods, the core method of an ethnography is always observation. Observations should be done at different times of day and on different days of the week so that the researcher can be assured that what he or she is seeing isn't shaped by any specific organizational schedule. For example, I was confused at first by the way people dressed on Fridays at the engineering firm. I noticed that sometimes people were dressed in standard business attire, sometimes they wore casual clothes, and often there was a mix of business and casual attire. It took me several weeks to learn that the company had a specific program that involved casual dress: on *some* Fridays, there would be a fund-raising event for a charitable organization. Individual employees would contribute money to the organization in return for permission to dress casually on that day, but the program wasn't mandatory. This meant that on Fridays when there was no event, everyone had to dress formally; when there was an event, some people would participate and others would not, leading to the inconsistency in attire.

Although this example may seem to have focused on an irrelevant detail, ethnographic observation *requires* constant attention to detail and an almost obsessive ability to record that detail. Although many discussions of observation suggest taking notes longhand (Glesne, 1999; Doheny-Farina & Odell, 1985), I used a laptop computer to take field notes. Given that laptop computers have become commonplace, it seems unlikely that they would be a distraction in most organizational settings appropriate for ethnographic research in technical communication.

Once my participants got used to my presence, they did not seem at all distracted by my note taking, although occasionally someone would ask what I could possibly be writing. The answer to that question was "everything." I made notes about the layout of the offices, the pictures on the wall, the clothes that the participants and their coworkers were wearing, the amount of time spent on particular tasks, what those tasks were, who called on the phone, how long conversations lasted, what documents people wrote or read, what reference materials people checked, and whom they called when they had a problem. I made notes about who attended various meetings, what they discussed in those meetings, and how people interacted and reacted in those meetings. I made notes to myself about questions to ask the participants or my colleagues, about ideas that I would need to investigate further, and about connections that might be made to earlier observations. Although I have not used all of this information in my reports of this study, it did create the "thick description," which allowed me to see patterns, create categories, and understand what I was observing. (For more details about conducting ethnographic observation, see Doheny-Farina and Odell, 1985, pp. 512–522; Glesne, 1999, pp. 43–56; Lindlof, 1995, pp. 132–162.)

The ethnographer needs to devise some type of system for *citing* those field notes. The most common method is a simple system of abbreviations—"ON" for observational note, "MT" for meeting, "IN" for interview—and the date of the event recorded. There is some controversy about the citing of these field notes. Herndl (1991) has warned that the citing of irretrievable field notes "appropriates the same documentary power" as the citing of published works (p. 326) and that it is a positivistic gesture that separates the observer from the observed. Although it may well be that the ethnographer's citing of field notes is a nod toward a more scientific tradition of evidence, its role in an ethnographic account is as a rhetorical device that helps establish the credibility of the researcher. Doheny-Farina (1993) suggests that such a device is ethical *as long as it is identified as such* (p. 263). From personal experience, I know that academic journals in our field are unlikely to accept ethnographic research without those citations of "irretrievable" field notes.

In addition to taking notes during observation, I often audiotaped meetings. Conversations (meetings and interviews, as noted below) that are recorded electronically must be transcribed, which is a difficult and tedious process. Because it is often especially difficult to transcribe tapes with multiple speakers, I also took notes during meetings, usually indicating such things as the names of the attendees, the order of speakers, unfamiliar terminology or acronyms, and noticeable body language or facial gestures.

Many researchers hire transcriptionists to tackle the arduous chore of transcription. I chose to do my own transcription because, quite simply, as a graduate student, I couldn't afford to pay someone else to transcribe the many hours of tape I had collected. However, I found that listening to the tapes carefully enough to transcribe them allowed me to remember the conversations more clearly. When it came time to do analysis, I had the ability to recall a great deal of what I had heard, when I had heard it, who had said it, and in what context it had been said. Even now, many years later, I can still remember an amazing amount of detail from my data. This vivid recall was invaluable for synthesizing information and "seeing" categories during analysis.

Interviews

In my study, I conducted four different types of interview: preparatory, observational, coworker, and discourse-based interviews. Brief descriptions of the first three types of interview, and a somewhat longer description of the discourse-based interview, should provide an idea of the role and value of each.

- *Preparatory interviews* gave me information about the newcomers who were the primary focus of my observations (their educational and work experience, their expectations about the new job, and so forth) and about the managers who would work with them and/or had hired them (their expectations for the newcomers, their descriptions of the positions these newcomers held, their description of the writing requirements, etc.). The preparatory interviews were semistructured—I began with a list of questions, but allowed the information I heard to shape additional questions within each interview.

- *Observational interviews* were informal, often spontaneous, conversations that typically occurred at the beginning or end of an observational session. I would ask the participant what he or she planned to do that day, follow up on events that had occurred during a previous observation, or ask for explanations of behaviors or activities that I had observed that day that were unclear to me. These interviews were also an opportunity for me to test what Doheny-Farina (1993) calls the "practical validity" (pp. 260–261) of research: as I started to come to some conclusions about what was happening in the setting, I would bounce my ideas off the participants to see if my interpretation of events matched their own perceptions.

- *Coworker interviews* were conducted when one of the participants interacted with a coworker, and I had questions about that coworker's response to or understanding of the interaction. For example, I conducted interviews with several supervisors after their first review of an early document written by one of the newcomers to get their reactions to those texts. These interviews were usually semistructured. As with the observational interviews, the coworker interviews were also opportunities to test the practical validity of my interpretations.

- *Discourse-based interviews.* Although the discourse-based interview has application in many fields, it is the only research method that I am aware of that was created specifically for research on writing in nonacademic settings. For this reason, and because it is somewhat difficult to design, it deserves a longer explanation. A discourse-based interview seeks to uncover the tacit information that writers use when they write for organizational purposes. The interview takes the form of a structured series of questions based on texts that the writer has written or with which the writer is familiar. Thus the first step in creating a discourse-based interview is the analysis of a significant number of texts. The analysis should reveal organizational discourse conventions, which the interviewer can then use to create questions. The questions are not pointed "why did you do this?" questions, which could result in defensive or inappropriate responses. Rather, the interviewer offers the writer alternative versions of specific parts of the text and asks about differences between the two.

Questions can take several different forms. The interviewer can show the participant alternative versions of common aspects of text and ask which one would be preferred in a final document; rewrite sections of a document the participant has written and ask if it would be acceptable to substitute the revision for the original; ask if the participant would be willing to move highlighted paragraphs or sections to a different (specific) point in the document; and ask the participant what the effect would be if highlighted words or phrases were left out completely.

A more specific example may help at this point. At the government auditing agency where I observed four newcomers, the primary document that the auditors produce is called an audit report. Audit reports consist, in part, of a series of "findings." Each finding is supposed to be a one-sentence statement of a problem that the auditors uncovered during their audit. The report also contains "background" and "recommendations" sections that provide pertinent information about each finding and explain what the organization that has been audited should do to correct the problem. As one part of my discourse-based interview with the new auditors, I showed them a series of paired findings. One of the pair was a finding taken from an actual audit report, and one of the pair was a version that I had rewritten. I asked them to tell me which of the two versions they thought would be preferred by the managers in the organization. Their answers told me whether they had absorbed the organization's discourse conventions for writing findings. I also did these same discourse-based interviews with several managers, which enabled me to compare the newcomers' explanations with those of seasoned veterans of the organization. (For more information about creating and conducting discourse-based interviews, see Odell, Goswami, & Herrington, 1983, and Odell, Goswami, Herrington, & Quick, 1983.)

Although discourse-based interviews are difficult to create, I found that some of the most insightful responses and informative data that I collected came from this source. The participants in my study actually seemed to enjoy explaining their documents to me in this way. However, it is possible that discourse-based interviews create a type of "observer effect." By asking questions about texts, I brought certain features to the attention of the participants—I made participants aware of aspects of text that they might not otherwise have thought about; in some instances my questions made tacit knowledge explicit. It is impossible to judge how this new and unusual awareness affected the members of the organization.

Because there is the possibility of encouraging "observer effect," discourse-based interviews should be reserved for late in the study. Waiting until near the end of the study also allows the researcher to become more familiar with the organization and its conventions, to gather more written documents to use as a basis for the interviews, and to recognize the difference between organizational discourse conventions and individual idiosyncrasies.

Even though the tape recording of interviews is extremely beneficial, I did not audiotape the preparatory or observational interviews. As Doheny-Farina and Odell (1985) point out, recording devices can "intimidate and/or irritate participants" (p. 524), so I chose not to record in the early stages of my study or during the more informal observational interviews. I did, however, audiotape many of the coworker interviews and all of the discourse-based interviews. I did not use a video recorder during this study, in part because of the discomfort expressed by participants. However, if participants are willing, video recording could be very useful for catching body language and facial expressions that are so important to our understanding of personal interaction.

Textual Analysis

Thomas Lindlof (1995) tells us that "[b]y themselves, documents are of limited significance. When related to other evidence, however, they have much to offer the analyst" (p. 208). Throughout my study, I collected a variety of documents, including reports, memos, letters, and forms. Because I was focusing on how newcomers learn to write, I often collected multiple drafts of their written work, and in most instances I was able to copy versions containing reviewers' comments. One of the primary uses for these documents was the construction of the discourse-based interviews described earlier, but they also provided a wealth of detail about the aspects of text that were the focus of the review process.

THE HARD PART: ANALYSIS

In many types of research, surveys, for example, the hard part is the design of the study. Once the instrument is created and tested and the data are collected and entered into the appropriate software, a computer can give you the "results," and the "analysis" is relatively easy. With ethnographic research, however, the data collection, although time consuming, is the relatively easy part. The hard part is figuring out what all that data mean. And what makes it even worse is that no one can really tell you how to do it—they can give guidelines and suggestions, but they can't be very specific about what an individual researcher should look for. (I think the best discussion of analysis and interpretation can be found in Goetz and LeCompte, 1984, pp. 164–207. For a concise discussion of problems with interpreting qualitative data, see Lauer and Asher, 1988, pp. 46–48.)

With ethnography, data collection and data analysis are not two distinct steps in a process. The researcher continuously uses new data to generate new questions and test old questions, thinks about the relationship between observations and theory, and looks for connections between current and prior observations. (See Dautermann, 1993, p. 101, for a time line that demonstrates how the various aspects of an ethnographic study overlap one another.) But at some point, data collection stops and the researcher's principal focus becomes analysis and interpretation.

Despite all the thinking and evaluation that take place during data collection, it is unlikely that the researcher will have a clear idea of what to do next once the collection phase has ended. In my case, I was overwhelmed by the nearly two thousand pages of information (observational notes, transcripts, and documents) I had collected. I knew that I had gained a great deal of insight into how newcomers learn to write, but my "insight" was nebulous and chaotic.

The first thing I did was sit down and read through all of my observations and transcripts several times. I had kept separate notebooks for each of my six participants, so reading each notebook was reading the "story" of what I had observed about that participant over the nine months of my observations. The first time, I just read each notebook without trying to make notes or see categories—I was just refreshing my memory and trying to see each person's notebook as a (more or less) coherent whole. As I read the second time, I used colored markers to try to segregate categories of information. The third time I read through the notebooks, I made notes about specific events that seemed important.

What all this reading allowed me to do was create a mental "thick description" of these individuals within their organizational contexts. However, it did nothing to relieve the chaos. At this point, Lee Odell suggested that I sit down and free write about what I had learned and the kinds of questions that I thought my data could answer. In forty-five minutes, I typed seven pages of questions or ideas that might become topics for analysis—approximately one hundred possible topics or categories. Although this exercise made me feel incredibly productive and gave me a profound and more specific sense of what I had learned, it did nothing to relieve my feeling that I was irretrievably lost in a sea of data.[3]

At this point, Lee made an inspired (or perhaps experienced) suggestion. He told me to choose any of the topics or questions I had noted and free write about it for as long as I could. When I ran out of things to say, I was to pick another topic and repeat the process. As I wrote, two things happened that were crucial: I learned what I was most interested in writing about, and I learned that no matter what topic I chose, I always ended up writing about the review process. Although I was not yet out of the woods, and I certainly don't want to give the impression that the rest of it was easy, at least I had a focus. I read through all of my notebooks again, this time specifically looking at what had happened during and as a result of the review process. My dissertation (Katz, 1996) and subsequent book (Katz, 1998a) provide a close examination of the nonacademic review process and describe how it differs from an academic review process, as well as how it benefits both newcomers and their organizations.

A more systematic approach to data analysis may appeal to researchers who are uncomfortable with the somewhat messy holistic approach that I used. Miles and Huberman (1994), for example, recommend creating codes before beginning data collection. These codes can be based on your conceptual framework, your research questions, and variables that you anticipate will be relevant to the study. As the study progresses, the codes can be refined to better reflect what is observed. The data can thus be gathered and coded almost simultaneously, which would make the task of analysis more manageable.

Furthermore, many researchers (see, e.g., Cross, 1994a, 2000) use computers to assist with the analysis of qualitative data. Once the data have been coded, it can be entered into a software program and sorted. The sorting process itself gives the researcher an excellent overview of the types of data that recur frequently, thus helping focus the analysis. The database also provides an efficient way to retrieve specific types of information, which would support not only the analysis of the data, but also the production of reports and articles.

CURRENT CONCERNS WITH ETHNOGRAPHIC RESEARCH

As with any method, there are always concerns about the validity and reliability of ethnographic research. However, there are also some concerns that have been raised about ethnography that are seldom raised about other methods (although many of them could as easily be raised about other types of qualitative or quantitative research). A brief description of some of these concerns will alert researchers and readers to questions they should ask before conducting or while reading reports of ethnographic research.

Validity and Reliability

As Lauer and Sullivan (1993) eloquently explain, validity and reliability are social constructions, "not transcendent, self-evident characteristics inherent in the nature of empirical research" (p. 163). Simply put, validity pertains to the credibility of the research design and reliability pertains to the rigorous collection and analysis of data, but how "credibility" and "rigor" are defined are usually discipline specific.

Geertz (1983) suggests that ethnographers can enhance the validity and the reliability of their studies by means of triangulation: the use of multiple data sources, multiple theoretical perspectives, multiple investigators, and/or multiple methods. In addition, ethnographers should check with participants throughout the study to make sure the world they are creating on paper is recognizable to the people who live in that world, and they should check with colleagues to make sure that they are not falling prey to unreasonable assumptions or overzealous interpretations. Ethnography cannot help but be collaborative, but it should be explicitly so. (For additional suggestions on enhancing validity and reliability, see Breuch, Olson, and Frantz, this volume.)

Claims

There are serious limitations to what an ethnographer can claim. These limitations on claims fall into two categories: claims of cause and effect and claims of generalizability. Ethnographers are not experimenters, creating control groups and testing variables. Rather, ethnographers record events as they take place in complex organizational environments. Thus it is virtually impossible to claim that a specific action or event caused some other action or event. Ethnographers *can* speculate about what may have contributed to a particular outcome. In my own work, I suggest that the writing review process was an important component in the socialization of newcomers. Further, I speculate about the types of interaction within the review process that affect socialization and provide opportunities for the newcomers. I cannot, however, claim that specific actions (e.g., the way newcomers responded to review of their writing) led to specific outcomes (e.g., their success within the organization).

Another limitation affecting the claims that ethnographers can make is that the data gathered are not based on large, randomly sampled populations. Rather, ethnographers observe small, purposeful samples (Patton, 1980)—"particular subjects ... [chosen] because they are believed to facilitate the expansion of the developing theory" (Bogden & Biklen, 1982, p. 67). Thus ethnographers cannot make claims about the generalizability of their findings. No two organizations—or even groups within an organization—can be identical, so the observation of an action, event, or series of actions or events in one place does not mean that it can, will, or should occur in any other environment.

However, that does not mean that ethnographers don't have something to offer to their colleagues at the end of the day. Ethnographers "can claim to have identified recurrent behaviors that are significant to the life of the group" (Doheny-Farina & Odell, 1985, p. 531). With this identification come questions about why the behaviors are significant, how the behaviors are perceived by insiders and/or outsiders, whether they do occur in other groups, how they are modified by those groups, whether the behaviors support or weaken existing theory, and so forth. In my study, I observed a recurrent behavior—writing review meetings—enacted by newcomers and their supervisors in two different organizations and under a variety of circumstances. My investigation allowed me to make some claims about that recurrent behavior and suggested implications for individuals in organizations that enact similar types of review, for scholars in at least two fields (organizational communication and professional communication), and for teachers of writing.

Narrative Choices

In research, quantitative and qualitative alike, there is always the question of what gets reported. What kinds of choices does the researcher make when he or she sits down to "write up" the study? How does the method—and the researcher's disciplinary agenda—constrain or enable the report? We all recognize that a major constraint comes in the form of audience, specifically the scholarly audience of our discipline in the form of colleagues, journal editors, and those who decide on promotion and tenure. But, as Doheny-Farina (1993) points out, there are other audiences as well: The participants in the study and other practitioners are audiences, and I would suggest that these are audiences that may be overlooked. Furthermore, Judy Segal and her coauthors (1998) tell us that some of those audiences may not be interested in hearing what we have to say.

We also have to consider the role of audience in shaping what the ethnographer reports. As mentioned at the beginning of this chapter, the researcher has to make choices about what to report. In Doheny-Farina's (1993) discussion of these other audiences, he demonstrates how the

choice of audience (e.g., participants in the study vs. disciplinary colleagues) may place certain constraints on the information that is included
in any report of the research. For example, in the report I wrote for the participants in my study, which was given to all of the newcomers and their
supervisors, I was very careful to protect the identities of those participants.
My report did not mention or describe the activities or behaviors of any
individual or organizational group of individuals, rather it described what
newcomers (in general) need to know about organizational writing conventions and how newcomers (in general) learn those things they need to
know. I later revised that report into an academic article (Katz 1998b &
1998c)—and in that revision process I inserted many examples of specific
observations of specific individuals because my new audience required evidence to support the claims I was making. (The participants didn't need
as much evidence because they recognized the validity of my claims—I was
making explicit things that they already knew tacitly.)

In addition to considering the effect of audience on the final narrative,
most scholars suggest that ethnographers need to report multiple perspectives in those narratives, not just their own observations (see Breuch,
Olson, and Frantz, this volume). Furthermore, they need to make explicit
what those perspectives are. Or, as Linda Brodkey (1987) suggests, the ethnographer's "ultimate concern" is "how best to represent the relationship
among observers, observational methods, and the observed" (p. 30). There
are several ways to do this, among them:

- Let the participants speak for themselves as much as possible, using sections of transcripts from interviews or meetings. These pieces, often in
  scriptlike form, can give the reader a sense of the "voice" of the participants.

- Include the comments and observations of other actors at the site in addition to the direct participants. (In my study, I frequently interviewed
  the supervisors of my newcomer participants and included their "voices"
  along with those of the participants themselves.)

- Explicitly describe your own perspective as the researcher and your reasons for choosing the methods you have employed (see also Lay, 1991).

Purpose

Although it is all well and good to say that we are trying to "figure out
what the devil they [participants] think they are up to" (Geertz, 1983, p. 58),
there is some considerable discussion about what we should do with

the information once we have figured it out. As Geertz's comment suggests, anthropologists who devised ethnographic methods were primarily interested in describing and interpreting other cultures. As their methods were adapted by compositionists, the goal shifted to a focus on informing composition pedagogy. More recently, researchers who see ethnography as inherently "activist" (Lay, 1991, p. 361) suggest that a goal (in ethnographic and other types of research) should be "to investigate the ideological work and the struggles that occur within professional discourse" (Herndl, 1993, p. 361)—or, as Ralph Cintron (1993) succinctly frames it, "to critique the social order" (p. 373). (See also Herndl and Nahrwold, 2000.)

These and other scholars recognize the power of ethnographic observation to uncover the structures, relationships, and conventions within organizations that may not be obvious to the people who work there, and they argue strongly for a critical ethnography that can influence what we teach to the next generation of organizational members, as well as what we share with the participants themselves. Segal and her coauthors (1998) suggest that we should try "to connect with, but not necessarily convert" the subjects of our investigations within organizational contexts (p. 83). Based on their experiences in a variety of settings, Segal, Paré, Brent, and Vipond (1998) make "specific suggestions about how rhetoricians might approach disciplinary work while avoiding the missionary position" (p. 84). These suggestions, which I will only briefly highlight here, can provide guidance for researchers who choose to approach their ethnographic studies from a critical framework. (See Segal et al., 1998, pp. 84–88 for a fuller discussion of these suggestions.)

- Take your time. Just as you would not expect to become fluent in a foreign language quickly, you cannot learn the conventions, behaviors, idiosyncrasies, jargon, values, and relationships of any group quickly. It takes months, if not years, to begin to see things from the perspective of the insider.

- Respect your participants and their organizational culture. Just as many of us now believe it to be inappropriate to impose western culture on the rest of the world, it is inappropriate to impose your personal goals and values on the organizational culture you observe. You don't have to come to agree with them, but you do need to try to see things from their perspective, to understand why they do things the way they do. You may eventually choose to critique that culture (and, in fact, it would be nearly impossible not to critique it in some way), but that critique should be informed by your experience within the culture, not as a complete outsider to it.

- If you want to solve problems, solve the problems that are important to the participants. Again, it is inappropriate to usurp the organizational members' authority over their lives, goals, and values. What you see as problems may be insignificant, unimportant, or valued traditions to them. If you stay with them long enough, pay close attention to them, and gain their trust, you will be able to see things from their perspective—and you *may* be able to persuade them to take a look at things from your perspective as well.

- Participate in their culture and their conversations. As suggested earlier, think of them as an audience in addition to thinking of them as "subjects." Consider writing articles, presenting reports, or creating workshops that will allow you to give something back to the community you have been studying.

LIFE AFTER ETHNOGRAPHY

I spent more than a year of my life planning my research and collecting data, and another year analyzing that data and writing an initial report of my findings. Even though it was grueling work and much more difficult than I had anticipated, I would really like to do it again. The reality is, however, that it is unlikely that I will be able to do another ethnography unless I win a major grant (or the lottery). Ethnography is a research method that doesn't co-occur easily with the day-to-day responsibilities of academic life, especially during the early years of an academic career when the demands of earning tenure dictate the rapid production of tangible results. I am fortunate that the data I gathered have allowed me to produce a variety of reports for a variety of audiences without any further fieldwork. However, with hindsight, I also know that I could have done a better job in some aspects of my study. Specifically, I would recommend that anyone conducting an ethnography incorporate the following ideas as they plan their own research:

- Don't allow your need for supportive data to shape the notes that you write to yourself. Although my field notes were accurate records of what I observed at each site, my notes to myself during data collection and during analysis focused on *similarities* between sites and among participants. The differences—perhaps based on gender, discipline, organization, work schedule, collegiality, and so on—might have generated some interesting ideas about the life of professionals in the workplace.
- Find a system of transcription that accurately reflects all the nuances of oral discourse. David Silverman (1993) describes such a system, allowing for features such as pauses, intonations, and overlapping speech. This type of transcription will improve your ability to read those transcripts with greater accuracy at the distance of several years.

- Make arrangements to stay in touch with the participants to allow for the possibility of a follow-up study at a later date (recognizing, of course, that this would involve another exchange with your IRB). Only one of my six newcomers is still employed by the organization where I did my study, and several of the supervisors have moved on as well. A follow-up study with the same individuals would provide valuable insight into how the newcomers affected their organizations—and how those organizations affected them.

One of the advantages of ethnographic research is the wealth of data that the researcher gathers. And perhaps inherent in that boon are two other advantages: the new questions that arise and the renewed motivation to investigate those questions that come from immersing oneself in the data.

NOTES

1. The results of this study can be found in Katz (1996 and 1998a). The most significant difference between these two documents is that the dissertation (1996) has a much longer section on methods.

2. Beverly Moss (1992) provides an insightful discussion about the special problems that inhere when researchers choose to study sites with which they are truly familiar or communities to which they belong.

3. As I write this chapter, I am reminded of the emotional roller coaster that I lived on for those months of analysis. I am sure that I whined a great deal. I am grateful to Lee and my fiancé, Paul Organ, for their patience and support throughout that period.

REFERENCES

Bazerman, C., & Paradis, J. (Eds.). (1991). *Textual dynamics of the professions*. Madison: University of Wisconsin Press.

Bogden, R.C., & Biklen, S.N. (1982). *Qualitative research for education: An introduction to theory and methods*. Boston: Allyn & Bacon.

Brodkey, L. (1987). Writing ethnographic narratives. *Written Communication*, 4, 25–50.

Cintron, R. (1993). Wearing a pith helmet at a sly angle, or, can writing researchers do ethnography in a postmodern era? *Written Communication*, 10, 371–412.

Cross, G.A. (1994a). *Collaboration and conflict: A contextual exploration of group writing and positive emphasis*. Cresskill, NJ: Hampton Press.

Cross, G.A. (1994b). Ethnographic research in business and technical writing: Between extremes and margins. *Journal of Business and Technical Communication*, 8, 118–134.

Cross, G.A. (2000). Collective form: An exploration of large-scale group writing. *Journal of Business Communication*, 37, 77–100.

Dautermann, J. (1993). Negotiating meaning in a hospital discourse community. In R. Spilka (Ed.), *Writing in the workplace: New research perspectives* (pp. 98–110). Carbondale: Southern Illinois University Press.

Dautermann, J. (1997). *Writing at Good Hope: A study of negotiated composition in a community of nurses.* ATTW Contemporary Studies in Technical Communication, vol. 2. Greenwich, CT: Ablex.

Doheny-Farina, S. (1993). Research as rhetoric: Confronting the methodological and ethical problems of research on writing in nonacademic settings. In R. Spilka (Ed.), *Writing in the workplace: New research perspectives* (pp. 253–267). Carbondale: Southern Illinois University Press.

Doheny-Farina, S., & Odell, L. (1985). Ethnographic research on writing: Assumptions and methodology. In L. Odell & D. Goswami (Eds.), *Writing in nonacademic settings* (pp. 503–535). New York: Guilford.

Duin, A.H., & Hansen, C.J. (Eds.). (1996). *Nonacademic writing: Social theory and technology.* Mahwah, NJ: Lawrence Erlbaum Associates.

Geertz, C. (1973). Thick description: Toward an interpretive theory of culture. In C. Geertz, *The interpretation of culture* (pp. 3–30). New York: Basic Books.

Geertz, C. (1983). From the native's point of view: On the nature of anthropological understanding. In C. Geertz, *Local knowledge: Further essays in interpretive anthropology* (pp. 55–70). New York: Basic Books.

Gilbert, G.N., & Mulkay, M. (1984). *Opening Pandora's box.* Cambridge: Cambridge University Press.

Glesne, C. (1999). *Becoming qualitative researchers: An introduction.* New York: Longman.

Goetz, J.P., & LeCompte, M.D. (1984). *Ethnography and qualitative research design in education research.* New York: Academic Press.

Heath, S.B. (1983) *Ways with words.* Cambridge: Cambridge University Press.

Herndl, C.G. (1991). Writing ethnography: Representation, rhetoric, and institutional practice. *College English, 53,* 320–322.

Herndl, C.G. (1993). Teaching discourse and reproducing culture: A critique of research and pedagogy in professional and non-academic writing. *College Composition and Communication, 44,* 349–363.

Herndl, C.G., & Nahrwold, C.A. (2000). Research as social practice: A case study of research on technical and professional communication. *Written Communication, 17,* 258–296.

Herrington, A.J. (1985). Writing in academic settings: A study of the contexts for writing in two college chemical engineering courses. *Research in the Teaching of English, 19,* 331–361.

Katz, S.M. (1996). *The dynamics of writing review: Opportunities for socialization and individuation in nonacademic settings.* Unpublished doctoral dissertation, Rensselaer Polytechnic Institute, Troy, NY.

Katz, S.M. (1998a). *The dynamics of writing review: Opportunities for growth and change in the workplace.* ATTW Contemporary Studies in Technical Communication, vol. 5. Greenwich, CT: Ablex.

Katz, S.M. (1998b). How newcomers learn to write: Resources for guiding newcomers. *IEEE Transactions on Professional Communication, 41,* 165–174.

Katz, S.M. (1998c). Learning to write in organizations: What newcomers learn about writing on the job. *IEEE Transactions on Professional Communication, 41,* 107–115.

Lauer, J.M., & Asher, J.W. (1988). *Composition research: Empirical designs*. Oxford: Oxford University Press.

Lauer, J.M., & Sullivan, P. (1993). *Validity and reliability as social constructions*. In N.R. Blyler & C. Thralls (Eds.), Professional communication: The social perspective. Newbury Park, CA: Sage Publications.

Lay, M.M. (1991). Feminist theory and the redefinition of technical communication. *Journal of Business and Technical Communication*, 5, 348–370.

Lindlof, T.R. (1995). *Qualitative communication research methods*. Thousand Oaks, CA: Sage Publications.

Lofland, J. (1971). *Analyzing social settings: A guide to qualitative observation and analysis*. Belmont, CA: Wadsworth.

MacNealy, M.S. (1999). *Strategies for empirical research in writing*. Boston: Allyn & Bacon.

Maxwell, J.A. (1996). *Qualitative research design: An interactive approach*. Applied Social Research Methods Series, vol. 41. Thousand Oaks, CA: Sage Publications.

Miles, M.B., & Huberman, A.M. (1994). Qualitative data analysis (2d ed.). Thousand Oaks, CA: Sage.

Moss, B.J. (1992). Ethnography and composition: Studying language at home. In G. Kirsch & P.A. Sullivan (Eds.), *Methods and methodology in composition research* (pp. 153–171). Carbondale: Southern Illinois University Press.

Murray, D.E. (1985). The composing process for computer conversation. In L. Odell & D. Goswami (Eds.), *Writing in nonacademic settings* (pp. 203–227). New York: Guilford.

Odell, L. (1985). Beyond the text: Relations between writing and social context. In L. Odell & D. Goswami (Eds.), *Writing in nonacademic settings* (pp. 249–280). New York: Guilford.

Odell, L., & Goswami, D. (Eds.). (1985). *Writing in nonacademic settings*. New York: Guilford.

Odell, L., Goswami, D., & Herrington, A. (1983). The discourse-based interview: A procedure for exploring the tacit knowledge of writers in nonacademic settings. In P. Mosenthal, L. Tamor, & S.A. Walmsley (Eds.), *Research on writing: Principles and methods* (pp. 220–236). New York: Longman.

Odell, L., Goswami, D., Herrington, A., & Quick, D. (1983). Studying writing in nonacademic settings. In P.V. Anderson, R.J. Brockmann, & C.R. Miller (Eds.), *New essays in technical and scientific communication: Research, theory, practice* (pp. 17–40). Farmingdale, NY: Baywood Publishing Company.

Patton, M.Q. (1980). Qualitative evaluation methods. Beverly Hills, CA: Sage Publications.

Rogers, P.S. (1993, March). How researchers gain access to organizations. *Bulletin of the Association for Business Communication*, 56, 42–47.

Segal, J., Paré, A., Brent, D., & Vipond, D. (1998). The researcher as missionary: Problems with rhetoric and reform in the disciplines. *College Composition and Communication*, 50, 71–90.

Silverman, D. (1993). *Interpreting qualitative data: Methods for analysing talk, text, and interaction*. London: Sage Publications.

Spilka, R. (Ed.). (1993). *Writing in the workplace: New research perspectives*. Carbondale: Southern Illinois University Press.

Sullivan, P., & Spilka, R. (1992). Qualitative research in technical communication: Issues of value, identity, and use. *Technical Communication*, 39, 592–606.

ACKNOWLEDGMENTS

The author would like to thank Lynda Aiman-Smith, Lee Odell, Anthony Paré, and Dorothy Winsor for predraft discussions of this chapter and Laura Gurak, Mary Lay, Nancy Penrose, Lee Odell, and several anonymous reviewers for their suggestions for revision of early drafts.

CHAPTER

Analyzing Everyday Texts
in Organizational Settings

Carol Berkenkotter

> The presence and significance of documentary products provides the
> ... [researcher] with a rich vein of analytic topics, as well as a valuable
> source of information. Such topics include: How are documents writ-
> ten? How are they read? Who writes them? Who reads them? For what
> purposes? On what occasions? With what outcomes? What is recorded?
> What is omitted? What is taken for granted? What does the writer
> seem to take for granted about the reader(s)? What do readers need
> to know in order to make sense of them?
> —Hammersley and Atkinson, 1983

This chapter begins with a bit of text that is from an organizational communication. The excerpt is from a memo drafted Spring Term, 1999, when
my former department's Graduate Studies Steering Committee was
wrestling with the issue of just what kinds of courses could be counted as
satisfying the "Research Methods" requirement:

Approaches to Research/Methods

To qualify as a research methods course, the class materials must include
both a significant segment in which the primary aim is instruction in *a structured and systematic approach* to the analysis of some body of data or texts
(oral, visual, written, or electronic) and/or the study of competing methodologies (rhetorical analysis, critical theory/cultural studies, discourse
analysis), and a project where students apply such relevant methods (and
theories) to a set of such texts. (Memo from the Graduate Studies Steering
Committee, Rhetoric and Technical Communication Program, Humanities
Dept. Michigan Technological University; italics added.)

I've used italics to emphasize what strikes me as the criterial phrase in this memo to graduate faculty members: "a structured and systematic approach" to the analysis of some body of data or texts. Structured and systematic tends to mean different things in different disciplines; however, researchers with an empirical orientation will generally agree that structured and systematic procedures are those that can be communicated or taught to other researchers for the purposes of replication and/or independent confirmation or disconfirmation. Within an empirical tradition (as opposed to a critical theory or cultural studies tradition) of qualitative research methods, "textual analysis," as I use the term in this chapter, includes methods of systematic observation[1] for analyzing content, linguistic form and its function, genre and text organization, rhetoric, and the role of texts within an organization's communicative system. Underlying the examination of all these techniques will be a consideration of (1) what questions these techniques are designed to answer, and (2) what kinds of problems would lead the researcher to pose and answer those questions through the use of specific analytical techniques.

Bear in mind that textual analysis is but one kind of qualitative research technique belonging to a repertoire of data collecting and analyzing methods which may include field notes that researchers use to keep a running account of their observations, interviews with various people in the setting being observed, audiotaped recordings of interactions such as meetings, conferences, client interviews, and so on. Qualitative researchers may also use photographs or sketches to capture elements peculiar to the setting such as artifacts, physical arrangement of furniture, and so on. They may, as well, use graphics such as flowcharts or other graphic designs (circles, triangles, etc.) to represent patterns of activity in the setting (see Gunnarsson, 1997b). Thus, collecting and analyzing organizational documents is one of many research techniques in a researcher's repertoire.

This chapter is concerned with three approaches to textual analysis: rhetorical analysis, as developed within the context of rhetorical criticism and theory; discourse analysis, as developed within the context of applied linguistics; and, finally, genre analysis, as developed in both rhetorical theory/criticism and applied linguistics contexts. These three approaches are quite different, and I could easily write an entire essay on these differences. Yet all three share a common concern with understanding the relationship between text and context. To briefly make some basic distinctions between the three approaches, a strictly rhetorical analysis is concerned with the strategies through which arguments are made in written, oral, or electronic texts. The analyst has available a rich array of concepts in classical and contemporary rhetoric to draw on for conducting the analysis. For example, the analyst might be concerned with the *kairos* (the opportune moment for persuasion) of a scientific paper (Miller, 1992), with the appeals an author (or speaker) makes based on *ethos* (or credibility), *pathos* (the emotions of the audience), or to *logos* (the consistency and substantiality of the claims). Not only is the rhetorical analyst concerned with the nature or character of arguments in texts, but the analyst also pays attention to the situational, sociohistorical, and discursive contexts in which the text appears. The analysis is interpretive and based on the analyst's bringing the tools of rhetorical criticism to bear on the text or texts in question.

Like rhetorical analysts, discourse analysts are often concerned with the argumentative or persuasive character of a text. However, discourse analysts pay close attention to the linguistic/grammatical elements in that text, developing coding schemes for analyzing syntactical, grammatical, morphological, and other kinds of linguistic features. Thomas N. Huckin (1992) aligned the goals of discourse analysis with those of qualitative research by suggesting that text analysis aims at *plausible interpretation* rather than *absolute reliability,* as one might expect within the quantitative research paradigm. Huckin's account of the procedures of discourse analysis includes the following strategies: selecting an initial corpus, identifying salient patterns, selecting a study corpus, a subset of the original corpus, verifying the patterns (through the use of a coding scheme, and/or using an independent rater to corroborate or disconfirm the findings) (pp. 90–93). In short, discourse analysis relies on procedures that are empirical; however, the researcher's identification of salient patterns in a corpus is most certainly an interpretive process in the sense that it involves selection.

Discourse analysts have been criticized as being as too narrow and reductive in their approach, as it tends to focus on textual phenomena per se, and not to attend to context. However, in the last ten years a number of researchers, including Huckin and myself, have combined participant-observation and case study techniques with fine-grained, linguistic analyses of written texts (Berkenkotter & Huckin, 1995; Berkenkotter, Huckin, & Ackerman, 1988, Freedman & Smart, 1997).

Following Carolyn Miller's (1984) seminal essay on genre as social action, a number of scholars and researchers in rhetoric and composition studies and in applied linguistics have become interested in describing professional, disciplinary, and organizational genres. These researchers have used a variety of rhetorical and discourse analysis techniques, often in combination, to better understand how and why certain texts in various historical and professional/disciplinary contexts evolve over time (Atkinson, 1999; Bazerman, 1988; Yates, 1989), become stabilized, or combine with other genres to become hybrids, or, in still other cases, become obsolescent. More than rhetorical analysis or discourse analysis, genre analysis is an interdisciplinary specialty; some researchers use the analytical tools of both rhetorical analysis and discourse analysis (Atkinson, 1999; Berkenkotter & Huckin, 1995; Swales, 1990).

TEXTS AS DOCUMENTARY PRODUCTS

Unlike literary studies, in which works belonging to the literary canon (or challenging that canon) are the object of study, the objects of study in technical communication research are everyday texts. By "everyday texts," I mean the mundane bureaucratic, institutional, and organizational documents that might typically include patient files, statistical records, records of official proceedings, Web sites, and so on.

In the last fifteen to twenty years, a relatively small cluster of groups of researchers from different disciplines have been analyzing organizational and institutional texts in order to better understand the work of various different professions. Some useful essays to read in this regard are Devitt's 1991 analysis of the intertextual relationship between tax forms used by accountants; Freedman and Smart's (1997) analysis of written documents in the Bank of Canada; Gunnarsson's (1997b) research on writing and organizational roles in a local government office in a small city; Engeström's (1999) study of physician's communication difficulties over organizing a patient's primary and tertiary care (the division of medical labor), during a period of transition in a Finnish health care delivery system; and Ravotas and Berkenkotter's (1998) study of psychotherapy case notes (see also Berkenkotter and Ravotas, 1997).

A related strand of inquiry in scientific and technical communication has been concerned with analyzing various *canonical* scientific texts: Watson and Crick's 1956 essay in nature on the double helical structure of deoxyribose nucleic acid (Bazerman, 1988); Gould and Lewinton's essay, "The Spandrils of San Marcos and the Panglossian Paradigm" (Selzer, 1993) or Darwin's *Origin of the Species* (Gross, 1990, 1996). My concern in this chapter, however, is not with the analysis of canonical scientific texts, but rather the mundane, everyday texts that technical communication researchers are most likely to encounter in various workplace settings.

Paperwork as Constituting "Documentary Reality" in Organizational Settings

Over the years that I've taught qualitative methods in communication research, I've found that novice researchers—in producing accounts of complex, literate organizational worlds—can become so focused on their observations of the actors in the setting that they forget to consider that "the collective organization of work is dependent on the collective memory that written and electronic records contain" (Atkinson and Coffey, 1997, p. 46). However, I can't overestimate the importance of paperwork[2] in contemporary organizational culture. As Atkinson and Coffey have recently argued,

> It goes virtually without saying that this quintessentially modern kind of social formation is thoroughly dependent on paperwork. Administrators, accountants, lawyers, civil servants, managers at all levels, and other experts or specialist functionaries are all routinely, often extensively, engaged in the production and consumption of written records and other kinds of documents. If we wish to understand how organizations function, then we also need to take account of the role of recording, filing, archiving and retrieving information. (p. 47)

Indeed, the functioning of organizations is *so* dependent on the production and consumption of written records and other organizational texts that Bloomfield and Vurdabakis (1994) propose, "Textual communicative practices are a vital way in which organizations constitute 'reality' and the forms of knowledge appropriate to it" (p. 456). The notion of textual, or "documentary reality," and how it is constituted through organizational paperwork are central conceptually to this chapter. This notion suggests the social constructionist basis of many current analyses of written texts. For example, in our study of the functions of psychotherapists' paperwork in a mental health clinic setting (1997, 1998), my co-researcher, clinical psychologist Doris Ravotas, observed that therapists in conversation would sometimes refer to their clients by the diagnosis assigned to that client in their written records—that is, as "Borderlines," or "Bipolars," or other diagnostic labels, thereby conflating the client with his or her diagnosis.

A few methodological caveats are necessary here. First, researchers should avoid using documentary sources or organizational paperwork as surrogates for other kinds of data. We cannot, for instance, learn through records alone how an organization actually operates day by day. The competent qualitative researcher "follows the actors" in the setting as well as "following the texts." The researcher needs *many* sources of data to corroborate his or her observations; these sources might typically include field

notes, audiotapes of meetings and conferences, and printouts of e-mail correspondence or collaborative group work (see, for example, Yates, Orlikowski, and Renneker, 1997). A second caveat is that researchers should
not treat organizational records and other forms of documents as being "official" or transparent—that is, as solid evidence of what they report, as is
illustrated in the example of psychotherapists inadvertently labeling their
clients based on information in the clients' records.

ARTICULATING MAJOR METHODOLOGICAL ASSUMPTIONS

Any research project, quantitative or qualitative, is grounded in often
unstated assumptions that shape many of the researcher's methodological
choices. In the past, in those disciplines using traditional empirical, quantitative procedures, students were not necessarily familiar with the assumptions that informed the methods they learned (cf. Campbell and
Stanley, 1966). In the wake of the influence of postmodernism in the social sciences and humanities, however, there is much interest in identifying epistemological assumptions undergirding research methods, as the rise
of "methodology" courses attests. I find it important therefore to describe
at the outset a number of core concepts constituting a theoretical framework that informs my approach to qualitative textual analysis:

- *The concept of "documentary reality."* This concept is based on a social constructionist view of the importance of symbolic systems and discourse to
  our perceptions of reality. This is to say, following Gunnarsson, Linell,
  and Nordberg, that an individual's "cultural knowledge and representations of reality are interactionally constructed, socially transmitted, historically sedimented and often institutionally congealed, and finally
  communicatively reproduced *in situ*" (Gunnarsson et al., 1997, p. 2). For
  example, what to a naive observer may seem perfectly "natural" (a Bali-
  nese cockfight, a psychiatric intake interview with a new client) is, to an
  experienced researcher, rife with meanings that are deeply contextual,
  that is, historical, institutional, ideological, and interactional.

- *The concept of intertextuality.* The concept of intertextuality has been of
  major importance in such fields as literary theory, linguistic anthropology, critical discourse analysis, and rhetoric and composition. In the
  context of understanding the intertextual functions of everyday texts
  in organizational settings, this concept foregrounds the notion that documents do not stand alone. Atkinson and Coffey (1997) conjoin the concepts of documentary reality and intertextuality when they suggest that
  institutional/organizational texts "do not construct systems or domains

of documentary reality as individual [or] separate activities. Documents ... also refer to other documents, and in this process to other domains and realities. The analysis of documentary reality must therefore look beyond separate texts and ask how they are related" (pp. 55–56; see also Bazerman, 1993; Berkenkotter, 2001; Berkenkotter & Huckin, 1995; Devitt, 1991).

- *The related concept of "genre system" or "genre set."* First used by Devitt, 1991, in her analysis of tax accountants' work, the concept is a few years later elaborated upon by Bazerman, 1994, 1999, in his examination of U.S. patent applications. From his perspective in critical discourse analysis, Fairclough (1992) as well conceptualizes "genre system" in a comparable fashion, suggesting that "a society or a particular institution or domain within it has a particular configuration of genres in particular relationships to each other, constituting a system. And of course the configuration and system are open to change" (p. 126). Examples of genre systems are those systems of texts that distinguish from each other the professions of law, medicine, psychiatry, and so on as these professions are constituted in different cultural contexts, for example, trial law in the United States compared with trial law in India. To give an even more specific example, Latour and Woolgar's ethnography, *Laboratory Life* (1986), characterized knowledge production in a molecular biology lab in terms of the texts it produced. The authors conceived these texts as networks of interrelated genres which functioned to link actors, laboratories, experimental animals, and equipment in the service of accumulating a field's stock of knowledge, or "credit" (capital).[3]

The concepts of intertextuality and genre system lead me to a summative theoretical formulation: *The professions are organized by genre systems and their work is carried out through genre systems.*

I now turn from the rather abstract, theoretical realm to the very practical and concrete business of conducting a textual analysis. Before I do, however, I need to make one important point: Research does not take place in a vacuum! The choices we make regarding research methods—our research questions and the design of the study (case-study, participant-observation, nonparticipant observation, etc.)—and the analytical tools we use (discourse analysis, rhetorical analysis) are all shaped and guided by our theoretical framework. There is an intimate relationship between such a methodological decision as using a particular coding scheme for analyzing data and the research questions that direct our inquiry. In turn, those research questions (which themselves reflect decisions) help shape the research design, are guided by our theoretical orientation.

That being said, the best place to begin qualitative inquiry is with the research questions that will drive the researcher's investigation and help her or him to determine the unit of analysis—in the broadest sense, the conceptual entity that is the focus of the investigation. A unit of analysis can be as narrow as the life history of an individual, or as capacious as an organization, including its objectives, rules, genres, artifacts, and constitutive activities unfolding over time (see Engeström, 1993; Russell, 1997).

DEVELOPING THE RESEARCH QUESTIONS

What the researcher collects as data and the manner in which he or she collects the data will depend on the research questions with which the researcher starts the project. Furthermore, research questions are often related to issues and concerns appearing in the published literature (in our discipline or area of inquiry), and this material can help the researcher to better understand issues of concern in the field. On the other hand, it can help to have formulated one's own a list of questions with which to begin. The questions below are very general, and they assume that the researcher has selected a research site and has gained access to that setting.

In that spirit, here are some questions for initiating inquiry:

- How are texts (oral and written) carrying out the work of this setting?
- What are the kinds of texts (genres) that are being used in this setting?
- What kinds of purposes do they accomplish?
- What are the interrelationships between oral, written, and electronic genres?
- What are the ways in which oral, written, and electronic genres interact with each other to carry out projects (work) within the setting?
- How does one text reformulate or recontextualize material in other (oral, written, or electronic) texts?
- What are the notable grammatical, syntactical, or graphical features of the texts?
- How does this text (these texts) function to influence audience?
- What type of social action does the text, or texts, carry out, in what kind of situation, and in what recognizable form?
- How does this text (these texts) fit into a larger system of organizational practices?

The importance of research questions is that they give the researcher an orientation to choosing the texts that he or she wants to analyze and perhaps, as well, suggests a method of analysis. In the next segment of this chapter, I focus more closely on the very important issue of the scope of the project: how narrow or inclusive the researcher's choice of texts should be.

CHOOSING TEXTS TO ANALYZE

Determining the Scope of the Project

The scope of a research project and the texts the researcher decides to analyze inevitably depend on a number of factors. MacNealy (1999) makes a strong case for thinking early on about the scope of the project, suggesting that

> Sometimes a researcher will want to analyze certain texts as part of a case study or ethnographic study of some community.... Other times a researcher may devote his or her entire research effort to the analysis of certain texts as a way of answering a particular question.... The scope of the project often determines how many pieces of discourse a researcher will examine and the method of examination. When a large body of possible texts for analysis exists, a researcher will want to use random sampling techniques to select the portions for analysis. (p. 128)

To cite just one example of a carefully chosen data set based on the scope of the project, applied linguist Dwight Atkinson (1999), in his historical study of the changes in the scientific research article as seen in essays in *Philosophical Transactions of the Royal Society* (PTRS) of London, 1675–1975, had a gigantic corpus of texts written over a three-hundred-year period to examine, and thus had to initially make some important choices regarding the scope of his project. Atkinson began with a set of 481 texts selected from increments of fifty years over the total period of examination: 1675, 1725, 1775, 1825, 1875, and 1925. He performed two kinds of analysis, rhetorical analysis and multi-dimensional analysis (or MD analysis, see Biber, 1988), only the first of which will concern us here. To conduct a rhetorical analysis of the "original articles" from the volumes under study (all of which had been photocopied), Atkinson began with the 1675 volume and then read through each article in each volume, noting all potentially relevant textual features, and writing brief commentaries on each article. On finishing an analysis of each volume's original articles, he proceeded to write a "summary characterization" (a brief description suggesting key observations) of these articles in terms of their rhetorical and textual features. On completing this procedure for all seven *PTRS* volumes under analysis, he then compared the summary characterizations of each volume's material, identifying the most prominent recurring features and developmental trends. As a final step, he checked his overall impressions against his commentaries on the individual articles in

each volume, and, where necessary, the actual articles themselves
(p. 60).

Atkinson's use of systematic procedures and his choice of texts were
guided by several very broad questions that focused on what he perceived
to be rhetorical issues growing out of previous investigations of scientific writing. These questions, in turn, shaped the analytic procedures
he used:

1. What different text types or genres of scientific research writing are iden-
    tifiable within each sampling period? What are the formal and informal
    semantic characteristics of these genres?
2. To what degree do these genre types appear to be standardized, or *con-
    ventionalized* (D. Atkinson, 1991) within each period?
3. What is the relationship of theory to data in each of the articles exam-
    ined? How stable does the relationship appear to be within and across
    periods?
4. What are the principles of "design coherence" (Phelps, 1985), or "top
    level" discourse structure (Horowitz, 1987; Meyer, 1985) within and
    across articles?
5. What aspects of the scientific discourse community (Swales, 1990) ap-
    pear to be indexed in texts across periods? That is, what can the rheto-
    ric of the articles themselves tell us about the social relations among
    their authors and other researchers?
6. Are there formal aspects of articles which appear to be shaped by the
    cultural "thought styles" (Fleck, 1979) or "conventions for construing
    reality" (Bizzell, 1982) that constitute the discourse community's base
    links between standardized rhetorical form(s) and scientific epistemol-
    ogy or epistemologies? (Atkinson, 1999, p. 61)

Atkinson's questions drove his selection of methods for his rhetorical
analysis; his choice of specific procedures enabled him to operationalize his
questions as he examined a large body of texts. However, had he not first
limited the scope of his project, the sheer number of texts to be examined
would have made his project very unwieldy.

Although there are a number of studies in scientific and technical communication research using large corpora (Bazerman, 1988; Berkenkotter
and Huckin, 1995, Gunnarsson, 1997a; Valle, 1999), the advice I give to
students beginning textual analysis projects is that it's generally better to
start small. In workplace or in disciplinary contexts, the segments of text
the researcher chooses to analyze are likely to be limited to a particular
set of data such as memo correspondence, multiple-authored proposals or
promotional literature and revisions, requests for proposals (RFP), and so
on.

Choosing the Most Appropriate Method for Conducting a Textual Analysis

Many of my students over the years have asked about the "right method" for conducting textual analysis. I inevitably respond that there is no single "right method." Each researcher has to decide what techniques to use. These decisions are based on specific disciplinary training, research questions, the theoretical framework guiding those questions, and the scope of the study. In fact, in order to limit the scope of this essay, I chose out of a larger array the three areas of textual analysis with which I am the most familiar: rhetorical criticism/theory, discourse analysis, and genre analysis, the latter often combining a rhetorical/contextual orientation with the fine-grained, discourse-based textual analysis. Rhetorical researchers have used such concepts as *kairos*, or appropriate timing (Miller, 1992); Toulmin argument (a structure of argument-constituted claims based on grounds and informed by warrants); rhetorical stases of fact, definition, and value; exigency (a situation or set of conditions requiring immediate action); and *ethos*, *pathos*, and *logos*. Other researchers have used non-rhetorical concepts such as speech act theory (Austin, 1962; Searle, 1969; see, for example, Bazerman, 1994, 1999; Berkenkotter & Huckin, 1995; Gross, 1990, 1996) or genre theory and analysis (Atkinson, 1999; Bazerman, 1988; Berkenkotter & Huckin, 1995; Dudley-Evans, 1994; Freedman & Smart, 1997; Gunnarsson, 1997a; Swales, 1990) to form the basis of the categories they developed to analyze their data. As one can see, there are several rich resources for creating coding categories, which are the basis of the kind of textual analysis that we turn to next.

A Systematic Approach to Analyzing Texts

Although one can find many different approaches developed in the areas of rhetorical criticism, genre analysis, and discourse analysis, what these methods have in common is categorization, that is, researchers develop a set of coding categories for systematically conducting their analyses.[4] For example, when Tom Huckin and I analyzed the peer review correspondence of a biologist who was revising a paper for a professional journal in her field (Berkenkotter & Huckin, 1995), we first developed coding categories based on Searle's (1969, 1979) taxonomy of speech acts (see also Van Eemeren & Grootendorst, 1983). We read each of the letters in the exchanges between the biologist, the journal editor, and two peer reviewers first to get a sense of the major issues that were raised by the participants. Then, using our initial coding categories, we coded the individual letters (by the sentence) to determine which of the various types of speech act in Searle's taxonomy were used by the participants and toward what rhetorical end. In this instance the coding categories provided by Searle's taxonomy of speech acts provided valuable information about the profoundly rhetorical nature of peer review in the set of texts Huckin and I examined. We could not, however, generalize beyond the texts we examined other than to say that certain utterances in the letters of each correspondent had a performative function of a particular type according to Searle's taxonomy.

Other rhetorical researchers (Gross, 1990, 1996, 1996; Bazerman, 1999) have used a speech act taxonomy as an analytical tool in examining scientific peer review correspondence (Gross) and patent applications and adjudications for incandescent light technology (Bazerman). Bazerman's and Gross's findings can be compared with (see Katz on methodological triangulation, this volume) Huckin's and my own, thus either corroborating (or contradicting) our respective observations regarding the performative functions of texts within the genre systems of peer review and patent applications.

ANALYZING TEXTUAL DATA: AN ILLUSTRATIVE CASE

To further illustrate the importance of analytical tools such as coding schemes and the unit of analysis that develops out of the researcher's questions, I next describe a recent study I conducted with a clinical psychologist, Doris Ravotas. We were particularly concerned with the discursive strategies that several therapists in the study used to represent their clients in the documents they wrote after an initial meeting with the client. This text, called "Psychosocial Assessment," is written to fill several institutional purposes.[5] Psychosocial Assessments are often the first text in an institutional record of a client's history, that is, the case history; it is used for billing purposes and to help keep the therapist appraised of the client's progress while in treatment. It may also be used in court at some future time, or it may be passed on to other therapists whom the client sees at some future time, or the assessment may serve as the basis for a referral the therapist writes to a psychiatrist, should the client need medication as part of the treatment plan (only psychiatrists, who are MDs, can prescribe drugs).

Because Ravotas and I were not examining the oral interaction in the initial interview, our analysis in this study was confined to therapists' written texts. Our concern, therefore, was with *the only information available to readers of therapists' reports*, readers not privy to the oral interaction and who, therefore, had no basis for comparing what was actually said in session and the written report that follows. We began our investigation with the question, What is it about the lexicon, syntax, and grammatical constructions in the written records that make it possible for readers from different professional communities (other therapists, psychiatrists, physicians, insurance company reviewers) to engage in the inferring activity that they do? (This question was closely linked to our theoretical framework, as described earlier in this chapter.)[6]

To answer this question, we adapted Harvey Sacks's (1972, 1995) concepts of *membership categorization devices* (MCDs) and *category-bound activities* (CBAs) to our examination of therapists' notes and reports.[7] Sacks sought to characterize what he called "some very central machinery of social organization" (1995, p. 40) which he observed occurring in social interactions between people getting to know each other by asking questions that enabled them to draw on stores of inferences, for example, Where are you from? and What do you do? From these observations he speculated that people routinely describe individuals vis-à-vis "families," or category sets such as race, gender, age, class, occupational group, mental status, and so on. These category sets he called "membership categorization devices," suggesting that our use of such devices activates implicit common, cultural norms shared with others in the same culture or community of practice.

Sacks developed a number of "hearers rules" (conventions and/or attitudes tacitly agreed upon by members of a discourse community) to flesh out his concept of membership categorization devices. Two of these are relevant to my discussion:

- *The economy rule:* If a speaker/writer uses any single category from any membership categorization device to describe some population of persons, for example, use of the term "daughter" from the collection "family," or "Borderline Personality" from the collection "Personality Disorders" (as appearing in the American Psychiatric Association's *Diagnostic and Statistical Manual of Mental Disorders*, 4th ed. [DSM-IV]), they can be recognized to be doing *adequate reference* to a person (1972, p. 333). Other features or characteristics of that particular category, "Borderline Personality," are implied by therapists, who use such descriptions as "Mary is *manipulative* in the group session."

- *Category-bound activities:* Certain activities are, through social typification, attributed to or bound to certain categories: "*babies cry,*" "*anorexics starve themselves,*" "schizophrenics *hallucinate,*" "borderlines *manipulate* other people." Many stereotypes are thus predicated on speakers' or writers' references to category-bound activities and the inferences that may be made from such references.

The same client might be described by a therapist-writer in any one of the following ways: (1) "a survivor of sexual abuse"; (2) "a local school teacher and mother of five"; (3) "an obese woman with bulimia"; or (4) "a twenty-four-year-old Native American woman with a depressed affect and a somewhat unkempt appearance." Each description carries a different set of associations and functions to frame the subject within a particular category set. In other words, each of the above categories is "heard" (or read) by listeners or readers as deriving from some *collection of categories*. In the example ,"local school teacher and mother of five," the category, "mother," belongs to the larger MCD, *family*; "teacher" belongs to the MCD, *occupation*.

Sacks (1972) suggested that the only way to bypass MCDs, CBAs, or other category-bound descriptors is to explicitly contradict the activity or quality that is associated with the category by implication. For example, in the sentence, "My aunt is ninety-two years old, *but she ran in a marathon last year*," the clause " ... *but she ran in a marathon last year*" is intended to contradict the category-bound activity of being sedentary. Without this disclaimer, the sedentary nature of a ninety-two-year-old would be inferred by readers or listeners, thus backgrounding (or eliding) other major aspects of this particular woman's life.

This process of inferring can be observed in therapists' use of diagnostic nomenclature. When a therapist speaks or writes, "The client is a Borderline," other therapists "hear" that this person is manipulative, clingy, fears being abandoned, has self-destructive tendencies, and is unable to maintain intimate relationships. Thus the term Borderline functions as an *adequate reference* that supplies the hearer of the professional community with a clinical picture of the client which serves to objectify and, I would argue, *pathologize* the person. In fact, the reification of diagnostic categories is so ubiquitous that even with an explicit contradiction of the above descriptors (e.g., "She has a supportive relationship with her husband"), many therapists would be skeptical (e.g., "Her marriage only *appears* to be supportive").

Although MCD analysis has been used primarily in the analysis of oral genres (see Hester & Eglin, 1997, for a review of these studies), it has also been used in the analysis of written genre conventions, such as newspaper headlines (Hester & Eglin, 1997, pp. 35–46). We believe it to be useful as well for enhancing our understanding of microlevel representational activity in therapists' written reports, keeping in mind that what occurs at the microlevel is shaped by the genre in which it appears. Like Harré (1985), we found therapists' written reports of oral interactions to be filled with the lexical items and nominalized constructions of a formal professional register that Harré described as "file speak" (p. 178). An MCD analysis of these items and constructions revealed how the client's densely contextual "raw material" (as seen in the therapist's session notes of the initial interview) became recontextualized into the therapist's nominalized psychiatric categorizations in the Psychosocial Assessment. Often these nominalizations were cast in the terminology used in the *DSM-IV* to describe symptoms of various mental disorders.

Now to summarize: I've described at considerable length the approach to textual analysis that Ravotas and I took with psychotherapy texts to illustrate how important it is that the choice of the unit of analysis and the analytical tool(s) (MCD analysis in the above instance) follow from the research question or questions. In turn, our research questions were shaped by interview data gathered from several therapists who worked for a local community mental health clinic. Because one of us (Ravotas) had been a therapist at this clinic, we drew on her knowledge of the organizational context and the daily routines at the outpatient clinic in developing our interview questions. Only after we had interviewed these therapists whose description of their case history writing practices (session notes, initial assessments) formed the basis of the study could we determine what we needed to attend to most closely in investigating their written texts. Even then we first "eyeballed the data," reading through our informants' paperwork, noting the common grammatical and lexical features of the texts, as well as any significant departures in individual texts from those conventions that seemed to be normative.

CONCLUSION

I want to return briefly to the notion of organizational texts as documentary products (Hammersly and Atkinson, 1983), a theoretical construct I believe to be central to our understanding of the ways in which everyday texts accomplish so much of organizational work. Rather than thinking of individual texts or groups of texts or actors as the unit of analysis, a perspective that tended to dominate research on scientific and technical communication in the late 1980s and 1990s (see Bazerman & Paradis, 1991; Blyler & Thralls, 1993, as representative collections), researchers are now turning to theoretical frameworks—and concepts within those frameworks—which make it possible to reconceptualize the unit of analysis in terms of entire systems of texts/genres. In turn, the texts in a genre system, such as psychotherapists' case notes and written reports in the system of written records in a mental health clinic, can be seen to circulate within and across organizations. For example, in the study I have just described, a therapist's case notes and progress reports are initially written to be used by the therapist and within the clinic in which the therapist is practicing. But it is also the case that these notes and reports may be transferred to a court of law, if, for example, a client's case history is subpoenaed in an involuntary commitment hearing. In this latter respect, psychotherapy texts accomplish particular kinds of organizational and interorganizational work. Such a view suggests that we must closely examine our initial impressions of what such texts mean in the larger discursive contexts in which they at times perform multiple functions.

Documentary products, as Atkinson and Coffey (1997) suggest, "construct their own kind of reality. It is therefore important to approach them as *texts*. Texts are constructed according to conventions that are themselves a part of a documentary reality" (pp. 60–61). Unpacking these conventions (genres) in order to ask questions about the form and function of the texts, genres, and genre systems in institutional and organizational contexts is the province both of rhetorically trained researchers and discourse analysts trained in applied linguistics. It is my hope that the next generation of technical communication scholars/ researchers will become proficient in the methods and technical vocabulary of both disciplines.

NOTES

1. By "systematic observation" I mean techniques capable of being replicated and confirmed (or disconfirmed) by independent observers for purposes of triangulation (see Katz, this volume).

2. "Paperwork," as I am using the term, refers to both print and electronic texts.

3. In our discussion of the production of scientific knowledge (1995), Thomas Huckin and I used a flowchart to graphically represent the processes through which "lab knowledge," through the production and dissemination of texts, becomes a part of the genre systems linked to the activities of journal peer review and grant seeking.

4. Using coding categories doesn't necessarily guarantee objectivity; the selection of the categories is itself an interpretive act. However, researchers develop coding categories to reduce a morass of textual information to salient patterns or themes that can be tracked as well through interviews and other participant-observation techniques; this process differs from the researcher's doing an impressionistic reading of texts that is the basis of textual analysis in literary studies and some rhetorical studies.

5. These texts are alternately called "Initial Assessment Progress Notes," "Screening Summaries," or some type of discipline-bound assessment ("Psychological Assessment," "Psychiatric Assessment," or "Social Work Assessment").

6. For a detailed discussion with examples of how we used these coding categories, see Berkenkotter and Ravotas, 1997.

7. See Ravotas and Berkenkotter, 1998, for a description of a coding scheme used to track therapists' uses of reported speech (speech representation of the client) in their session notes and Initial Assessment texts. For a detailed description of coding and transcription activities in discourse research, see, for example, Lampert and Erving-Tripp, 1993. A caveat is necessary here: Developing coding categories is best accomplished under the supervision of an experienced instructor who has background and training in using coding schemes in qualitative studies. The base discipline of this faculty member is not as important as is his or her ability to guide novice researchers through the vicissitudes of analyzing, coding, and transcribing written, oral, or electronic data.

REFERENCES

Atkinson, D. (1991). Discourse analysis and written discourse conventions. *Annual Review of Applied Linguistics*, *11*, 57–76.

Atkinson, D. (1999). Scientific discourse in sociohistorical context: *The Philosophical Transactions of the Royal Society of London*, 1675–1975.Mahwah, NJ: Lawrence Erlbaum.

Atkinson, P., & Coffey, A. (1997). Analyzing documentary realities. In D. Silverman (Ed.), *Qualitative research: Theory, method, and practice* (pp. 45–62). London: Sage.

Austin, J.L. (1962). *How to do things with words*. Cambridge, MA: Harvard University Press.

Bazerman, C. (1988). *Shaping written knowledge: The genre and activity of the experimental article in science*. Madison: University of Wisconsin Press.

Bazerman, C. (1993). Intertextual self-fashioning: Gould and Lewontin's representations of the literature. In J. Selzer (Ed.), *Understanding scientific prose* (pp. 20–41). Madison: University of Wisconsin Press.

Bazerman, C. (1994). Systems of genres and the enactment of social intentions. In A. Freedman & P. Medway (Eds.), *Genre and the new rhetoric* (pp. 79–104). London: Taylor & Francis.

Bazerman, C., & Paradis, J. (Eds.). (1991). *Textual dynamics of the professions: Historical and contemporary studies of writing in professional communities*. Madison: University of Wisconsin Press.

Bazerman, C. (1999). *The languages of Edison's light*.

Berkenkotter, C. (2001). Genre systems at work: DSM-IV and rhetorical recontextualization in psychotherapy paperwork. *Written Communication*, *18* (3), 326–349.

Berkenkotter, C., & Huckin, T. (1995). *Genre knowledge in disciplinary communication: Cognition/culture/power*. Hillsdale, NJ: Lawrence Erlbaum Associates.

Berkenkotter, C., Huckin, T., & Ackerman, J. (1988). Conventions, conversations, and the writer: Case study of a student in a rhetoric Ph.D. program. *Research in the Teaching of English*, *22*, 9–44.

Berkenkotter, C., & Ravotas, D. (1997). Genre as tool in the transmission of practice over time and across professional boundaries. *Mind, Culture, and Activity*, *4*, 256–274.

Biber, D. (1988). *Variation across speaking and writing*. New York: Cambridge University Press.

Bizzell, P. (1982). Cognition, convention and certainty: What we need to know about writing. *Pre/Text*, *3*, 211–245.

Bloomfield, B.P., & Vurdabakis, T. (1994). Re-presenting technology: IT consultancy reports as textual reality constructions. *Sociology, 28*, 455–78.

Blyler, N.R., & Thralls, C. (Eds.) (1993). *Professional communication: The social perspective.* Newbury Park, CA: Sage.

Campbell, D.T., & Stanley, J.C. (1966). *Experimental and quasi-experimental designs for research.* Boston, MA: Houghton Mifflin.

Devitt, A.J. (1991). Intertextuality in tax accounting: Generic, referential, and functional. In C. Bazerman and J. Paradis (Eds.), *Textual dynamics of the professions: Historical and contemporary studies of writing in professional communities* (pp. 336–357). Madison: University of Wisconsin Press.

Dudley-Evans, T. (1994). Genre analysis: An approach to text analysis for ESP. In M. Coulthard (Ed.), *Advances in written text analysis* (pp. 219–228). London: Routledge.

Engeström, Y. (1993). Developmental studies of work as the test bench of activity theory: The case of a primary care medical practice. In S. Chaiklin & J. Lave (Eds.), *Understanding practice: Perspectives on activity and context* (pp. 64–103). Cambridge: Cambridge University Press.

Engeström, Y. (1999). Making expansive decisions: An activity-theoretical study of practitioners building collaborative medical care for children. Paper presented at the Annual Meeting of the Society for Social Studies of Science, San Diego, CA.

Fairclough, N. (1992). *Discourse and social change.* London: Polity Press.

Fleck, L (1979). *Genesis and development of a scientific fact.* Chicago: University of Chicago Press.

Freedman, A., & Smart, G. (1997). Navigating the current of economic policy: Written genres and the distribution of cognitive work at a financial institution. *Mind, Culture, and Activity, 4*, 237–255.

Gross, A. (1990, 1996 2nd ed.). *The rhetoric of science.* Cambridge, MA: Harvard University Press.

Gunnarsson, B.L.(1997a). On the sociohistorical construction of scientific discourse. In B.L. Gunnarsson, P. Linell, & B. Nordberg (Eds.), *The construction of professional discourse* (pp. 99–126). London: Longman.

Gunnarsson, B.L. (1997b). The writing process from a sociolinguistic viewpoint. *Written Communication, 7*, 139–188.

Gunnarsson, B.L, Linell, P., & Nordberg, B. (1997). Introduction. In Gunnarsson et al., *The construction of professional discourse* (pp. 1–12). London; Longman.

Hammersley, M., & Atkinson, P. (1983). *Ethnography: Principles in Practice.* London: Tavistock.

Harré, R. (1985). Situational rhetoric and self-presentation. In J.P. Forgas (Ed.), *Language and social situations* (pp.175–186). New York: Springer-Verlag.

Hester, S., & Eglin, P. (Eds.), (1997). *Culture in action: Studies in membership categorization analysis.* Lanham, MD: University Press of America.

Horowitz, R. (1987). Rhetorical structure in discourse processing. In R. Horowitz & S.J. Samuels (Eds), *Comprehending oral and spoken language* (pp. 117–160). San Diego: Academic Press.

Huckin, T. (1992). Analyzing talk about writing. In Kirsch, G & Sullivan, P.A. (Eds.), *Methods and methodology in composition research.* Carbondale: Southern Illinois University Press.

Jönsson, L., & Linell, P. (1991). Story generations: From dialogical interviews to written reports in police interrogations. *Text, 11*, 419–440.

Lampert, M.D. & Erwin-Tripp, S.M. (1993). Structured coding for the study of language and social interaction. In J.A. Edwards and M.D. Lampert (Eds.), *Talking data: Transcription and coding in discourse research* (pp. 169–206). Hillsdale, NJ: Lawrence Erlbaum Associates.

Latour, B., & Woolgar, S. (1986). *Laboratory life: The construction of scientific facts*. Princeton, NJ: Princeton University Press.

Linell, P. (1998). Discourse across boundaries. On recontextualizations and the blending of voices in professional discourse. *Text, 18–2*, 143–157.

MacNealy, M.S. (1999). *Strategies for empirical research in writing*. Boston, MA: Allyn & Bacon.

Miller, C.R. (1984). Genre as social action. *Quarterly Journal of Speech, 70*, 151–167.

Miller, C.R. (1992). *Kairos* in the rhetoric of science. In S. Witte, N. Nakadake, and R. Cherry (Eds.), *A rhetoric of doing: Essays in honor of James L. Kinneavy* (pp. 310–372). Carbondale: Southern Illinois University Press.

Meyer, B.J.F. (1985). Prose analysis: Purposes, procedures and problems. In B.K. Britton & J.B. Black (Eds.), *Understanding expository text: A theoretical and practical handbook for analyzing explanatory text* (pp. 11–64). Hillsdale, NJ: Lawrence Erlbaum Associates.

Phelps, L. (1985). *Composition as a human science*. New York: Oxford University Press.

Ravotas, D., & Berkenkotter, C. (1998). Voices in the text: The uses of reported speech in a psychotherapist's Notes and Initial Assessments. *Text, 18–2*, 211–39.

Russell, D. (1997). Rethinking genre in school and society: An activity theory analysis. *Written Communication, 14*, 504–554.

Sacks, H. (1972). On the analyzability of stories by children. In J.J. Gumperz & D. Hymes (Eds.), *Directions in sociolinguistics: The ethnography of communication* (pp. 325–345). Oxford: Blackwell.

Sacks, H. (1995). *Lectures on conversation* (G. Jefferson, Ed.). Oxford: Blackwell.

Sarangi, S., & Slembrouck, S. (1996). *Language, bureaucracy, and social control*. London: Addison Wesley Longman Limited.

Searle, J.R. (1969). *Speech acts: An essay in the philosophy of language*. Cambridge: Cambridge University Press.

Searle, J.R. (1979). *Expression and meaning: Studies in the theory of speech acts*. Cambridge: Cambridge University Press.

Selzer, J. (Ed.). (1993). *Understanding scientific prose*. Madison: University of Wisconsin Press.

Swales, J. (1990). *Genre analysis: English in academic and research settings*. Cambridge: Cambridge University Press.

Valle, E. (1999). *A collective intelligence: The life sciences in the Royal Society as a scientific discourse community*. Unpublished doctoral dissertation, University of Turku.

Van Eemeren, F.H., & Grootendorst, R. (1983). *Speech acts in argumentative discussions*. Dordrecht, Netherlands: Foris.

Yates, J.A. (1989). *Control through communication: The rise of system in American management*. Baltimore: The Johns Hopkins University Press.

Yates, J.A., Orlikowski, W.J., & Renneker, J. (1997). Collaborative genres for collaboration: Genre systems in digital media. In Proceedings of the Thirtieth Annual Hawaiian International Conference on System Sciences. Washington, DC: IEEE Computer Society Press.

CHAPTER 4

Historical Methods for Technical Communication

Teresa Kynell and Bruce Seely[1]

Technical communicators are likely to find that historical methods have great utility, for historians and technical communicators have more in common than might initially meet the eye. First, and perhaps most important, both disciplines consider clear writing as their most essential concern. Both also recognize writing as a translation exercise in which they must make ideas understandable to audiences of nonexperts. Technical communicators may do this more often and much more explicitly, but many historians also write for general and lay audiences and for colleagues working in distant subfields. Finally, technical communicators are quite likely to encounter projects where they will be as interested as historians in gathering information about past or even current events. To be sure, the goals of technical communicators and historians are not the same; at the most obvious level, historical writers are concerned with the past, whereas technical writers usually seek to explain contemporary events. Even so, historical methods and information-gathering approaches have clear utility for technical communicators (Tebeaux, 1998, 125–52; Adams, 1993).

It will be useful to consider historical work as having two dimensions. As historians attempt to find out what happened in the past, they gather information using a variety of sources and research strategies. Often they feel as though they are detectives or puzzle solvers, but most historians enjoy the challenge of seeking material, from which they can build a picture of the past. The goal is an accurate account, but inevitably there are holes in the historical record. Moreover, the meaning of incomplete information may not be obvious. These situations separate historians from mere reporters of past events, and mark the second stage of historical work. Imperfect knowledge requires analysis and interpretation of just what historians have learned. This combination of chasing information and making sense of it in a consistent, accurate account makes doing history fun and exciting for its practitioners.

Technical writers face rather different tasks and challenges. Only rarely will they need to "do" history in the same way as professional historians. But it is highly likely that technical communicators will undertake projects that involve learning something about past events. Moreover, the information-gathering approaches of historians are generally applicable to many situations, so we devote substantial attention to where technical writers can turn for information and sources. It is the second aspect of historical work, however—making sense of the past—that poses the most challenging methodological issues for those undertaking historical work. So our approach in what follows will be to first examine the basic assumptions that historians bring to unraveling the past, before discussing some historical information-gathering approaches and historical sources that might prove useful to technical communicators. We conclude with a case study that demonstrates the use of these methods—a history of technical communication itself.

THE HISTORIAN'S METHODS:
INTERPRETATION OF THE PAST

In a senior undergraduate seminar in the mid-1970s, one of the authors remembers discussing a story—perhaps apocryphal—about Leo Tolstoy, the novelist whose work rested on Russian history. The story goes that the novelist awoke in anguish from a bad dream, explaining to his wife that he had forgotten to include three horsemen in one of the cavalry charges in *War and Peace!* Tolstoy's agitation stemmed from his belief that historical writing required knowing everything that had happened. Professional historians of a century ago echoed this claim, for they envisioned history as a "scientific" discipline comparable in its goals to economics or physics. Their intent was to let the facts speak; they aspired to balance and evenhandedness; they sought truth. Their outlook assumed that history was an "objective" enterprise and that the patterns of history "are 'found,' not 'made'" (Novick, 1988, p. 26). Most practicing historians today realize that they can never "know" everything that happened, nor are they sure they can find "the truth." Given the differing perspectives of, say, slaves *and* Virginia planters, absolute truth can be elusive. This tendency has been reinforced by recent social theories, whereas ideas from the sociology of knowledge have eroded expectations of finding universal patterns in the past or elsewhere. Historians today still aspire to Tolstoy's goals, and have not forsaken a concern for accuracy and detail, but they acknowledge that the same events look very different to slaves and planters, men and women, or immigrant laborers and capitalists. As a colleague explains to introductory American history classes, there has not been a single "American experience."[2]

The basic problem is that the facts cannot speak for themselves. Therefore history is not a simple matter of assembling information to show exactly what happened in the past. In fact, far too many high school students never experience what history is really about, as they struggle to digest a seemingly endless list of names, events, dates, and personages. History comes alive when we recognize that it is really about attempting to understand those people, events, and places as actors in a process of change over time. And most practicing historians will tell you that seeing history as a process of change over time requires them to interpret what happened in the past. By this, they mean they try to make sense of the information they have gathered by offering as coherent account of the events they are examining as they can.

Methods supporting this way of doing history are of potential utility to technical communicators who need to gain an understanding of events past or present. They, too, will discover the difficulty of determining with absolute certainty what happened in a particular situation. So how to start? First, one must learn to ask questions of the sources of information. To do this, researchers must acquire an understanding of the surface content of documents being studied for their historical information. Then one must explore the deeper context of those events and the individuals involved, attempting to understand the social setting and the intellectual world in which they were situated. In addition, historians may have to ask what the documents might have said but did not. Analysis, not simple narratives of events, thus becomes the main goal of a historical exercise. But it should be instantly apparent that this process of analyzing the past, and the sources into that past, rests on the questions one asks.

Indeed, this is the most important step in any effort to gather historical information. Documents only come alive when we bring informed questions to them. But how does one pick the questions to ask? Remember that the questions *not* asked can be as important as those that are. Care is required, for we might ask questions that never occurred to the original participants. The 20/20 hindsight available to a historian who knows how things turned out can certainly affect how we view a historical episode. An event that was completely trivial at the time can be magnified into crucial importance by the different lens we turn on a situation from the future. So the process of historical interpretation must proceed with care.

Most historians approach the past with questions that seem important from our own time. There is a real danger here of reading the present into the past, of attributing to actors in the past ways of thinking that simply did not exist in their time. But this tendency is almost unavoidable—this link between the past and the present is a vital element in why people are interested in history. Done well and with care, this interpretive approach begins with a critical eye and not as simply an attempt to find the origin of current views and ideas. The goal is not to make the past tell the story you want it to tell. For many historians, the influence of the present is apparent in guiding the topics they choose to study, as historians gravitate to past events that resonate with us now. But historical writers balance this concern from the present by first seeking to understand the past on its own terms. What motivated those people? What were their main concerns? This balancing act is the essence of interpretation. But it almost certainly means that no universally correct understanding of the past can be achieved, for rival interpretations can exist.

The difficulties of interpretation were made visible to nonhistorians in 1995 by the Smithsonian Institution's Air and Space Museum's effort to display the aircraft that dropped the first atomic bomb on Japan. The furor unfolded around the exhibit script, with controversy centering on the differing interpretations that various groups brought to the plane and its history. Different actors understood the significance of this artifact quite differently. Veterans groups and some in Congress were most interested in telling a story of brave airmen, soldiers, and sailors who ended a war and saved lives. The museum curators wished to focus on the long-term impact of the weapon dropped by that plane, including its immediate effect on the people of Hiroshima. The highly visible debate that followed opened to view another interpretative question: Did the American government need to drop the bomb at all? To many veterans and others, the question was simply ridiculous. Everyone knew that the Japanese were not going to surrender and an invasion would have been extremely costly in Japanese and American lives. The bomb was the only chance to end the war quickly. But historians had explored this issue at length, and knew many factors shaped President Truman's decision, including being new in office and operating under the shadow of Franklin Roosevelt, the existence of weapons that had cost more than $2.2 billion to develop, the Japanese sneak attack that opened the war and the merciless conduct by both sides, and fear of the Russians in a postwar world. The desire of some nuclear scientists to demonstrate the bomb before using it was also a factor, although the navy believed it could starve Japan into submission with a blockade. Finally, there is evidence that the Japanese government was moving toward surrender when the bombs were dropped in August 1945. In other words, different interpretations of the past explained much of the controversy about the Enola Gay exhibit.[3] In part this happened because we can never know what the primary actors really thought. Historians believe that the more thorough the research, the more confident one can be that an account mirrors reality, but universal certitude is just not possible.

How might knowledge of interpretation affect the work of technical communicators? Most are unlikely to immerse themselves deeply in historical exercises, but it is useful to remember that even simple historical queries can generate surprisingly complex and even multiple interpretations. Take, for example, the question: When was the National System of Interstate and Defense Highways created? Reference books explain that President Eisenhower officially created this road network in 1956. But one can also find a more complex story, for the first funds for an interstate system were provided in 1952, for a road system identified on official maps by 1947. In fact, legislation passed in 1944 created a system of express interregional highways, based on a report from a presidential committee formed in 1941 to consider a report issued in 1939. So the simple answer of 1956 is not wrong, but the detailed interpretive answer is the massive federal road program that began in 1956 was the product of much preliminary activity.

This example indicates how the question asked can influence the answer. In many fields, theory helps sort out the key questions to ask: What about in history? It may be surprising to learn that many historians do not approach this task with a formal, detailed, or well-worked-out set of theories. Political scientists, other social scientists, and even some humanists see a primary goal of their work to be correcting and adjusting theories so they better describe reality. Few historians explicitly adopt this approach. Rather, if they address theory explicitly, usually it will be at the end of the work. This order is important, for it suggests that the story is the key, and that theory must conform to the historical account and the author's analysis. Similarly, it is unusual to identify historians by their theoretical stance, in the way that sociologists might be known as Parsonian or Weberian, or economists as members of the Chicago School. A notable exception involves historians who build their work on the theoretical base of Karl Marx. But such "grand theory" has not typically occupied center stage. The limited importance of formal theoretical discussions does not mean that theory is unimportant to historical researchers. Indeed, theories have found wide acceptance among historians. American historians are introduced to Frederick Jackson Turner's theory that American society, including its democratic institutions, was influenced much more by the existence of a frontier unoccupied by European settlers than by the ideas that those Europeans brought with them. More recently, feminist theory and theoretical approaches from the sociology of knowledge have gained significant influence. But as one observer noted, "historical narrative usually incorporates many theories rather than just one" (Davidson & Lytle, 1992, p. 71). And many of these might as easily be labeled frameworks, for many are not rigorously fully worked out. Often they take the form of analogies, as when historians of technology adopt the language of evolution to talk about technological innovation (Basalla, 1988). The concept of an industrial revolution is another form of midlevel theory that has become almost universally used by historians, although the term has recently come in for substantial debate by historians concerning its validity and utility (Mokyr, 1993).[4]

However historians approach theory, they cannot escape it. The authors of a book on historical methods observe, "historical theory encompasses the entire range of a historian's training, from competence in statistics to opinions on politics and philosophies of human nature. It is derived from formal education, from reading, even from informal discussions with academic colleagues and friends." Later they note, "without it, researchers cannot begin to select from among an infinite number of facts; they cannot separate the important from the incidental; they cannot focus on a manageable problem." Albert Einstein put the proposition succinctly. " 'It is the theory,' he concluded, 'which decides what we can observe' "(Davidson & Lytle, 1992, pp. 71–72, 92). It is also true that theories are "usually part of a historian's mental baggage before he or she is immersed in a particular topic. It encourages historians to ask certain questions, and not to ask certain others; it tends to single out particular areas of investigation as worthy of testing, and to dismiss other areas of inquiry as either irrelevant or uninteresting." In this way, theory is a "pervasive influence" in all historical work. But for all its pervasiveness, "many historians work with theory more intuitively than explicitly"(Davidson & Lytle, 1992, pp. 71–72). This point demarcates an important difference between history and most of the social sciences.

HISTORICAL RESEARCH: GATHERING INFORMATION

With these general points in mind, we can turn to a discussion of historical research methods that might prove useful to technical communicators. Our assumption is that technical communicators will find themselves in situations where knowing how to gather information about past events, people, and places will be important. History, however, is a multifaceted enterprise with many different approaches, not one.

To be truthful, historians tend not to be as concerned about methodology as some social sciences and humanities scholars. This situation may seem to parallel the seemingly casual attitude of many historians toward theory. But equally important is a basic pragmatism among many historians about the issue of methods—use the methods that will most help you obtain the kind of information you need. Put another way, few historians tackle a question simply because of the methods with which they are most familiar; rather they identify questions and a subject and then proceed to use the methods that fit. This attitude connects to another tendency in the way that historians perceive methodological issues. Historians, because they are concerned about almost anything one can imagine, often touch and intersect the work of scholars in other fields in the humanities and social sciences. Often they discover that methods used by scholars in those fields have utility for historical research. Notable examples of this approach in recent decades include attention to the approaches of economists beginning in the 1960s. An approach labeled *cliometrics* emerged, based upon detailed quantitative analysis of statistical data in the manner of econometricians.[5]

Many social historians were similarly eclectic in borrowing quantitative methods from sociology and the social sciences. Voter records and census data, analyzed using statistical tools, opened new dimensions for social history.[6] Other historians developed psychohistory using techniques and understandings from psychoanalysis and psychotherapy.[7] In other words, historians have never been shy about adopting methodological tools from other disciplines. In this, historians and technical communicators potentially have a great deal in common.

Technical communicators may not need to adopt these specialized historical methods for gathering information, although they may borrow the work of those who have. Communicators who need historical information are, however, likely to share with historians a very basic methodological concern: How does one gather information from historical documents? Only the critical study of historical materials allows one to piece together stories about the past. It seems so easy and straightforward, but in fact is a demanding task.

It may seem surprising that one must learn to use and read documents. At its most basic, reading documents critically requires careful attention to detail and concern for accuracy in both note taking and in recording citations about the sources. All writers know this, but it bears repeating. But beyond these surface matters, learning to read historical documents critically and ask questions of the sources is a basic skill.

Scholars in a great many fields, not simply historians, must master this technique. But many historians were started down this road early in their careers by professors and mentors, who turned graduate students loose in the archives. This approach reinforces the traditional sense the documents speak by themselves, but there is, in fact, no other way to do history. Gathering historical data usually requires working in archives or with published records.

Many historians have noted that such historical research is analogous to detective work. For example, those pursing the past very quickly learn the documentary record is never complete. There are always missing records or records that were never produced. To overcome the frustrating incompleteness of the historical record, one learns to cast a wide net and utilize a range of sources, as well as to read for inferences, hints, and clues. But one also learns quickly that not all members of society left records of equal thoroughness or volume. Scholars therefore make educated guesses and assumptions, occasionally acknowledging they simply cannot know what happened.

What kinds of records are we talking about? Historians have always placed priority on *primary sources*, which are contemporary information, such as original letters, diaries, memoranda, and corporate and government documents. Found in libraries and archives, such documents remain the foundation on which historical research is based. Using such documents can require special skills, such as the ability to read foreign languages or scripts no longer in use, or the ability to translate difficult-to-read handwriting. Historians are among the people most grateful for the introduction of typewriters and carbon paper!

Archival records are widely scattered on the landscape. Most exist in library repositories, which range in size from the massive holdings of the Library of Congress and the National Archives to small collections of personal papers in smaller libraries and state or local historical societies. The National Archives remains the primary location for government records, both in Washington, and in its regional centers; it also oversees the various presidential libraries. The World Wide Web again makes access to this material much easier (http://www.nara.gov). The difficulty of finding relevant archival records in other collections is eased by the National Union Catalog of Manuscript Collections, an important mechanism for identifying collections based on subjects. Begun in 1959, the catalog was updated at regular intervals through 1993, and is now accessible in a microfilm edition.

Technical communicators may find themselves with one important advantage over historians when it comes to working in corporate document repositories. Many companies maintain closed collections that historians would love to see, but cannot. In recent years, many business corporations have begun to establish their own archives with greater public access. A few, like the Dupont Corporation, have long given their records to libraries. Use of any archives, but especially corporate records, requires knowledge of the entity being studied. When fortune smiles, researchers will discover finding aids that provide an overview of the entity, basic background information, and an overview of the collection itself. Encountering uncatalogued records can be very discouraging, for sifting masses of material for a few nuggets of information is truly frustrating. Still, primary documents provide the soundest base upon which to build historical accounts.

Historical researchers approaching documentary sources must always remember to maintain a critical eye. The problem almost never involves outright fraud or forgery, although that can happen, as Seymour Hersh recently discovered. He found that letters supposedly connecting John Kennedy to Mafia activities in Cuba via Marilyn Monroe were forgeries.[8] Usually, problems are more subtle than that. One must always remember that the authors of documents were fallible individuals with incomplete knowledge of events and circumstances. The descriptions and accounts provided in their correspondence and other documents must always be checked and corroborated against other sources. Not infrequently, discrepancies will emerge in different sources that defy easy resolution, leaving the final call to the researcher's knowledge and judgment. Like lawyers, historians know only too well that even eyewitness accounts of a given event never agree. The preference of historical researchers for documents helps explain why history used to focus upon political and diplomatic events. These were the events best recorded in archival sources. But after the Second World War, a few historians began to suggest that documentary sources did not provide information about all parts of history. Left out of stories told from traditional documents were those individuals who could not produce written documents—in other words, most people for most of human history. The most obvious disparity in American history concerns slavery, which is recorded in some letters and diaries of slaveowners, and the records of slave markets, plantations, and other businesses. But very few manuscript records were produced by the slaves themselves, a fact that certainly biases many interpretations of slavery.

This situation highlights the most maddening problem of historical research—gaps in the records, either from missing documents or an incomplete series, or from the failure of contemporary observers to record events.

Many historians have wished for access to a time machine to see for themselves what was happening at a remote time and place! The only solution is to find alternate sources of information.

In recent decades, the array of possible sources has expanded well beyond traditional documents. Material culture represented an early field where researchers found useful nondocumentary information. Museums and museum curators developed techniques for reading artifacts, just as historians read documents.

Archaeologists face similar problems, and their interpretive efforts offer another guide to comprehending artifactual evidence. Materials, workmanship, and social context all can be inferred from such materials. Tool marks can tell many things about an object.

Blending documentary evidence with studies of objects often is the most helpful strategy. An important resource in this regard is trade catalogs and trade cards, which some libraries have collected explicitly and which others maintain in their vertical files of ephemera. Both contain a wealth of information, both visual and text, about the objects that constitute our material environment. Because technical communicators often deal with the physical world as well, attention to how historical scholars "read" objects might prove worthwhile (Lubar & Kingery, 1993).

A similar exercise in learning to read is required to incorporate photographs into the historical records. Obviously limited to more recent events, photos provide vital information about many events. As one observer commented, "from the moment in 1839 when the French pioneer Louis Jacques Daguerre announced his discovery of a process to fix images permanently on a copper plate, observers repeatedly remarked on the camera's capacity to record reality. More than anything else, the seeming objectivity of the new medium caught the popular imagination" (Davidson & Lytle, 1992, pp. 180–81). But rarely do images constitute an objective record of the past, so they, too, must be read with care. Researchers have to remember that cameras have not recorded everything. For example, they could not record motion at first because of long exposure intervals. Later, the cost of photos made photography accessible to the upper and middle classes. Most important, photographers control the composition of the image. Even "documentary" photographs must be examined carefully, for their makers brought a point of view and a goal to their work. Researchers must understand those purposes in order to properly interpret their images.[9]

Movies constitute a very special type of photographic image that can prove useful to historical researchers. They also can be a very problematic source. Certainly Hollywood's commercial films offer one way of understanding society at any given point in time. Even fictional films about historical events can open the time period to view. But there are difficulties as well. For example, James Fenimore Cooper's novel, *The Last of the Mohicans*, was made into successful, but very different, films by George Seitz in 1936 and Michael Mann in 1992. Seitz cast Randolph Scott in the lead, while Mann had Daniel Day-Lewis as Hawkeye and Russell Means of the American Indian Movement as Chingachgook.

Documentary films may hold more potential as tools for understanding the past, as Ken Burns has demonstrated with his very successful productions. His studio's long string of critically acclaimed productions has touched on topics as diverse as the Brooklyn Bridge, the Civil War, and Frank Lloyd Wright. The power of motion pictures becomes most evident when words, images (including contemporary film footage), and people come together with a good subject. Burns makes special efforts to work with historians, but even at their best, documentary films rarely convey the complexity underlying most historical narratives. Burns has acknowledged this problem by publishing well-illustrated historical texts alongside almost all of his large film projects.[10]

An increasingly important source of information for historians and technical communicators alike is the oral interview. The value of these sources is quite clear, but they, too, must be used properly. For example, some of the most important evidence of the lives of slaves was recorded in interviews during the New Deal. These came as the last survivors of the slave era were passing on. Several university archives pursue oral histories specifically to retain the memories of key principals in large and important projects and events. Events such as the Manhattan Project have been the focus of more than one oral history effort, but many others have been pursued as well.

But if interviews are valuable, they also pose very difficult challenges for users. An earlier comment about discrepancies in eyewitness accounts applies here. Additionally, the frailties of human memory become apparent, especially when subjects describe events that occurred years before. Interviewers also must remember that subjects inadvertently filter their recollections through various interpretive lenses, which might include desires to enhance—or diminish—their own roles in events, or an attempt to protect—or blame—other actors for the events or their aftermath. Oral histories must always be checked carefully against other sources of information, and nearly always force researchers to use one individual's account of the past with great care. For all that, the effect is often well worth the effort, for the words of firsthand participants reaching across the years have a very special power.[11]

All these sources of historical information, traditional and otherwise, constitute the primary sources researchers have preferred to utilize. But for many technical communicators who seek to utilize history, *secondary sources* may prove more important. Secondary works are the product of other writers and historians in the form of scholarly articles, books, and monographs, and let's face it—it's often easier to learn what one needs from the expert on a subject. Electronic card catalogs greatly ease the difficulty of finding titles that may prove useful, although books remain easier to identify than journal articles. And as the number of databases for serial publications expands, it will be some time before these extend to the years before 1980. A few printed indexes help make serial literature more accessible, but only a few journals or mass circulation serials—historical or otherwise—are completely indexed.

With that said, important historical sources for technical communicators are professional and trade journals. Matching the general increase in published literature over the past 150 years, the number of serial titles catering to highly specialized audiences in individual industries has expanded enormously. Many titles instantly identify their subject; Ice Cream Age is a particular favorite. Because many of these publications appeared weekly, they had a voracious appetite for information, and editors used anything they could get in print. Speeches by leading figures in the industry were often run in their entirety or abstracted. Most issues contained editorials that offered snapshots of the thinking of the field's leading opinion shapers, as well as coverage of legislative developments and the activities of key players. Trade journals thus provide information about almost any technical development since the end of the nineteenth century. They are a "primary source" in their own right, and constitute a vital source of information.

In sum, then, technical writers seeking to add a historical dimension to their work face the same challenges confronting historians—how do I understand the past? It is crucial to learn both the approaches and the sources used by historians. Communicators may find that they share something else in common with historians working on twentieth-century topics, for in these cases the biggest problem is not a shortage of information, but too much material. The increasing volume of printed words threatens to overwhelm researchers the closer they come to the present.

So how does the technical communicator facing the challenges just noted embark on historical research into the foundations of the discipline? Although historical study has as its primary motivation the uncovering of facts, events, and trends that, taken together, reveal insights about the past, such investigation, when employed as a means of inquiry into a particular field, may also yield significant detail about the emergence of the field. Such is the case in technical communication, a relatively young discipline which was fully conceptualized in this country by the post–World War II period. Research into the pedagogical past of technical communication was both revealing and challenging. Evaluating the process of conducting historical research, as the following case study highlights, provides insights into the difficult but rewarding job of applying historical methods in studying the roots of a discipline.

A CASE STUDY

Revealing Technical Communication's Pedagogical Past

Although technical communication is taught at both the undergraduate and graduate level in virtually every academic institution in this country, little has existed historically on the evolution of the discipline. Indeed, works often cited on the history of discipline were either article-length pieces (Connors, 1982, pp. 329–52; Kynell, 1999) articles on specific individuals (Kynell, 1995; Moran, 1993) or book-length works on the European antecedents of technical communication (Miller & Saidla, 1953) Even though all this material was potentially useful in understanding more about the discipline, few attempted to trace the formative pedagogical period in technical communication's evolution. One of the authors of this chapter, thus, set out to study and evaluate the antecedents of the discipline in America, a project that culminated in both *Writing in a Milieu of Utility* and *Three Keys to the Past: The History of Technical Communication* (Kynell, 2000; Kynell, 1999). To do so meant employing many of the strategies discussed earlier in this piece. The process also meant, however, seeking a variety of other sources for missing information. This section of our look at historical methodology presents details on the search that led to two historical works, how historical sources are evaluated, and how contextual considerations are paramount when studying the history of any discipline. Perhaps the single most important consideration in tackling a historical project is the critical question that will drive the research. To undertake the detective work implicit in studying the antecedents of a discipline means far more than simply reporting information. Many who read history, in fact, are under the mistaken impression that history is little more than a compilation of facts, dates and events. Indeed, such information is relevant to historical methodology, but not without a fundamental context within which to establish a framework or raison d'être for the project. If one, for example, sought to study the history of technical communication with only that—a broad, sweeping timeline of people and events—as a goal, how would such a researcher begin? The history of technical communication involves people, trends, events, pedagogy, other disciplines, science and technology, and so on. In order to pursue history, then, the writer must settle on the one question that will motivate the search. The fundamental question for the coauthor of this chapter was simply this: Pedagogically, how did technical communication evolve in this country? More specifically, did technical communication grow out of experiments in other disciplines? Evidence of technical communication, as historians have already indicated, exists as early as the Romans (Miller & Saidla, 1953, pp. 13–67). But how did we begin teaching it as a distinct discipline in the colleges and universities of this country? Are we, in essence, a product of the events that historical research will reveal? The question is vital in this sort of inquiry, particularly when so little has been written on the history of the topic. Initiating the search, though, involves the more difficult task of preparing for a kind of historical detective work, a combination of isolating key sources and a little serendipity.

Initiating the Search

After establishing a foundational question that will guide the course of historical inquiry, perhaps the second most important aspect of the search is a natural curiosity, a desire to piece together bits of evidence that will suggest the course or pattern of events. For example, if the explicit primary question for research involves the pedagogical evolution of technical communication, then certainly the implicit, secondary research question must involve the series of events or curricular shifts that led to the professionalization of the field. Thus, in initiating a historical search the researcher must be clear about the goals of the search. That is not to say that the search and subsequent evidence will confirm the researcher's original supposition. Indeed, often the evidence points in a completely different direction. The historian, though, follows the varying threads with a critical eye and allows the pattern to reveal itself.

Initiating a search does require some specific attention to purpose or goal. In trying to determine the pedagogical evolution of technical communication, for example, the researcher would want to ask some of the following questions:

1. Given the nature of the discipline, with its emphasis on science and technology, where would experiments in technical communication likely have occurred?

2. One such curriculum—engineering—has seen considerable change since it emerged as a professional academic program in the late nineteenth century. Will shifting engineering curricular patterns reveal changes as well in writing instruction?

3. If the educational and pedagogical patterns of engineers is a fertile hunting ground for evidence of early experiments in technical communication, at what time in this country's history would such experiments begin?

4. Which documents would highlight those changes in both engineering education and in shifting experiments within an engineering curriculum? Can those documents be interpreted in such a way so as to make sense of the information and also demonstrate a consistent pattern?

5. What kinds of material will reveal—either explicitly or implicitly—early attempts at professionalizing the field? Will such a study rely more upon primary or secondary sources for information?

6. Who are the key individuals who played a leading role in curricular experiments?

If, for example, students are undertaking historical research into specific, professionally related topics, they might consider questions like these:

1. What role did major social and/or political events play in workplace requirements that changed the dynamics for technical communication?

2. What do early experiments in writing for and about traditionally gender-specific activities reveal about the role of women in technical communication?

3. How did corporations, both before and after World War II, treat functional documentation and did the shifts in emphasis and expectations reveal trends that hint at future experiments in workplace writing?

4. Can public policy writing and/or industry-related documentation in the role of technology suggest the future role of the technical communicator?

Establishing questions like these, prior to the search for information, presupposes the vital role of context and interpretation in the process of historical detective work. Researchers must generate a framework around which to work; otherwise, without such a framework, the search would be an aimless exercise in collecting documents and materials with no guiding questions to provide that critical contextual foundation.

The evidence may not support the original questions. Good historians not only don't always know the answer, but also they often ask the wrong questions at first. Ideas and foundational questions must be discarded when it is clear the evidence will not support the original premise. This is not, of course, unlike any critical research that begins with a hypothesis and sometimes ends with evidence that reveals an unexpected answer. The difference for historians is the presumption of the unexpected. The previous questions may well have guided an initial search that turned up little on experiments in writing instruction, but the search may have included a wealth of information on seemingly unrelated areas: faculty involvement in curricular change, a shift in emphasis on the liberal arts, or the role of literature in the curriculum. Indeed, engineering education provides only one means for evaluating potential experiments in writing instruction that may have led to a technical communication pedagogy. Primary research questions may have focused on the role of writing instruction in medical, scientific, or agricultural programs, whereas secondary questions may have focused on the role of business writing or corporate influences on the curriculum. The point, essentially, is that a set of good questions can provide the best framework possible for initiating historical research. Once the framework has been established, the researcher must evaluate the vast diversity of materials available and begin the task of historical detective work.

Evaluating the Available Sources

As was noted earlier in this chapter, both primary and secondary resources may be useful to anyone undertaking historical research. Evaluating the validity and usefulness of those resources, however, constitutes one of the most time-consuming and difficult aspects of historical research because virtually anything might potentially illuminate the topic. To undertake such research involves a tacit agreement to follow leads, to trace sometimes incomplete data back to original sources, to follow one footnote to another in order to verify information. For historical research into the pedagogical development of technical communication in this country, though, there are categories of sources that may prove more useful avenues of inquiry. Please note that the following discussion of sources is in no way exhaustive. Evaluating, for example, technical communication's historical antecedents in Europe would involve a far different search and potentially archaic texts.[12] The following groups or types of sources are those typically drawn upon by historians evaluating educational and/or pedagogical shifts in this country.

Archives.   One of the single most useful sources of primary (letters, diaries, memoranda, and corporate documents) is an archive, whether university, corporate, or municipal. Indeed, archives, because they so often house primary documents, can reveal specific information regarding trends, key individuals, and influences. To study the pedagogical and professional evolution of technical communication, for example, meant focusing on the role of writing instruction in an engineering curriculum. Connected to that strand, though, was the role of corporate writing concerns and subsequent in-house experiments in technical writing. The archives of companies such as General Electric, Westinghouse, and General Motors would likely house a rich body of primary materials related to technical communication.

Municipal libraries are also potentially important sources of primary and secondary information. For example, in the process of researching one key individual in the evolution and professionalization of technical communication, Sada A. Harbarger, a computer search revealed a book in a small Ohio library that was not one of Harbarger's textbooks. Upon further inquiry, the book turned out to be a collection of Harbarger's articles, selected letters, her obituaries, and miscellaneous other materials. This gold mine of information was available in no other known form. Given the speed and thoroughness of contemporary computer searches, municipal and small-city libraries can be significant sources of material.[13]

Societies.   Occasionally the proceedings of societies, particularly when those proceedings have been carefully compiled for an extensive period of time, can reveal a good deal about key shifts and trends in a discipline. Of particular usefulness in studying the pedagogical evolution of technical communication were the proceedings of the Society for the Promotion of Engineering Education (SPEE). This society, which first met in 1893, addressed all manner of engineering education and curricular questions. Indeed, no other society really demonstrated such consistent attention to engineering curricular matters as the SPEE. Studying societal proceedings is an invaluable means of following a timeline as well. From its inception until it became the American Society of Engineering Education in the late 1940s, SPEE reprinted papers presented at annual meetings, the proceedings of subcommittee gatherings, and the opening addresses of key speakers. Tracing the role of writing instruction in an engineering curriculum through SPEE proceedings provided an important piece of the evolving technical communication puzzle. The number of societies with potentially useful proceedings related to technical communication is too numerous to list here. Some proceedings may, by now, even be available on the Internet.

Perhaps the best reason for studying societal proceedings is their ability to reveal growing trends over time. In fact, as was the case with the SPEE, many societies also publish in their proceedings transcripts of "discussion" groups wherein several members gather to debate specific issues. These discussion transcripts can be extremely revealing of imminent trends or shifts.

Journals.   Academic journals are perhaps the most obvious source for researching the history of technical communication, as well as for verifying material contained in proceedings or elsewhere. Carefully consider how and why certain journals might be useful. For example, as secondary resources to support material located in proceedings or archives, journals like *Educational Review, Journal of Engineering Education*, and *History of Education Quarterly* are all potentially good sources. Remember, however, that few English-related journals published much on technical communication until the late 1960s and early 1970s. Engineering journals published material on writing instruction, but a journal such as *College English* would contain little on technical communication. Subsequent specialty journals such as the *Journal of Technical Writing and Communication, The Technical Writing Teacher, Journal of Business and Technical Communication*, and *Technical Communication Quarterly* are, naturally, rich secondary sources about primarily modern trends.

Textbooks.   Naturally any inquiry into the pedagogical growth of technical communication would have to include the textbooks that emerged in support of the evolving discipline. Textbooks, in fact, are not only useful in tracing specific curricular trends, but in the case of technical communication, those early textbook authors were, in many cases, influential figures in the early growth of the discipline in this country. Although this is in no way an exhaustive list, the following texts provide a good introductory look at the growth and development of technical communication pedagogy in this country. Ray Palmer Baker's (1919) *Engineering Education: Essays for English* is an early example of collected essays (a reader) for engineering students. T.A. Rickard's (1931) *Technical Writing*, another early example, was essentially a technical editing text, and Sada A. Harbarger's (1992) *English for Engineers* was a popular text that went into several editions. Two texts that also reveal a good deal about the growth of technical writing in science and engineering curricula are Reginald O. Kapp's (1948) *The Presentation of Technical Information* and Sam F. Trelease and Emma S. Yule's (1937) *Preparation of Scientific and Technical Papers*.

Perhaps the most important reason to study textbooks for hints at the pedagogical past of a discipline is that textbooks are market driven. As the discipline of technical communication, for example, evolved beyond the constraints of an engineering writing requirement, texts moved away from specifically engineering concerns (the case in Harbarger's text) and to a more discipline-specific emphasis (such as Joseph Ullman's (1952) *Technical Reporting*). The use of texts, in fact, demonstrates one of our earlier points. Historians use those sources that are most relevant to the history being written.

Studies and Dissertations.   Studying the pedagogical growth of technical communication in this country and its roots in an engineering curriculum meant also considering some of the major educational reports associated with engineering. Two very important reports, William E. Wickenden's (1923–1929) *Report of the Investigation of Engineering Education* and H.P. Hammond's (1940) *Report on Aims and Scope of Engineering Curricula*, provided a good deal of information on the place of English (writing) instruction in an engineering curriculum. These reports are potentially important to historians for two reasons. First, they accurately summarize the concerns about engineering education at the national level and in so doing, reveal as well concerns about the relative inability of engineers to write well. Those concerns, in part, led to experiments in writing instruction. Second, the reports also look at the role of English instruction (specifically literature) in building the status of the engineer, long perceived as a vocational career choice. Thus, those discussions on English and status-related concerns bring to bear secondary issues the historian must consider—issues that can raise new questions. How did preoccupation with status concerns impact the development of a technical communication curriculum? If literature is associated with status but engineers are not writing effectively on the job, can those two distinct pedagogues be resolved? These and other questions result directly from careful scrutiny of a variety of sources.

Evaluating sources, then, means carefully considering the vast number of sources and types of materials available. Another potentially invaluable avenue for historians is the dissertation. Sometimes formally published and sometimes simply housed in university libraries, dissertations can provide a wealth of information because the topics are naturally narrow enough in scope and focused closely on a specific topic. A case in point is the (published) dissertation of A.M. Fountain, (1938) *A Study of Courses in Technical Writing*. This relatively obscure dissertation provides very specific information on the growth of technical communication, including survey material that Fountain gathered on class size, faculty, core curriculum, and so on. Few sources before Fountain revealed so much about the development of technical writing as a pedagogical alternative in this country.

Whether primary or secondary sources, whether archaic manuscripts or corporate archives, the technical communicator undertaking historical research, after establishing the foundational question that will guide research, should consider anything—carefully. Evaluating sources means viewing them with a critical eye, checking sources against other sources, and verifying information, when possible, against primary materials. With a certain measure of good fortune, the sources will confirm the presupposition that initiated the historical research in the first place. But this is only a portion of historical methodology. When materials are gathered in support of the inquiry, the historian begins what is arguably the most difficult and misunderstood aspect of the research—providing a contextual framework for the completed project by interpreting the data, establishing the relevance of the data, and determining predominant patterns.

Providing a Contextual Framework

Rather than simply reporting the collected facts, the technical communicator writing history must place those facts, dates, events, and people into a contextual framework. That is, the historian must have some sense about the context within which something took place. The historian, therefore, is just as interested in the events on the periphery of the research as those events at the center of the research. Why? History, by its very nature, is contextual and predicated on linkages. The whole issue, for example, of status concerns, English education, engineering curricular choices and the growth of technical communication is the result of a series of linkages placed in the context of (1) the political milieu of the country, (2) the burgeoning middle class desirous of a college education, and (3) the growth and development of technology and weaponry. And this is only a portion of the framework.

Establishing a contextual framework also has something to do with the theoretical background from which each individual historian works. Theory, though not explicitly a facet of historical detective, is present in the way that the historian views human nature, social institutions, and power relationships. For example, in studying the pedagogical growth of technical communication in this country, one narrow area of focus would certainly be the role of women (Durack, forthcoming). Although few women opted for an engineering education, many women taught the composition service course in land grant universities, thus affording the opportunity for experiments in technical writing. Thus, a feminist approach to the historical role of women in the discipline might focus on issues of status and prestige. A social constructionist might evaluate the ways in which small

communities of individuals make meaning and establish a lingering hege-
mony within a given discipline. The point, regardless of the predilections
of the historian, is that theory not only informs our practice, but also it informs the ways in which we regard the world. As such, theory is always an
implicit aspect of the job of the historian. One way in which historians
demonstrate their individual sense of the world involves interpretation of
data. Very simply, interpreting data is the historian's "take" on the material, the way in which the material supports or, in some cases, refutes the
original hypothesis. Because there are always holes or gaps in any historical search and because complete documentation on anything is rare, the
historian pieces together what is available and attempts to interpret the
full body of material in light of both the original question and the contextual framework within which the material will be evaluated. Among
other issues, interpreting the data means paying careful attention to some
of the following points:

- From what valid source was the material gathered? If a secondary source,
  can the material be verified against another, primary source?
- Who is the writer of the material? Is this individual key to the study or a
  peripheral figure? Is there any evidence that this individual may have had
  an agenda?
- Is the material recorded "fact" (a transcript, letter, memoranda, etc.), or is
  the material from a secondary source unrelated to the primary area of study?
- Does the material "fit" into the contextual framework created for the
  study? That is, does certain evidence clearly contradict already established patterns? Does this constitute a secondary consideration that warrants further inquiry?
- If the evidence leads to no clear conclusions, what can be pieced together
  based on interpretation?

These questions, although not exhaustive, demonstrate the difficulty
that historians face when trying to make sense of the collected evidence.[14]
Indeed, interpreting the data is only part of the equation. Even when data
have been verified and interpreted in light of the overall contextual framework, historians must then establish the relevance of data to the completed
project.

Establishing Relevance

In essence, not all collected data, evidence, and peripheral materials will
be relevant to the study undertaken. In studying the pedagogical growth
of technical communication in this country, for example, one fascinating,

though somewhat irrelevant sidelight involved the growth and development of business communication with distinct pedagogical concerns and
emphases. That is not to say, however, that such seemingly irrelevant material should be discarded. For the purposes of an individual study perhaps,
but such evidence can be useful for future research or for footnotes that
other scholars may wish to follow.

Establishing the relevance of data, therefore, means carefully considering how collected and interpreted materials will be reflected in the completed project. Occasionally a series of documents or quotes will seem very
revealing of a period or trend but in fact are distractions from the main
thread being followed. As tempting as it may be to include such material,
the tendency to include everything may result in a shift in focus. For any
historian carefully piecing together a series of events, remaining focused
on the careful development of the topic is vital for determining predominant patterns and trends.

Determining Predominant Patterns

Studying the growth and evolution of technical communication as a
discipline in America meant ultimately evaluating and interpreting materials in search of a discernible pattern. Most historians are concerned
with patterns of growth and development because, again, such patterns
reveal a good deal about human nature, social institutions, and power relationships (regardless of the field of inquiry). Determining patterns is a
very fruitful area of study for technical communication due to the preva-
lence of technical documents historically. Are all such documents "technical writing"? Evaluating verifiable shifts, for example, in the ways in
which humans write "how-to" documentation is demonstrable proof of
increasing levels of sophistication in technology. Evaluating verifiable curricular shifts is just as revealing of the growth and evolution of a distinct
discipline.

Thus, patterns are important for the historian in that they emerge—
with hard work and little serendipity—out of the interpreted and verified data. The development of patterns, the roles of key individuals, the
shifts and trends along the way all tell a story and, in many ways, history
is about just that—telling a story. Although the research itself is often
painstaking and difficult, there is also a great deal of joy to be had during the discovery process. Historical methodology, therefore, is a relevant field of inquiry to technical communication research because the
discipline, as we now teach and study it, is still so new. History exists as
a choice for those who wonder where we came from, why we've estab-

lished consistent pedagogical practices, how we have evolved, and where we are headed in the twenty-first century. Because the future is rooted in the past and because we, today, are a product of past experimentation, historical methodology is a vital and relevant research alternative for anyone with a healthy curiosity who seeks to understand the growth, development, and subsequent professionalization of the discipline of technical communication.

NOTES

1. Authors are listed alphabetically and contributed equally to this chapter.

2. For more discussion of interpretation, see Davidson & Lytle, 1992, pp. 45–67.

3. For information on the Enola Gay controversy, see Bird & Lifschultz, 1999; Harwit, 1996; Linenthal & Englehardt, 1996. A much larger literature exists on the decision to drop the atomic bomb. See the highly readable account by Rhodes, 1986; Sherwin, 1975; and Alperovitz, 1985.

4. The phrase seems to have been coined by Toynbee.

5. The most noted examples of work were Fogel, 1972b; Fogel & Engerman, 1974; also Fogel, 1972a.

6. An important work in this area was Kleppner, 1970; see also Dollar, 1971.

7. Erikson's famous psychobiography of Martin Luther was a very early effort in this direction; others have followed. See Erikson, 1958; Kakar, 1970; and Mazlish, 1990. Good introductions to this subject are Lifton, 1974; and Gay, 1985.

8. The book was Hersch, 1997; for a discussion of his difficulties with sources, see *History: A warts and more look at Camelot*, 1997.

9. Historian James Curtis studied the famous Farm Security Administration photographers who recorded the lives of rural Americans caught in the Great Depression and found evidence that photographers moved objects in rooms, posed individuals, and in general worked carefully to convey certain attitudes and feelings. See Curtis, 1989. General overviews on the nature of photography can be found in Sontag, 1977; Tractenberg, 1979; and Newhall, 1964.

10. See Burns, 1981; Burns, 1990; Burns, 1994; Burns, 1997; Burns, 1998. The accompanying books are Duncan, 1997; Ward, 1990; and Ward, 1994.

11. See Sitton, 1983; Ritchie, 1995; and Shumway, 1971. See Robert J. Connors, "The Rise of Technical Writing Instruction in America," *Journal of Technical Writing and Communication* 12, pp. 329–352; and Teresa Kynell, "Technical Writing from 1850–1960: Where Have We Been as a Discipline?" *Technical Communication Quarterly* (summer 1999).

12. See, for example, Tebeaux, 1998.

13. Thanks to the Ohioana Library in Columbus, Ohio, for assistance in locating an important collection of Sada A. Harbarger's papers.

14. For an example of "collected evidence" evaluated in a historical work, see Longo, 2000.

REFERENCES

Adams, K. (1993). *A history of professional writing instruction in American colleges*. Dallas: Southern Methodist University Press.

Alperovitz, G. (1985). *The decision to use the bomb and the architecture of an American myth*. New York: Penguin.

Baker, R. (1919). *Engineering education: Essays for English*. New York: Wiley.

Basalla, G. (1988). *The evolution of technology*. New York: Cambridge University Press.

Bird, K . & Lifschultz, L. (Eds.). (1999). *Hiroshima's shadow: Writings on the denial of history and the Smithsonian controversy*. Stony Creek, CT: Pamphleteer's Press.

Burns, K. (Producer). (1981). *The Brooklyn Bridge*. (Documentary Film).

Burns, K. (Producer). (1990). *The Civil War*. (Documentary Film).

Burns, K. (Producer). (1994). *Baseball* (Documentary Film).

Burns, K. (Producer). (1997). *Lewis and Clark: The journey of the corps of discovery*. (Documentary Film).

Burns, K. (Producer). (1998). *Frank Lloyd Wright*. (Documentary Film).

Connors, R. (1982). The rise of technical writing instruction in America. *Journal of Technical Writing and Communication*. 12, 329–352.

Curtis, J. (1989). *Mind's eye, mind's truth: FSA photography reconsidered*. Philadelphia: Temple University Press.

Davidson, J. & Lytle, M. (1992). *After the fact: The art of historical detection* (3d ed.). New York: McGraw-Hill.

Dollar, C. (1971). *Historian's guide to statistics, quantitative analysis and historical research*. New York: Holt, Rinehart, and Winston.

Duncan, D. (1997). *Lewis and Clark: An illustrated history*. New York: Knopf.

Durack, K. (forthcoming). Instructions as inventions. In T. Kynell & G. Savage. *Power, status and legitimacy in technical communication*. New York: Baywood.

Erikson E. (1958). *Young man Luther: A study in psychoanalysis and history*. New York: Norton.

Fogel, R. (1972a). *The dimensions of quantitative research in history*. Princeton: Princeton University Press.

Fogel, R. (1972b). *Railroads and American economic growth: Essays in econometric history*. Baltimore: Johns Hopkins University Press.

Fogel, R., & Engerman, S. (1974). *Time on a cross: The economics of American negro slavery*. 2 vols. Boston: Little, Brown.

Fountain, A. (1938). *A study of courses in technical writing*. Raleigh: University of North Carolina Press.

Gay, P. (1985). *Freud for historians*. New York: Oxford University Press.

Hammond, H. (1940). Report of committee on aims and scope of engineering curricula. *Journal of Engineering Education*. 30.

Harbarger, S. (1928). *English for engineers*. New York: McGraw Hill.

Harwit, M. (1996). *An exhibit denied: Lobbying the history of the "Enola Gay"*. New York: Copernicus.

Hersch, S. (1997). *The dark side of Camelot*. New York: Little, Brown.

History: A warts and more look at Camelot. (1997, November 17). *Time*. p. 40.

Lubar S. & Kingery, D. (1993). *History from things: Essays on material culture*. Washington, DC: Smithsonian Institution Press.

Kakar, S. (1970). *Frederick Taylor: A study in personality and innovation*. Cambridge: MIT Press.

Kapp, R. (1948). *The presentation of technical information*. London: Constable.

Kleppner, P. (1970). *The cross of culture: A social analysis of midwestern politics, 1850–1900*. New York: Free Press.

Kynell, T. (1995, fall). Samuel Chandler Earle and the Tufts experiment. *Journal of Technical Writing and Communication*.

Kynell, T., & Moran, M. (Eds.). (1999). *Three keys to the past: The history of technical communication*. Stamford, CT: Ablex Publishing Corporation.

Kynell, T. (1999, summer). Technical writing from 1850–1960: Where have we been as a discipline? *Technical Communication Quarterly*.

Kynell, T. (2000). *Writing in a milieu of utility: The move to technical communication in American engineering programs, 1850–1950*. Stamford, CT.: Ablex Publishing Corporation.

Linenthal, E. & Englehardt, T. (1996). *History wars: The "Enola Gay" and other battles for the American past*. New York: Metropolitan Books/Henry Holt and Co.

Lifton, R. (Ed.). (1974). *Explorations in psychohistory*. New York: Simon and Schuster.

Longo. B. (2000). *Spurious coin: A history of science, management and technical writing*. New York: SUNY Press.

Mazlish, B. (1990). *The leader, the led, the psyche: Essays in psychohistory*. Hanover, NH: University Press of New England.

Miller, W., & Saidla, L. (Eds.). (1953). *Engineers as writers: Growth of a literature*. New York: Van Nostrand.

Moran, M. (1993). The road not taken: Frank Aydelotte and the thought approach to engineering writing. *Technical Communication Quarterly*. 1, 161–175.

Mokyr, J. (Ed.). (1993). *The British industrial revolution: An economic perspective*. Boulder, CO: Westview Press.

Newhall, B. (1964). *The history of photography from 1839 to the present*. New York: Museum of Modern Art.

Novick, P. *That noble dream: The "objectivity question" and the American historical profession*. New York: Cambridge University Press.

Rhodes, R. (1986). *Making the atomic bomb*. New York: Simon and Schuster.

Rickard, T. (1931). *Technical writing*. New York: Wiley.

Ritchie, D. (1995). *Doing oral history*. New York: Twayne Publishers.

Sherwin, M. (1975). *World destroyed: The atomic bomb and the grand alliance*. New York: Knopf.

Shumway, G. (1971). *Oral history in the United States: A directory*. New York: Oral History Association.

Sitton, T. (1983). *Oral history: A guide for teachers (and others)*. Austin: University of Texas Press.

Sontag, S. (1977). *On photography*. New York: Farrar, Straus and Giroux.

Tebeaux, E. (2000). The voices of English women technical writers, 1641–1700: Imprints in the evolution of modern English prose style. *Technical Communication Quarterly* 7, 125–152.

Tebeaux, E. (1998). *Emergence of a tradition*. New York: Baywood.

Tractenberg A. (1979). Introduction. In U.S., National Archives. *The American image*. New York: Pantheon Books.

Trelease, S. & Yule, E. (1937). *Preparation of scientific and technical papers*. Baltimore:
    Williams and Wilkins.
Ullman, J. (1952). *Technical reporting*. New York: McGraw.
Ward, G. (1990). *The Civil War: An illustrated history*. New York: Knopf.
Ward, G. (1994). *Baseball: An illustrated history*. New York: Knopf.
Wickenden, W. (1923–1929). *Report of the investigation of engineering education*. Pittsburgh:
    American Society for Engineering Education.

CHAPTER

Surveys and Questionnaires

Daniel J. Murphy

The purpose of any kind of research is either to learn something that one does not already know, or to analyze more closely something one believes to know for the benefit of trying to see it from a different perspective. What phenomena are investigated will, of course, be as varied as there are topics that interest people. It is not uncommon, especially in communication research, for queries to be precipitated by some problem that has to be overcome. Other queries arise by some situation or event(s) that needs to be improved. The goals of communication research may also involve substantiating what one *assumes* to be true by employing some sort of quasi-scientific measurement or procedure that will hopefully help to support or refute prior assumptions. Based on the outcomes, the investigators should then be in a better position to make more informed decisions to improve processes or to overcome problems. One frequently used practice to achieve these ends involves the use of surveys or questionnaires, even though survey research will more often involve attempts to describe events rather than to explain them. Nevertheless, surveys can be used to explain events and can also be used in experimental and quasi-experimental research (Bowers & Courtright, 1984). Indeed, survey/questionnaire research is arguably the most popular form of social inquiry, due primarily to efficiency, versatility, and generalization, but caution must be taken with respect to sampling, measurement, and overall design, or the effort is likely to fail (Schutt, 1996).

The social sciences have a substantial literature addressing formal, "scientific" theory building and model development involving inductive and deductive approaches in the conduct of inquiry. Outside of the university, however, and certain specialized research agencies whose procedures are necessarily rigorous, there is considerable interest in conducting surveys and questionnaires not so much as to build theory, but rather with a view toward practical application of these approaches for commonplace organizational issues. The purpose of this chapter is to offer guidelines and resources to individuals who are interested in collecting communication-related data, especially in organizational settings, and who desire to use questionnaires and survey instruments as primary research tools. From the outset, it must be acknowledged that employing sophisticated empirical approaches to investigate communication-related phenomena is too vast a subject to be treated in detail in a single chapter. The breadth and complexity of these topics are substantial. Entire volumes have been written on these areas, and the list of references at the end of this chapter offers a variety of sources to guide those technical communicators who are interested in some of the more advanced aspects of communication research methods. For our purposes, however, the more modest goal offered here is to discuss practical strategies and to offer useful pointers to help guard against errors in survey design and in sampling methodologies. The focus is to simplify the questionnaire/survey process for those who may be undertaking it for the first time and to assist those who may wish to improve processes already in place. I begin with a brief discussion of what elements constitute survey and questionnaire research, touch briefly on some of the theoretical foundations upon which such approaches rest, and illustrate salient points with references to a study of previous survey research involving aerospace scientists and engineers (Murphy, 1997).

ROLE OF THEORY

Sound research is grounded upon theory insofar as it is part of the "inductive/deductive cycle": Individuals observe the world around them and generalize as to its substance and order (induction) and then, based on these observations, try to state the nature of the relationships hypothesized to exist among the various phenomena in ways that can be tested (in this case, by using surveys and questionnaires). This is done with a view toward developing revised ways of thinking and then applying what one has learned (deduction). It is this cycle of observing, stating, testing, and revising followed by more observing, stating, testing, and revising that pushes back the frontiers of knowledge and constitutes what we claim to "know" about a given subject. Much of the research that has been done in organizational settings will not necessarily be grounded in theory, but some will.

The dichotomy between research that is grounded in theory, and that which is not, goes to the heart of investigation and affects the research questions themselves in terms of formality or informality in the scientific sense.

For example, nearly ten years ago I began initial groundwork for related studies of online communication well before the notable exponential growth of the "e-factor" in organizations. The scientific and theoretical rigor that was required over time to assess the dimensions of communication media, its uses, and its associated costs had to be fairly strict in formality and measures of association. One of the main reasons for this, other than for the purposes of scientific rigor, was that some managers at the time were insisting that all investments in computer systems needed to be justified with hard return on investment (ROI) figures, but most of the significant communication opportunities could not be evaluated in that way (Murphy, 1992). It became clear that computer-based information systems and electronic media had to be perceived as important in the achievement of organizational goals by top-level management to achieve successful IT implementation in the absence of ROI data. Apart from ROI considerations, it was only after more methodical analyses based on a priori theoretical assumptions of organizational environments and communication practices drawn from survey data that a clearer picture of electronic media use by aerospace specialists began to emerge (Murphy, 1997).

When it comes to deciding what factors need to be studied, if one can specify in a conjectural statement involving two or more variables the relationship that is to be tested, then that relationship can be rewritten as a hypothesis in the form of a declarative statement. This approach was used consistently in the communication media study referenced previously. In a typical conjectural statement such as "the greater the variety of tasks to be performed in a department, the higher the levels of uncertainty that will be experienced by the workers" implies that both task variety (variable 1) and levels of uncertainly (variable 2) can be measured given the proper research instrument, in this case, questions on a survey. It is up to the investigator to perform appropriate statistical tests to ascertain whether the null hypothesis is to be rejected or not rejected. Simply put, the null hypothesis (sometimes abbreviated H_0) implies that there is no real difference between the populations from which the samples came (Dooley, 2001). In the example cited, the null hypothesis is that levels of task variety have no bearing on levels of uncertainty. The researcher does not try to "prove" a hypothesis because it is not possible to prove something involving humans to be universally true at all times and in all places. Rather, the researcher looks to see if—based on the survey data—it is plausible to infer that there is a difference between populations based on the responses from the samples. If one can, with reasonable confidence, establish that there are significant differences tied to hypothesized relations among phenomena as the statistical tests indicate, then one "rejects" the null hypothesis. To reject the null hypothesis in the example is to decide that levels of variety do indeed influence levels of uncertainty. At that point, it is possible to devise plans to solve the problem or to overcome obstacles.

Aficionados of American movie history know that a stock plot in romantic comedies of Mickey Rooney and Judy Garland had the characters try to solve problems by proclaiming enthusiastically, "Let's put on a show!" As a modern parallel, if there is a problem to be overcome or a situation that needs to be better understood, a first inclination might be to say: "Let's do a survey!" Done correctly, survey research is a powerful analytic tool, but an investigator needs to be aware that the survey research project must be both feasible and based on sound rationale if it is to be successful (Dooley, 2001). For example, it would not make sense to try to learn about sensitive, specialized topics (such as brutality) by mailing out surveys. It would, however, make sense to use survey research to learn more about market studies, political forecasting, media use, organizational behavior, or satisfaction with established policy. Survey research can be a most useful approach and preferable to other types of data collection, such as face-to-face focus groups, for a variety of reasons: surveys are generally less costly, entail less risk on the part of those charged with gathering the information, and take less time to administer.

RESEARCH ON HUMAN SUBJECTS, INFORMED CONSENT, AND PRIVACY

Research involving human subjects will always be a sensitive issue. People are rightfully circumspect about having strangers investigate them no matter how noble the purpose. Even beyond individual reticence, departments or organizations as a whole may also be unwilling to participate in survey-based studies, so both individual and organizational concerns must be addressed. Either way, you need to follow guidelines on what constitutes "fair play" in information-gathering enterprises. There is an extensive literature that focuses on the ethical issues of research involving human subjects, and the topic is sufficiently detailed that a comprehensive summary is not necessary here. A helpful discussion of the topic is provided in this anthology by Breuch, Olson, and Frantz.

Let me emphasize here, however, that a major consideration the survey researcher does need to keep in mind pertains to issues of anonymity and/or confidentiality. Anonymity implies that no one, not even the researchers themselves, will know the identity of the respondents. Confidentiality implies that although the identities of the respondents may be known to the research staff, these identities will not be revealed without the respondents' consent. In both kinds of investigations, it is customary to report sets of scores, such as averages or medians, without identifying individuals. This issue will have different implications depending on how the survey is conducted, such as by mail or by telephone. Kerlinger (1986) pointed out that research involving telephone surveys is generally not recommended as it tends to limit what people will say to a stranger. In other words, phone calls from strangers to ask questions about one's opinions or practices are annoyances most people would avoid. Although they are discussed in more detail later, it is worth mentioning here that telephone surveys may compromise the anonymity of the respondent during data collection if the individual is requested by name because it may reduce the subject's inclination to speak candidly. However, if the caller assures the subject that the number was chosen by a random-dialing system so that the identities are unknown to the interviewer, then the respondent may be more forthcoming. You should also keep in mind that the respondent may not feel willing to converse freely if the telephone environment is not private.

If you want to gather information in an organizational or departmental environment, you should obtain permission in writing from a responsible authority before you can begin the survey. It is always preferable to secure such permission in writing before too much effort is expended prior to the data collection. Do not rely on handshakes or informal agreements and gestures of goodwill to gather the data. You probably have heard stories about research projects that proceeded on track up until the last few hours before data collection and then, seemingly out of nowhere, the project was terminated by people who heretofore were silent or uninvolved. In an organization, you may want to consider asking for the legal department's permission early in the process. It will pay dividends in the long run to secure all necessary written permissions in advance to avoid long delays or expensive, time-consuming changes later.

POPULATIONS AND SAMPLES

If you conduct communication research inside or outside of an organizational setting, it is usually impossible (due to expense, numbers of people involved, lack of time, etc.) to query every individual who could possibly be involved in the areas about which you are interested. You will instead have to survey a small part of the group or population and make your conclusions by extrapolating from your sample. The term *population* in this sense refers to the entire collective of individuals (often called the "universe") whose traits you want to understand with a given degree of confidence. These traits likely will include a variety of behaviors, characteristics, beliefs, attitudes, preferences, and so on. The researcher's sample, or smaller subset of the population, is therefore surmised to possess characteristics that are representative of the larger group.

Representativeness

You can use a survey or questionnaire to learn about the characteristics of your sample, and then use inference to arrive at a better understanding of the traits of the population. To have confidence in your inferences, it is important to ensure as much as possible that you have used a *representative* sample for findings to be reliable and valid with respect to the "true" nature of the population. If it turns out that the sample was not representative, then errors and/or biases are likely to occur in the research findings, and using flawed findings as the bases for decision making could possibly be more disastrous to one's purposes than doing nothing. What practical steps can the researcher use to minimize this problem? One of the best strategies to avoid sampling bias is to strive to have the sample drawn by *random* selection; simply put, it means that any member of your population should have an equally likely chance of being included in your sample. If you are familiar with the concept of the television industry's use of the Nielsen Media Research reports on estimation of audience size, then you can see how the principles of randomization and representativeness apply. Nielsen Media Research states that representative samples do not have to be very large to represent the population. Although a sample doesn't have to be large to represent the population, the sample does need to be selected in a way that gives all members of the population the same chance of being chosen (Nielsen Media Research, 1999). Dooley (2001) echoes the notion that a representative sample is more important than the sample's size. You should be aware there is some disagreement among researchers when it comes to fixing a sample size. For example, Sumser (2001) states that when it comes to determining sample size, one never needs a certain proportion of the population. On the other hand, Neuman (2000) suggests that for small populations (under 1,000), a researcher needs a sampling ratio of approximately 30 percent. There are numerous sources that provide probable deviation tables enumerating the desirable sample size given one's best estimate of the population. McDermott (1999) offers several such tables, as well as several equations that can be used to estimate sample size that are easy enough to use with a calculator. But because size alone is only one determinant of sampling adequacy, even larger sample sizes that are not randomly drawn have the possibility of being less representative than smaller samples that are truly random. So basically, the size of the sample is of less importance than the representativeness of the sample, and, in the end, the greatest determinants of sample size tend to be time and money (Sumser, 2001).

Collecting a truly random sample is not easy, and it is often more expedient to use a "convenience" sample, that is, to collect information from those individuals who are readily accessible. It may be convenient, but it does increase the likelihood of sampling bias. Also, be cautioned against using an arbitrary stratification process in subject sampling as is explained in the following example. Imagine the hypothetical case of an investigator employed in a university's research department who wanted to draw a sample from among the students who reside on campus. To simplify the selection, the researcher decided to poll residents by arbitrarily choosing students who live on the odd-numbered floors of the largest campus residence hall. Assume further that the particular hall chosen for the study just happened to separate its residents by gender, such that every other floor was either all male or all female. As an unforeseen result, the researcher would have unwittingly introduced a substantial sampling bias in the study by eliminating either all of the males or all of the females from the sample. Depending on the type of information being collected, this stratification could lead to serious sampling errors due to overrepresentation of one gender, and by extension result in poorly made decisions based on flawed data. The researcher would have been better off to have assigned a number to all of the students who live in the residence hall and then use a random-number algorithm or table to select the subjects. The example given is somewhat extreme, but it illustrates the danger inherent in sampling biases.

RESPONSE RATES

Improving the response rate you get from surveys is an important and necessary factor in effective research. It is normal for people to be circumspect about revealing information about themselves on a questionnaire, so the researcher must present a convincing argument as to why a respondent should bother taking the time to participate. In today's society, there is a sustained effort that seeks or demands some sort of response from every one of us on almost a daily level. We are told: buy this; subscribe to that; act now on something else. Effective survey research has to cut through the noise of competing voices in order to be heard. To help generate a representative sample, I indicated that it is desirable to obtain the highest possible response rate, but this introduces the question as to what constitutes an "acceptable" response.

As explained earlier, when a statistic is calculated from a sample, one is estimating the population value. That is, we infer from the sample what the "true" parameter is in the population itself. For example, if all the employees in a large, international corporation were polled about whether they are in favor of or opposed to a newly proposed administrative policy, the outcome of such a poll would be the "true" population value. But because polling every person is expensive and time consuming, an alternate approach is to estimate that "true" value by polling a much smaller—but hopefully, representative—sample, and then inferring the "true" value from the sample. The variability as to what percentages constitute an "acceptable" response rate is therefore tied to a large degree to the number of respondents with respect to the size of the population. Sampling is based on probability theory and indicates that the tendency for error tends to decrease as more subjects are added. However, there comes a point on the curve where likelihood for error has flattened to such an extent that adding a few dozen or even a few hundred more subjects will not appreciably increase the confidence level. In such cases, the time and expense associated with increasing the sample size is met head on with the reality of increasingly diminished returns. For example, McDermott (1999) explains that at a 95 percent confidence level, a population of 10,000 can be studied with a sample size of 370; a population of 100,000 can be studied with a sample of 383, and a population of infinity with a sample of 384. Thus, adding hundreds of more subjects is not necessary, depending on the margin of error that the researchers are willing to accept. It is nevertheless in the best interests of the investigator to achieve the highest response rate as can be reasonably managed, and toward that end, a few practical suggestions to improve one's chances for gaining compliance from the subject pool are offered here.

Common sense indicates that there is an inverse relationship between the response rate and the length of the survey instrument: the longer the survey or questionnaire, the fewer the number of people who will be inclined to cooperate. A survey that takes longer than a few minutes to complete will lose the interest of many participants, and if the time to complete the survey is beyond twenty minutes, the decline in response rate will be even more severe. So, keep it as short as is necessary to get to what you need to know. Researchers have also used incentives with some success, and the incentive need not necessarily be large. Even a small reward can increase one's response rate. As a side note, Leon Festinger's (1957) discussion of minimal justification in the cognitive dissonance literature explores the role of incentive in gaining task compliance. If the survey is administered by a means of a paper mailing, an important but frequently overlooked way to improve response is to include a postage-paid return envelope so that the respondent doesn't have to pay to send back the completed instrument.

A follow-up mailing can also help. After some time, perhaps two weeks, has passed since the original survey was distributed, send out a reminder, such as a postcard, to initiate another flurry of response activity. If there are sufficient funds, a third mailing that includes another complete questionnaire (in case the original was lost) sent to those who have not yet responded is ideal.

It is important to realize that the opinions of those who are inclined to respond quickly to surveys will likely be different from those who are inclined to not respond. Consequently, trying to get the cooperation of those less inclined to respond must always remain a goal. It may surprise you that simple, straightforward persuasiveness can help a great deal; just tell the unresponsive subjects that the survey is important and ask them to please reconsider their decision. Professional survey takers have said that in follow-up interviews, when previously uncooperative respondents were asked why they didn't answer the questions, they replied that the original query didn't make their participation sound very important or necessary. It is beneficial to impress on the respondents that you value their participation, and answering the questions is certainly worth their time.

INSTRUMENT CONSTRUCTION

Having made a case for drawing responses from representative samples and seeking robust response rates, consider the construction of the research instrument itself. Whether it is a written questionnaire or a phone or face-to-face survey or some combination, there are some general strategies you can follow that will be beneficial. First, consider written questionnaires, because they tend to be the least costly in terms of the researcher's time to gather the data from individual respondents. Also, questionnaires have traditionally been the most common approach so people tend to be familiar with them; however, in political polling particularly, the use of the telephone has been effective, and e-mail or Web-based surveys are also becoming more common.

Written Questionnaires

As indicated at the beginning of this chapter, because the goal of research is to learn something new or to see things from different perspectives, researchers need to clarify precisely the questions they want to study. One needs to know what the "*is is*." It is worth mentioning that, similar to our earlier discussion of sampling representativeness, poorly designed questions or flawed methods may be more destructive than doing no study at all, because use of a bad measure may lead to implementing decisions based on faulty assessment. Deciding how to develop the survey leads to a series of difficult tasks facing the researcher: Does one use a preexisting scale to measure a given variable or should one construct a new measure? There are a variety of publications that provide measures, as well as summarize and critique tests and measurement scales. The reader may refer to such sources as *Annual Review of Psychology, Applied Psychological Measurement, Communication Research Reports, Handbook of Social Psychology, Human Communication Research, Journal of Applied Communication Research, Journal of Educational Measurement, Psychological Abstracts, Public Opinion Quarterly,* and *Review of Research in Education* to name a few. One must realize that if no measure exists for the variable in question, or if existing measures are found to be unsuitable, then the researcher must either drop the variable from consideration or develop a new measure, which, as noted, can be a difficult task.

Question Design

If you must develop new measures to assess your variables, then you will need to construct a series of questions. Questions will fall into one of two category types: those that allow for a wide range of responses (open ended) and those that more strictly control the answers that are acceptable (closed). In the study of communication media use among aerospace engineers and scientists (Murphy, 1997), we tried to avoid open-ended questions, such as What do you think about getting e-mail messages at work? Instead, we favored closed questions, such as Do you get e-mail messages at work? It is easier to codify the responses in closed questions, but it may be more desirable to allow for more variability in the answers than simple binary Yes/No responses. A common strategy, therefore, is to employ the multiple-response answers often used on exams where the investigator has come up with a list of predefined responses. This style of questioning is generally referred to as Likert-scale scoring.

A frequently used method to collect data in the behavioral sciences is to employ tests or scales that are summed or averaged to measure one variable. A single question will not by itself give an adequate representation of the phenomena that is being investigated. Rather, the researcher should come up with more than one question that tries to get at the issue or elements that seem to lie at the core of the phenomena being investigated. In this way, one builds what might be called a "dimension" or multiple view of the variable.

For example, in the aerospace media study, in order to assess the differential amounts of task variety that were present in the workplace (i.e., the extent to which the types of tasks performed by the employees differed), we measured four separate items in the survey that all had to do with variety. Be careful not to have all of the items scored in the same direction. In other words, if the acceptable answers range from one to five, where one is "low" (also, "very infrequent" or "strongly disagree," etc.) and five is "high" ("very frequent" or "strongly agree," etc.), then word the questions so that a response set (a pattern where an individual just marks down one side or in the middle of the score sheet) is less likely to occur (Stacks, 1999). This strategy is called "reverse scoring" and needs to be understood by the individuals who analyze the data, but its use is not made known to the respondents. This principle, used in the aerospace media use study, is illustrated where "(R)" means that a question is reverse scored:

1. The work is routine. (R)
2. The tasks performed differ greatly from day to day.
3. We use repetitive activities in doing the work. (R)
4. Our tasks require the use of many skills.

Each of these items is measured with a five-point Likert scale ranging along a scale where 1 = Strongly Disagree; 2 = Disagree; 3 = Neutral; 4 = Agree; 5 = Strongly Agree. With the reverse scoring, 1 would be converted to 5, 2 converted to 4, 3 stays the same, 4 is converted to 2, and 5 converted to 1. The reason for the reversal is so that when the composite scale range of overall variety is computed by adding the items together, the "unweighted" sum (unweighted means no question receives a higher value than another question) of the scores for all items yields a number from four to twenty. That is, if 1 is scored for each of the four items and they are all added together, a 4 indicates the lowest level of variety. At the other end of the scale, if 5 were scored for each item to indicate the highest level of variety and then added together, a 20 as the top end of the scale would indicate the highest level of variety. If you subtract four from twenty, the range of the scale is sixteen, and you'd expect to see scores falling anywhere within the range, from a low of four to a high of twenty. (If you detect a score outside the top end of your range, such as 27 in this example, then you'd know there were errors in the tabulation. Scores below the range at the low end do not necessarily indicate tabulation errors, because the respondent may simply have skipped some of the items.) Although the questions are listed together here, they should actually be interspersed among other questions in the questionnaire that target different variables.

Faulty Questions

Another consideration in survey design is to avoid double-barreled questions or leading questions. A doubled-barreled question, as its name implies, hits the respondent with two things at once that serves only to cloud the issue and make it more difficult to reach a true determination. Consider a poorly designed question such as the following: Do you receive more than forty e-mail messages a day, and do you respond to the majority of them on the same day that they arrive? Clearly, there are at least three issues here: (1) whether the subject receives more than forty e-mail messages a day, (2) whether the respondent responds to more than half of them, (3) whether the responses are given on the day the messages arrive. The writer of such a question muddles several issues. What is the main point the question was intended to address? Does the researcher want to know if the e-mail load is higher than one message per hour on an average day? Or is the issue whether a majority of the messages receive a response on the same day that they arrive? One might further argue that a binary Yes/No answer to such a question would contain insufficient information to be genuinely useful, so that a Likert-type scale to assess several dimensions of the question (average message load, response frequency, and timeliness) would be the better approach.

Good question design also avoids "leading" questions such as: Don't you agree that it's better for our company to hire a different Internet service provider as the only way to avoid our frequent service interruptions? This is a badly designed question because it "leads" the respondent in several ways: (1) that there are indeed frequent Internet service interruptions; (2) that a different Internet service provider would provide better service; (3) that a different service provider is the only available option and hence the best one. Each of the three aforementioned questions could, by itself, be the topic for a more neutrally worded inquiry, such as: Indicate how often you experience Internet service interruptions in an average work week: 1 = never experienced an interruption; 2 = about one per week; 3 = two or three per week; 4 = four to ten per week; 5 = more than ten per week.

Other flaws to avoid in questionnaire design include using questions that are emotionally volatile, such as: Should we demote the overpaid chief technology officer? Also, phrasing questions in a way to make them sound more socially desirable can cause skewed results (Stacks & Hocking, 1999). If you were to ask people which publications they read regularly, and the list included titles such as the *New York Times* together with the *National Enquirer*, you would likely wind up with an overreporting of the *Times* and a lower than actual reporting of the *Enquirer* than actually exists in the population.

Remember also that as a researcher it is likely that you may differ from the population you are studying in important ways. As much as you can, try not to allow your education, experience, or personal background to exert an undue influence on the instrument. For example, if gathering demographic information about education levels, don't necessarily lump everyone who is "less than college graduate" into a single category. But this of course will depend on the population being studied. In the aerospace media use research, the assessment of education levels was divided into six levels with the stratification at the higher educational levels due to the high academic prerequisites normally expected of scientists and engineers (Murphy, 1994). Depending on the type of population being studied, such a question could feasibly place everyone into a single category, and this is less helpful than having clearer demarcations along the education continuum in this example. Also, avoid jargon, state your questions simply and clearly, and take care not to impose your views directly or indirectly on the content of the questions, or your results may not be as impartial as you'd hoped to obtain.

Practical Considerations

It should probably go without saying that a practical consideration in mailing questionnaires is to ensure that the survey instruments are usable and clearly understandable. There will not be someone on the research team looking over the respondents' shoulders to help them if problems arise. Those who choose to do questionnaire research should know and apply sound communication strategies. As previously mentioned, it is necessary to be persuasive to help in your response rate, so write a clear, concise cover letter or introductory statement, and hand sign it in ink if time permits. Explain as much as necessary the point of the research, the importance of each participant's response, your anonymity or confidentiality policy, and where the subject can obtain answers to questions if the need should arise. You might want to ward off the "Why me?" reaction by including a few words on how and why they were selected for the study. Be particular about the quality of the presentation overall. Ensure that the completed questionnaire and its accompanying cover letter are legible, printed on good stock with attractive text, carefully proofread, and free of errors. Be sure to close the letter or questionnaire with an expression of thanks for voluntary participation in the study. An important strategy that will help you to spot errors in your approach is to run a pretest trial (often called a "pilot study") on a small number of individuals. Done well enough in advance of the main study, the pretest or pilot study will provide input from persons far enough removed from the construction of the survey that they will be able to offer fresh points of view about wording, complexity, time of completion, and other necessary design considerations.

Assuming that you have a research instrument that has the appropriate characteristics, you need to determine whether it has reached the hands of the intended person. I recently received a paper questionnaire sent by a professional organization that drew names from its database based on a few parameters that marginally applied to me. There were enough parameters to include me in the mailing, but it was evident to me that I was not representative of the group they were interested in querying. It is useful to have a question right at the start that will help you determine whether a respondent's answers should be included in the data analysis. For example, suppose a researcher wanted to gather information about the billing rates of independent contractors. At some time in the distant past, an individual who indicated that he or she was a contractor on a membership roster of a professional society might be placed into a database to receive such a survey, but is that information still relevant? Is the person still an independent contractor? One of the first questions should be something along these lines: "Do you earn at least 75 percent (or whatever amount is deemed desirable for data gathering) of your income as an independent contractor?" If the response is "No," then the survey should either direct the respondent to some general demographic questions to answer at the end or otherwise skip to the instructions on how to return the survey. The researcher should not assume that all responses will automatically be included in the analysis. An early question to help ascertain suitability of subject inclusion is a good way to improve sample representativeness.

Phone Surveys and Face-to-Face Interviews

Phone surveys, because they are faster than paper questionnaires in turn-around time, now rank among the top of the most frequently used data collection methods. They can be more inexpensive than printing and distributing paper surveys, especially if the sample is local. However, unlike paper surveys, phone interviews involve considerably more "human hours" to conduct and are subject to the individual quirks of the persons doing the interviewing. This implies that training interviewers well is important to minimize bias or manipulation of points of view. Dillman (1978) enumerates several helpful suggestions regarding telephone research. This advice also applies to the administration of face-to-face interviews, which are more costly than phone interviews in terms of time and often take considerably longer to conduct. They pose more risk to the interviewer, because that individual has to interact with unknown persons in strange and perhaps even dangerous environments, depending on the sample and the types of questions being asked. But in terms of thoroughness, the face-to-face interview has the potential to yield some of the richest data because a trained and experienced interviewer can guide the conversation to get to important points that might be overlooked in the less personal phone conversation or even more impersonal paper questionnaire. Combining interviews with paper surveys is referred to as "triangulation" and gives the researcher greater opportunity to follow up in the interviews any issues or questions that may have been left unanswered or inconclusive in the survey.

Internet-Based Research

With respect to issues like cost and timeliness, using the Internet as a data-collection medium might seem ideal for some research efforts. Depending on the type of data being collected, this may be true and may increase in efficiency as technology diffuses in society. However, current Internet research may not allow random selection of subjects, because computers and Internet access are by far less ubiquitous, especially in the lower socioeconomic groups of the population, than are the presence of telephones or mailboxes for paper surveys. Also, even among those who have Internet access there lingers a sort of "black-box" suspicion surrounding Internet use. Stories of people being reticent to submit a credit card number are common, and the distrust of information technology with respect to privacy issues is also pervasive. Guarantees of anonymity and confidentiality are harder to impress on people when the media outlets carry more and more stories about passwords being compromised and hackers running amuck among even the most secure systems. As the technology diffuses and becomes more accepted, availability and reticence as limiting factors will likely decrease.

DATA ENTRY AND ANALYSIS

Once the data are collected, the numbers will need to be entered into a database or spreadsheet before generating a computer-based output. For less formal analyses, even a program like Microsoft Excel can provide basic statistics such as the mean and standard deviation. If you want to run any higher-level statistics, such as factor analysis, multiple regression, or an alpha coefficient of reliability, then it is preferable to use dedicated statistics software such as SPSS or SAS. Prior to analysis, the researcher will have to "clean" the data, meaning that it is necessary to inspect the numbers to ensure that they were not entered incorrectly. There are a variety of statistical tools that search for outliers (out-of-range numbers) that would flaw the analysis.

It must be emphasized, however, that when it is time to analyze the data, merely reading the output of a computer-generated statistic is not by itself the solution to the research questions or the communication problems because the statistic alone does not tell us what to do. Implementing change or devising a new strategy to cope with a problem remains a fairly high-ordered responsibility. The data obtained from the survey or questionnaire can offer insights into the characteristics of the population, and such insights form the basis for making better-informed decisions. Oftentimes, there is no "one right way" of responding to the problem. Successful planning to achieve beneficial results might begin with a survey or questionnaire, but it is no more than a beginning. Knowing what to do or what to say in a given situation is not in the statistics printout, but without the printout the knowing can be that much more difficult. Acquiring that kind of wisdom generally comes after considerable experience, reading, and learning, often including formal education in statistical analysis and research methods. There are a number of sources listed in the following references to help in your study, as well as those used within this chapter. Kerlinger (1986) is an especially recommended resource because the book offers good starting points and a sound overview of the entire research effort, as well as providing guidance in the use of more complex approaches.

In the end, one may wonder why survey research offers both an attractive and at the same time powerful approach. The simplest answer is probably this: If you want to know something about people, you should ask them questions. But, if you are interested in knowing what large numbers of people think, and you are not planning on talking directly to every person about whom you are interested (i.e., as in taking a census), then the most promising alternative is to do a survey of a representative sample. As an illustration, there are approximately six hundred thousand students in the Los Angeles County School System (Morse, 1998), and if a communication researcher wanted to know something about the beliefs, attitudes, behaviors, or communication competence of these students, the survey approach makes the most sense in terms of time, money, and effort. It is one of the most straightforward approaches: you ask questions, get answers, and analyze results. Furthermore, if one wants to influence a large audience, it is first necessary to know what most of that audience thinks, and the survey method allows you to sample a smaller group and then generalize those answers to the larger group (Frey, Botan, & Kreps, 2000). If the kind of information that you need involves large numbers of people, then survey research is the best approach. As Mauro (1992) pointed out, it is not necessary for a doctor to draw all of a person's blood to test for cholesterol or for disease, nor is it necessary for a chef to consume an entire pot of soup to make an informed judgment about it: rather, testing a sample will suffice, and if done properly, will yield significantly more information than if no sampling were done at all.

REFERENCES

Babbie, E.R. (1995). *Survey research* (7th ed.). Belmont, CA: Wadsworth.

Backstrom, C.H., & Hursh, G.D. (1981). *Survey research* (2d ed.). New York: Macmillan.

Blalock, H.M. (1979). *Social statistics* (2d ed.). New York: McGraw-Hill.

Bowers, J.W., & Courtright, J.A. (1984). *Communication research methods*. Glenview, IL: Scott, Foresman.

Cohen, J. (1988). *Statistical power analysis for the behavioral sciences*. Hillsdale, NJ: Lawrence Erlbaum.

Cronbach, L.J. (1951). Coefficient alpha and the internal structure of tests. *Psychometrika*, *16*, 297–334.

Denzin, N.K. (1970). *The research act: A theoretical introduction to sociological methods*. Chicago: Aldine.

Dillman, D.A. (1978). *Mail and telephone surveys: The total design method*. New York: Wiley.

Dooley, D. (2001). *Social research methods* (4th ed.). Upper Saddle River, NJ: Prentice-Hall.

Ferguson, G.A. (1981). *Statistical analysis in psychology and education* (5th ed.). New York: McGraw-Hill.

Festinger, L. (1957). *A theory of cognitive dissonance*. Stanford, CA: Stanford University Press.

Frey, J.H. (1983). *Survey research by telephone*. Beverly Hills, CA: Sage.

Frey, L.R., Botan, C.H., & Kreps, G.L. (2000). *Investigating communication: An introduction to research methods* (2d ed.). Needham Heights, MA: Allyn & Bacon.

Groves, R.M., & Kahn, R.L. (1979). *Surveys by telephone*. New York: Academic Press.

Hoinville, G., & Jowell, R. (1978). *Survey research practice*. London: Heinemann.

Kaiser, H.F. (1974). An index of factorial simplicity. *Psychometrika*, *39*, 31–36.

Kerlinger, F.N. (1986). *Foundations of behavioral research* (3rd ed.). Fort Worth, TX: Holt, Rinehart and Winston.

Kim, J., & Mueller, C.W. (1978). *Introduction to factor analysis.* Beverly Hills, CA: Sage.

Lissitz, R.W., & Green, S.B. (1975). Effect of the number of scale points on reliability. *Journal of Applied Psychology, 60*(1), 10–13.

Mauro, J. (1992). *Statistical deception at work.* Hillsdale, NJ: Lawrence Erlbaum.

McDermott, S.T. (1999). Quantitative/sampling. In D.W. Stacks & J.E. Hocking (Eds.), *Communication research,* 2d ed. (pp. 209–232). New York: Longman.

Morse, R. (1998, June 2). Back to school on shootings. *San Francisco Examiner,* p. A2.

Murphy, D.J. (1992). Electronic communication in smaller organizations: Case analysis from a theoretical perspective. *Technical Communication, 39*(1), 24–32.

Murphy, D.J. (1994). *NASA/DoD aerospace knowledge diffusion research project.* Report Number 30. Washington, DC: National Technical Information Service.

Murphy, D.J. (1997). The influence of analyzability, equivocality, uncertainty, and variety on communication in small, medium, and large U.S. aerospace corporations. In T.E. Pinelli, R.O. Barclay, J.M. Kennedy, & A.P. Bishop (Eds.), *Knowledge diffusion in the U.S. aerospace industry* (Part B; pp. 581–610). Greenwich, CT: Ablex.

Neuman, W.L. (2000). *Social research methods: Qualitative and quantitative approaches* (4th ed.). Needham Heights, MA: Allyn & Bacon.

Nielsen Media Research. (1999). What TV ratings really mean ... and other frequently-asked questions. http://www.nielsenmedia.com/whatratingsmean/.

Nunnally, J. (1978). *Psychometric theory* (2nd ed.). New York: McGraw-Hill.

Rummel, R.J. (1970). *Applied factor analysis.* Evanston, IL: Northwestern University Press.

Schutt, R.K. (1996). *Investigating the social world.* Thousand Oaks, CA: Pine Forge Press.

Stacks, D.W., & Hocking, J.E. (1999). *Essentials of communication research* (2d ed.). New York: Longman.

Sumser, J. (2001). *A guide to empirical research in communication.* Thousand Oaks, CA: Sage.

Young, R.K., & Veldman, D.J. (1981). *Introductory statistics for the behavioral sciences* (4th ed.). New York: Holt, Rinehart and Winston.

CHAPTER 6

Experimental and Quasi-Experimental Research

Davida Charney

ROLES FOR EXPERIMENTAL METHODS IN TECHNICAL COMMUNICATION RESEARCH

Our reasons for conducting research in technical communication are often practical and progressive. We seek to understand how communication works in technical and professional settings in order to make things better: to promote text designs that are easy for readers to use, to acculturate students into professional discourse communities, and to identify and promote effective and ethical communication practices in the workplace. All these goals may be furthered through experimental research methods. Technical communication researchers have used experiments to investigate such questions as these:

- Are structured abstracts for medical research articles easier to read than traditional abstracts? Do readers of medical journals prefer structured abstracts? (Hartley & Sydes, 1997).

- Are job recruiters willing to grant interviews to an applicant whose résumé contains grammatical errors, nominal sentence style, or irrelevant details? How do these features interact in forming a recruiter's judgment of a résumé? Do undergraduates assess these factors in the same ways as recruiters? (Charney, Rayman, & Ferreira-Buckley, 1992).

- As compared with working face-to-face, how does using electronic communication technologies from distant locations change the way a business team produces a written text, the quality of their report, or their satisfaction with the project? (Galegher & Kraut, 1994)

- Does oral feedback on a text differ from written feedback? When reviewers audiotape their feedback, do they provide comments on different topics or comments of different length, content, or style as compared with when they write out their comments? How do comments in oral or written media affect writers' revisions and attitudes toward the reviewers? (Neuwirth, Chandhok, Charney, Wojahn, & Kim, 1994)

Experimenters investigate the possible causes of a phenomenon. Experimenters work systematically to create situations in which different possible causes are present or absent. Then they observe how typical groups of people respond in each situation. In a "true" experiment, the situations are designed to be as similar as possible, differing only in the presence or absence of the causal factor under investigation. In the first example, some readers were given structured abstracts of a set of medical journal articles, while others read traditional abstracts of the same articles. Achieving the conditions of a "true" experiment often involves a high degree of control over the setting so that, for example, equal numbers of randomly chosen participants try out each causal factor. Quasi-experimental methods were designed for real-world settings where the controlled conditions necessary for "true" experiments are more difficult to arrange.

RESEARCH METHODS AND RESEARCH CLAIMS

To understand how experiments differ from other research methods, it is useful to think about the types of questions that research is used to address. A useful typology of research questions is the classical rhetorical system of stases, a sequence of questions that guides critical inquiry from the point when attention is drawn to a phenomenon to the point when we decide what to do about it. In Jeanne Fahnestock and Marie Secor's (1988, 1990; Fahnestock, 1986) formulation of the stases, five questions can be investigated:[1]

- Existence—whether a phenomenon exists or happened
- Definition—whether it belongs to some established (albeit fuzzy) category
- Cause—how it came about or what effects it has
- Value—whether it is to be considered good or bad
- Action—what should be done about it

The stases were originally formulated for use in courts of law, where lawyers argued over whether a crime took place, "whodunit," and so on. In recent years, rhetorical theorists have found the stases useful for analyzing and constructing arguments in a wide range of domains, private, public, and professional.[2]

The stases form a sequence; arguments at later stases build on consensus established from arguments at the earlier ones, even if agreement is provisional or accounts for only part of the audience.[3] The stases can be seen at play in a recent sequence of news stories about an astronomical phenomenon. Astronomers gained front-page newspaper headlines when they reported detecting a mysterious flash of light. They first sought grounds for agreeing that the flash in fact took place out in space and was not a local atmospheric effect. They worked to establish the timing, location, and intensity of the light, all claims at the stasis of *existence*. Then considerable debate ensued as astronomers attempted to determine what the flash was, to *define* it. A leading researcher eventually concluded that it was a special form of quasar, not a star and not something completely new. Finally, astronomers argued over what *caused* this quasar to behave differently from other more common quasars.

As a guide to inquiry, the sequence of stases is recursive and open ended rather than strictly linear. Progress in the sciences often involves revisiting earlier stases. For example, many years after agreeing that genes are *causal* agents in heredity and evolution, biologists launched the Human Genome Project to identify (or *define*) the sequence of genes in a human chromosome. The results of this project are expected to help researchers conduct further experiments about the causes of particular diseases and the effects of various medical treatments.

In some discourse contexts, such as a law court or a public policy debate, arguments are expected to range across the entire sequence of stases. But the entire sequence need not be addressed; a scholarly study often addresses an argument at a single stasis. Fahnestock and Secor (1988) analyzed the main argumentative focus of scholarly articles in literary and scientific journals. In literary criticism, they found that arguments often hinged on the stasis of value (such as the relative worth of an author or a text). In scientific articles, the argument focused on one of the three lower stases: existence, definition, or cause.[4]

Within the framework of the stases, research methods can be seen as standardized approaches that a discipline agrees on as suitable for supporting claims of certain types. Specific research methods are warranted for supporting arguments at specific stases. In most disciplines, descriptive and observational methods, whether qualitative or quantitative, including case studies, ethnographies, surveys, process-tracing, and textual analyses, are warranted for supporting claims of existence and definition. Experimental and quasi-experimental methods were developed specifically to warrant causal claims. Because the causes of a phenomenon often cannot be explored in a meaningful way until its nature is understood somewhat, descriptive and observational methods often precede experimental research. But, as noted earlier, research is best understood as recursive, with results at a "higher" stasis often leading to further work at a "lower" stasis. Similarly, within composition studies, Bereiter and Scardamalia (1987) describe how different "levels" of writing research (including practitioner observation, experimentation, and simulation) interrelate cyclically.

It is important to emphasize that using a standard method does not guarantee that findings will be accepted as true or important, merely that the arguments will be treated as worthy of serious consideration. Using a standard method of research opens up the work to scrutiny by others who are familiar with either the methods or the phenomena (Charney, 1996). In his history of the research article, Charles Bazerman (1988) describes how specific methods evolved as ways to anticipate and respond to challenges to experiments that were initially conducted in very public arenas. In the course of extending and challenging each other's work, specialists in an area develop, apply, and refine a repertoire of methods that they consider appropriate for certain types of inquiries. Over time, some methods gain credibility on the basis of their elegance and their reliability across many applications. When scientists introduce new and unfamiliar methods, they argue at length for their reliability and productivity (Thompson, 1993). But even though researchers rarely have to justify using a standard method, they do have to argue that they applied it appropriately because almost every application involves creativity and hard choices. Over the course of time, even standard methods are subject to challenge; advances in knowledge, technology, or methodological standards frequently alter the credence that scientists invest in specific methods and their interpretations of studies that employed them.

Experiments as Causal Inquiry

The basic strategies for causal inquiry derive from John Stuart Mill (1843, 1930) who advocated experimentation, active manipulation of a situation to observe the effects of an intervention in controlled circumstances. Mill proposed four methods for causal inquiry:

- Agreement: searching for relevant factors (candidate causes) that are always present before the outcome (or effect) occurs

- Disagreement: searching for a single relevant difference between situations, such that the factor is present whenever the outcome occurs and absent whenever it doesn't

- Concomitant Variation: searching for relevant factors whose strength or frequency is positively or negatively correlated with the outcome[5]
- Residues or Elimination: identifying the roles of multiple factors by systematically removing known causes to see if the outcome continues to occur

The first three methods, agreement, disagreement, and concomitant variation, may be carried out by observing natural events. A researcher may seek out all possible cases in which an outcome occurred and analyze which factors were present and which were absent. The final method calls for experimentation. Experimenters try to create conditions in which the outcome occurs and then vary those conditions to test the contribution of individual factors.

To see how factors can be tested systematically, consider a series of experiments conducted by psychologist Lynne Reder. She started with a seemingly simple question: Do students learn more of the central ideas in a standard introductory college textbook by reading fully elaborated texts (including explanations, evidence, restatements, and so on) or by studying the main ideas in isolation? Reder took chapters from several widely used textbooks and prepared summaries that were one-fifth as long. In her first experiment, she gave half the students the original chapter to read and the other half, the summary. Then she tested the students' comprehension and recall of the main points. Reder was surprised to find that the students who had read the summaries performed better on the tests than those who had read the full chapters. Her colleagues suggested a wide number of accidental reasons why she might have gotten these results. She eventually completed ten studies checking out these factors (Allwood, Wikstrom, & Reder, 1982; Reder, 1982; Reder and Anderson, 1980). She varied how soon the test was administered (immediately after reading or after delays of up to one year); what type of test questions were asked (true/false, short answer, or free recall); and how the outcome was measured (accuracy or speed). She also varied the reading conditions. In one study, students were allowed to take the materials home to read at their leisure; in other studies, the duration of the students' exposure to each main idea was carefully equated. Consistently, students who read the summaries learned the main points better. One factor that Reder did not vary in these studies was the kind of learning expected of the students. However, remembering facts is only one goal of learning. Students also need to know how to use new knowledge to solve problems. In our research together, Reder and I investigated whether a full text would produce better results when readers needed to *apply* what they learned. We prepared full and summary versions of a manual for a computer operating system and asked students to learn a set of basic commands. We found that students who had read manuals with certain types of elaboration performed better at a set of computer tasks than those who had read summary versions of the manuals (Charney, Reder, & Wells, 1988).

In their classic text *Quasi-Experimentation*, Thomas Cook and Donald Campbell (1979) explicitly relate experimental methods to causal argument and sensitively address recent philosophical concerns about causation (see also Cook & Shadish, 1994). Like many other researchers, they are cautious about making or accepting causal claims—and with good reason. As psychologists have repeatedly observed, most people are overly eager to infer causal connections between phenomena that simply occur together (perhaps by accident) and overly reluctant to say that some factor could not be a cause of some outcome, even when sufficient evidence for ruling it out is available (Kuhn, Amsel, & O'Loughlin, 1988). Because mistaken causal inferences can have serious social as well as scientific consequences, the standards for designing and reporting experiments are intended to encourage self-critical reflection and to maximize opportunities for public scrutiny of both methods and results.

Toward these ends, researchers have developed sophisticated protocols for conducting experiments. Cook and Campbell (1979) provide an excellent discussion of the general classes of experimental and quasi-experimental research designs. They also lay out some bases for judging an experiment by identifying a number of "threats" to validity that researchers routinely consider in designing their experiments and by explaining how specific research designs and practices can minimize these threats. Some of these strategies are sketched in the following sections (see also Shaughnessy, Zechmeister, & Zechmeister, 2000; Slavin, 1992).

PRINCIPLES FOR EXPERIMENTAL RESEARCH

An experiment is a comparison between a situation in which a putative causal factor is present and a situation in which it is absent. The aspects of the situation that are varied are called *independent variables*. Each independent variable has at least two levels, to reflect the presence or absence of the cause. For example, in Reder's (1982) study, the text variable had two levels: either many elaborations or no elaborations at all. Independent variables can also have more than two levels, allowing different degrees or kinds of the causal factor to be present. In our studies of computer manuals (Charney, Reder, & Wells, 1988), the text variable had several levels, including no elaboration, explanations of the syntax of the computer commands, and elaboration of the reasons for using the commands.

Other aspects of the situation, called *control variables*, are held constant or equated. In Reder's experiments, students were asked to learn the same set of main points, regardless of whether they saw them in the full chapter or in the summary. Reder also took steps to ensure that the summary and full-text groups were equally typical of the student body as a whole and that they studied the texts under similar conditions. Ideally, all aspects of the situation except the independent variables are controlled. But control does not always mean conscious regulation. Paradoxically, a variable can be controlled by letting it vary as freely or randomly as in natural settings. For example, if enough participants are chosen randomly from among the students on campus, they will vary naturally in height, weight, religious affiliation, amount of sleep the previous night, and so on.

The sequence of events in which the participants are presented with the materials is called the intervention or treatment. Participants carry out tasks in which they perform the activities or form the attitudes or beliefs that the independent variables are hypothesized to affect. The tasks might include reading, writing, answering questions, solving problems, or using a device. The effects of the independent variables are measured by tests administered before, during, or after the treatment. The ways in which performance on the tests is evaluated are called *dependent measures* or *dependent variables*. These may include correctness of response, speed of response, strength of preference on an attitude scale, quality judgments by raters, or frequencies of occurrence within a participant's response (e.g., length in words or references to the audience in a written passage). In Reder's (Allwood, Wikstrom, & Reder, 1982; Reder, 1982; Reder & Anderson, 1980) studies, the students' learning was measured in various ways, with different types of questions (true/false, short answer, or free recall). She measured how long students spent reading the texts, how long they took to answer individual questions, how many of their answers were correct (on true/false tests), and how many of the main ideas they wrote down (on free recall tests).

In analyzing the results, experimenters do not usually produce profiles of individual participants. Instead, they try to characterize the central tendency of each group, its average or most representative behavior pattern, as well as its range and variation. Reder's (1982) report that readers of summaries learned more on average than readers of full-length chapters was based on consistent findings that the average correctness score for the summary group as a whole was higher and their average response time was shorter. Statistical analyses are used to compare the patterns of scores to determine whether differences observed between the groups are robust enough to warrant a claim that they were not produced by chance, but instead were caused by the factor under study (Abelson, 1995). If so, the results are considered *reliable* or *statistically significant*. Statistical significance is expressed as a probabilistic confidence judgment rather than an assertion of fact. If none of the results of a study are statistically reliable, the researchers may modify the experiment to try to create conditions in which the results are reliable. Or they may ultimately conclude that the initial hypothesis was not tenable or that that particular experimental approach is not viable.

If the only systematic differences in the treatment of the groups are the levels of the independent variables and if there are reliable differences between the groups on the test scores (the dependent measures), then researchers may claim that changing the independent variable caused the difference in results. The results of a single experiment are rarely completely clear-cut. As described previously, Reder and her colleagues (Allwood, Wikstrom, & Reder, 1982; Reder, 1982; Reder & Anderson, 1980) conducted a series of ten experiments to check whether the superior performance of the summary group was due to specific aspects of how they had conducted the study. The consistent finding that the summary group performed better under a variety of conditions increased their confidence that isolating the main ideas in the summaries made them easier for students to understand and recall. At that point, experimenters weigh the pragmatic importance of the results for disciplinary or real-world issues. For example, if Reder had found that reading summaries reliably increased an average student's score by only 1 percent, this result might be considered real but unimportant. As Linda Flower (1989) has noted, statistical evidence has meaning only as part of a cumulative, communally constructed argument, in which "the special virtue of a claim that has earned the name 'result' is that it has been subjected to a given research community's more stringent rules of inference" (p. 300).

Experimental Designs

One common way to set up an experiment is to assign participants randomly to different treatments, in a *between-subjects* design. Then one (or more) group of participants receives *experimental* treatments, treatments that are hypothesized to cause a change. Reder's (1982) study employed a between-subjects design, because one set of students was assigned to read the summary and a different set to read the full-length chapter. A between-subjects design may also involve a *control* group. The control group participates fully in the study and is treated as similarly as possible to the experimental group, but does not receive a treatment that is expected to cause a change. In medical research, for example, patients in a control group may be given placebos (sugar pills) instead of medication. The control and experimental groups may receive their pills on exactly the same schedule, with neither patients nor staff members aware of who is receiving medication and who is receiving a placebo.[6] The control group provides baseline information about how this medical condition might proceed without medication, but with the same experiences as the medicated group of other aspects of health care, confidence in their doctors, and so on. A challenge for between-subjects designs is forming equivalent groups of participants. In many cases, randomly assigning participants to groups is sufficient; however, many research designers also recommend giving pretests so that the groups' starting points on the dependent measures may be directly compared.

A second way to design a study is to see how the same individuals respond to a variety of situations, both when the putative cause is present and when it is absent. In a *within-subjects* design, every participant eventually receives all the treatments. Fewer participants are needed in studies with within-subjects designs because the participants, in effect, serve as their own controls; they bring in the same mix of preferences, experience, and physical characteristics when they act in one condition as when they act in the other. The simplest way to implement a within-subjects design is to have each participant go through the same experiment twice. For example, in a study of the effects of familiar and distant audiences on children's writing styles (Cohen & Riel, 1989), each child took part in two sessions, in one, writing an essay to their teacher for a grade, and in the other, writing a letter on a similar topic to be posted to a child in a foreign country. Cohen and Riel found that when students wrote to distant audiences their essays scored higher in content, organization, and language use than when the same children wrote to their teachers. Cohen and Riel ruled out the possibility that the effects were due to the order of completing the assignments, by having half the students write to the teacher first and the other half write to the peer first.

A within-subjects design can be implemented within a single session. This kind of design can be illustrated with a study I conducted with two colleagues to investigate how writing features affect job recruiters' judgments of student résumés (Charney, Rayman, & Ferreira-Buckley, 1992). We asked job recruiters visiting campus to rate a set of thirty-six student résumés on a four-point scale, to indicate their willingness to interview the students for a job in mechanical engineering. The résumés were fictitious, but their content was drawn from real job application materials. The résumés were carefully constructed to vary four factors: sentence style (nominal or verbal), grammatical errors (present or absent), elaboration (no elaboration, object-based description, and function-based description), and relevance of previous work experience (low, medium, and high). The final set of thirty-six résumés comprised one of every possible combination of these four factors, so the same recruiters rated résumés in every condition. Other aspects of the résumés were held constant, such as format, grade point average, and degree program. Each recruiter gave only one overall score to each résumé. However, by sorting the scores for résumés representing the different factors (a task simplified by statistical computer applications), we could see the independent effect of each factor. For example, we calculated the average score for the eighteen résumés with grammatical errors and compared it with the average score for the eighteen correct résumés. We found that all the factors influenced the ratings. Our design allowed us to assess the strength of each factor and see how they interacted; for example, recruiters were sometimes harsher in penalizing mechanics errors from students whose résumés listed more relevant work experience.

Between-subjects and within-subjects factors can also be combined in a single study, for example, if different groups of participants perform the same tasks. In a later version of the résumé study, we compared job recruiters' ratings with those of technical writing students. In this comparison, participant status (student or recruiter) was a between-group factor, and the résumé variables (grammatical errors, elaboration, relevance) were within-subjects factors.

Strengthening Confidence in an Experiment's Validity

Because researchers try to control so many aspects of an experiment, there is often good reason to question whether the results are valid, to ask whether an experimental treatment really caused an apparent difference in the outcomes. Even if researchers find a big difference in the performance of two groups, it might not be due to the intervention. It might have been caused by some other factor or it might be an accident. Or researchers might see no difference in the outcome measures, even though the intervention actually caused a change—perhaps it was a change that the outcome measures were incapable of detecting. To help experimenters anticipate such challenges and design studies that avoid them as much as possible, Campbell and others developed a general list of threats to validity (and possible recourses) that researchers now routinely consider as they plan experiments

(Abelson, 1995; Cook & Campbell, 1979; Cook & Shadish, 1994; Shaughnessy, Zechmeister & Zechmeister, 2000; Slavin, 1992).

History and Maturation.   Unanticipated events may occur during the study. Or participants may simply change over time. Unless they are equally likely to affect all participants, these events and changes may produce spurious differences in the outcomes for the two groups. Randomizing assignment of participants to treatments, randomizing the order of tasks, and conducting studies in a controlled quiet setting can reduce these threats. For example, suppose that between the time Reder's (1982) students read the passage and the time they took the test, a large freshman dormitory on campus was flooded and the students who lived there went without a good night's sleep. If many of the participants in the full-chapter group were recruited from this dormitory, their poor performance might not be due to the chapter, but due instead to their intervening history. But if students recruited across campus were randomly assigned to groups, then students from this dorm should be equally heavily represented in both groups, so the detrimental effects of sleeplessness should balance out.

Testing.   A pretest may alter performance on a posttest, either because participants have a chance to practice or their attention is attracted to a key topic or strategy. Using a control group reduces the problem because the control and experimental groups should be affected equally by the pretest; differences detected on the posttest are then likelier to be due to the treatment.

Instrumentation.   The quality of the test may obscure differences between groups in several ways. First, the test might vary during the study, if, for example, a study involves networked computers and there is great variation in the speed of response. Second, multiple tests might not be equivalent. If, for example, the posttest is harder or less interesting than the pretest, then participants' gains from the treatment might not be detected. Third, the tests might be too easy or too hard. If a test is too easy, then the scores all bunch at the top of the scale (a ceiling effect). If the test is too hard, the scores bunch at the bottom (a floor effect). The tests may spuriously show no difference between experimental and control treatments because there is no way for the improvement to register. Pilot testing can prevent many of these problems.

Selection Bias, Attrition, and Regression to the Mean. These threats reduce the chances that groups of participants are functionally equivalent, when the groups should start off on average at the same ability level, with the same overall mix of attributes. Assigning participants randomly to groups avoids the problem of *selection bias*, such as steering the most "promising" participants to the experimental group (consciously or accidentally), which would spuriously increase the chances of finding that the intervention "succeeded." *Attrition* is a problem if participants drop out of one group more than another. If, for example, many women dropped out of the experimental group, then at the end of the study, the control and experimental groups would no longer be equivalent. Any differences in the outcomes may be due to gender differences rather than the treatment. *Regression to the mean* describes the probability that people who score extremely high or extremely low on a test will score closer to the average if given another test. The problem arises if researchers try to compare treatment groups chosen from the extreme ends of a scale, because participants at the bottom may spuriously appear to improve and those at the top may spuriously appear to regress.

Nonrepresentativeness, Artificiality, Reactivity. Researchers are often concerned that their findings will only represent the behavior of the specific group of participants from the local setting in which the study was conducted. In planning their studies, they may take several steps to increase confidence that the findings generalize to a larger population. Any argument for generalization is an assessment of plausibility. To increase plausibility that the findings apply to a general group, researchers try to recruit participants who are representative, create conditions that are realistic, and use measures that are stable. Participants are *nonrepresentative* if they are, as a group, unlike the larger population of interest. It is not enough for all the members of the participant pool to be members of the larger population. They are nonrepresentative as a group if they do not have the same mix of attributes as any other sample chosen at random from the population. The costs of a nonrepresentative sample may be great. In 1987, the IRS user-tested its new W-4 tax form on nontechnical IRS clerical staff, who the IRS assumed knew no more about taxes than any typical taxpayer; however, these employees were far more capable of understanding the form than ordinary taxpayers (Gutfeld, 1987). The forms turned out to be unusable and were recalled and redesigned at great expense. Random selection is the best way to avoid the problem of nonrepresentativeness. *Artificiality* is the problem that the conditions of the study were so unusual that the same results would not occur in other, more natural settings. Some artificiality is inevitable; researchers reduce the threat by conducting similar experiments under many kinds of conditions, as Reder (Allwood, Wikstrom, & Reder, 1982; Reder, 1982; Reder & Anderson, 1980) did. Some clearly artificial studies may be perfectly valid (Stanovich, 2001). For example, researchers studying the effects of visual feedback on writing style might legitimately ask students to compose on a computer with no monitor.

Tolerance for Threats to Validity.   Beginning researchers who read experiments sometimes take validity as a single-elimination contest—as if finding any weakness whatever makes a study entirely invalid. But some flaws are more serious than others. No study can test every factor; the conditions can never be completely controlled. Robert Slavin emphasizes that readers must apply "educated common sense" to judge a study: the results of a seemingly perfect experiment are not guaranteed to be valid and the results of a seemingly flawed study may yet be strong enough to serve as a basis for further research (1992, p. 22). The indeterminacy of scientific methods does not mean that anything goes. Keith Stanovich (2001) notes that theories can be rigorously evaluated on the basis of a large number of partially flawed experiments, especially when the limitations of one are addressed in another (see also Charney, 1996). Meta-analysis is one way to see if an effect consistently occurs across experimental studies, such as George Hillocks's (1986) meta-analysis of various writing pedagogies.

Random Selection, Random Assignment, and Random Ordering

In contrast to everyday parlance, doing something "at random" in an experiment does not mean being careless. Instead, randomization means relying on the laws of probability to reproduce naturally occurring mixtures of attributes. Experimenters randomize for two main purposes: to select a sample of participants that is, in aggregate, representative of a larger population and to divide this pool into treatment groups that are, in aggregate, equivalent to each other. Experimenters also frequently randomize the order of tasks or materials to avoid the threat to validity of history. For all these purposes, randomization works on the principle of giving everyone an equal opportunity to be chosen.

The rationale behind randomization is that individuals are unpredictable. Members of a particular population, such as active NBA basketball players, share many salient characteristics because of selection criteria, training, and acculturation. Even so, they vary in their personal traits, beliefs, politics, habits, moods, and current states of mind. Basketball players are obviously taller than male adults in the United States generally, but the heights of the individual players represent a range, with most players grouped around the average and a few who are quite a bit taller and a few quite a bit shorter than average. This kind of variation is what is "normal" about a "normal" bell curve distribution. To select a random sample of active NBA basketball players, we might take the official rosters of all the teams, start in an arbitrary spot, and select every sixth name. The resulting sample should mirror the range and variation of heights of the entire population, as well as their ages, fitness conditions, ethnicities, and a host of other attributes, none of which played any explicit role in the selection process. Random sampling does not ignore or suppress individual differences or commonalities; rather it treats them as too subtle and too complex to apportion and it gives them free play. If all members of a population have an equal chance to be selected, then common and rare attributes of the population should be represented as common or rare in the sample.

Some variations on random sampling can ensure that certain features of interest are included in the sample. Stratified sampling involves close analysis of some community in an effort to include some important constituency in representative proportions. So in constructing groups of taxpayers to test a new form, one might ensure that each group contained representatives of the various income brackets in the same proportions as the U.S. population. No matter how many categories are formed in a stratified sample, none may be reliably represented by only one person. The more individuals in the sample, the less any one participant may be mistaken as typical of the whole group.

Quasi-Experimental Designs

Quasi-experimental designs were developed for research in real-world settings where it is more difficult to randomly select participants or assign them randomly to conditions, such as schools, neighborhood literacy centers, nonprofit organizations, or workplaces. In a typical college classroom, for example, the selection of students is far from random; some take the course to fulfill a requirement, others out of interest, and others because it fits their schedule. The twenty-five students hardly represent a random sample of the entire student body, or of all seniors, or of all engineering majors. The considerations for avoiding threats to validity listed earlier apply even more strongly to quasi-experiments. As Cook and Campbell (1979) emphasize, because researchers using quasi-experimental designs cannot rely on random selection to avoid some of these threats and cannot control the conduct of the study as closely, they must analyze the situation much more closely to make the possible threats explicit and find ways to reduce them. Slavin (1992) provides a useful discussion of strategies for reducing threats in research in classroom settings.

Control groups are frequently used in quasi-experiments. When researchers are unable to select participants randomly or assign them randomly to conditions, they usually collect more detailed information on the backgrounds of the participants and pretest their abilities, in order to check as much as possible on the equivalence of control and treatment groups. Some quasi-experimental designs use strategies similar to the within-subjects design, by providing a sequence of phases in which treatment is provided, withdrawn, and repeated, with performance tests at the end of each phase. An argument for causation can be made if the outcome measures reliably change when the treatment is present and reverts to control levels when it is withdrawn. Another strategy in quasi-experiments is to administer the outcome test repeatedly over a period of time before and after the treatment. Rising and falling test scores at the predicted times might then show the time-course of any effect of the treatment.

In and of itself, the setting does not determine whether a study should be designed as an experiment or quasi-experiment. In Cook's recent discussion of quasi-experimental designs (Cook & Shadish, 1994), he emphasizes that experimental methods are widely applicable in real-world settings. The choice of design is more likely to depend on the experimenter's degree of access, matters of timing and convenience, and other aspects of the situation.

ETHICAL TREATMENT OF PARTICIPANTS IN EXPERIMENTS

Some people object to experimental research because participants are taken as "objects" of study, which critics assume must be dehumanizing. These critics also object to the distant, impersonal stance that experimentalists adopt—as compared with ethnographers. Many of these criticisms essentialize experimental researchers too hastily as cold and uncaring (Charney, 1996, 1997). For most experimentalists, impersonality is intended as a form of ethical behavior that preserves participants' freedom of action. An impersonal stance minimizes the chances that a researcher will (even unknowingly) pressure participants to adapt to his or her predispositions, as in placebo effects. Experimentalists, like everyone else in the world, are prone to biases. Practices that promote objectivity cannot train researchers out of their biases—rather, they reduce the effects of biases by limiting and systematizing interactions with participants and by making methods and results more available for scrutiny and replication by researchers with different sets of biases.

Experimental researchers plan out their interactions with participants ahead of time, and many even write out a "script" detailing all planned communications with participants—except, of course, for open-ended questions and comments. These plans and scripts avoid some threats to validity by ensuring that all participants are treated the same. They also prevent unethical exploitation of the participants. Written descriptions of how participants will be recruited and what they will be asked to do are submitted for external independent review to an Institutional Review Board (IRB), which at most universities is made up of faculty members and members of the public. Before any data are collected, the IRB checks the procedures for obtaining participants' informed consent, ensures that participants' right to privacy and right to withdraw are protected, and assesses the procedures' risks and benefits (and may require modifications). For a more detailed discussion of the IRB and its processes, see the Breuch, Olson, and Frantz chapter in this volume.

Although this planning and review process is the most visible arena for protecting the rights of participants, other important protection processes take place after the data are collected and an article is drafted or even published. At this point, the discussion moves from the institution in which the researchers practice to the discipline as a whole, where new standards of conduct might be developed. The method sections of an experimental research article opens the procedures to scrutiny by the research community at large, allowing problematic procedures to be challenged. For example, it is largely because of routine reporting of sampling procedures that feminists documented the unwarranted exclusion of women participants in some social science and medical studies, and it is because of such reports that ongoing reforms can be monitored.

Researchers must also take steps to protect participants when they describe their results. To protect participants' rights to privacy, researchers usually confine the data analysis to summaries of group tendencies, rather than to descriptions of individual participants. Because the scores are reported as averages rather than as individual scores, the participants in the study remain anonymous; their scores and their personal histories cannot influence future teachers or administrators. This approach limits the types of claims that researchers may make. Researchers may only make causal claims about how their factors influenced the tendencies of groups, not the behaviors of individuals. Generalizations about the central tendency of a group are not distributive to the members; in other words, claims about the group as a whole are not assumed to hold of each member. For example, a study of the effects of a Head Start program may report that children from the most economically disadvantaged groups make the greatest gains. Some students in the most economically disadvantaged Head Start group probably make no gains at all, and the progress of some might seem to be held back. Predictions or judgments of outcomes for individual participants, such as the likelihood of academic success for any particular child in the Head Start program, are not warranted. Unfortunately, average results are sometimes taken as "normal," even though there is no basis for concluding that children who did not benefit from Head Start are "abnormal." Normative interpretations can be and are challenged in disciplinary as well as public arenas. In fact, statistical conventions for reporting average scores and variances are designed to help researchers and readers assess a group's heterogeneity. Using large numbers of participants and discussing group tendencies can thus be a way of respecting individual differences and a way of resisting totalizing or deterministic conclusions.

RESEARCH IN REAL-WORLD SETTINGS

The common assumption that experimental methods are not possible in real-world settings is incorrect. Even though Cook and Campbell are credited with developing quasi-experimental methods, they increasingly advocate conducting true experiments whenever possible (Cook & Campbell, 1986; Cook & Shadish, 1994). And they argue strongly that true experiments can be conducted in more settings than one might expect. They cite many successful studies that use random assignment of participants to treatments in field settings, including schools, housing developments, and clinics. Conducting experiments may take additional imagination, planning, and effort, but we should not choose methods or research questions primarily on the basis of convenience. All important research skills, from foreign language learning to statistics, require specialized training that may take years to master. Many interesting causal questions remain in technical communication and they are worth pursuing.

NOTES

1. For an alternative formulation of the stases for scientific discourse, see Prelli (1989). I have chosen to follow Fahnestock and Secor (1988, 1990) because

they treat cause as an independent stasis. This seems justified, especially in the current discussion, because of the substantial attention experimentalists devote to causal arguments. In most important respects, the two systems are compatible.

2. Notably, these strategies for inquiry are in no way restricted to scientific research. Similar techniques appear in popular argument textbooks for first-year composition (e.g. Fahnestock & Secor, 1990; Lunsford & Ruszkiewicz, 1999; Ramage, Bean, & Johnson, 2000).

3. Certainty about a claim at any stasis is not necessary in order to go on with an argument. In fact, research at a higher stasis is often conducted in order to address continuing disagreements about the nature of a phenomenon. As Fahnestock (1986) and many others have observed, claims in scientific texts tend to be probabilistic with qualifiers giving explicit signals of the degree of the writer's degree of confidence.

4. Fahnestock and Secor (1988, 1990) note that scholarly arguments almost always address value, at least implicitly. In order to persuade colleagues to read their work and take it seriously (by challenging it, replicating it, or building on it), scholars have to argue that the work is important and relevant to ongoing work in the discipline. (For an analysis of how they do so, see Swales, 1990.) Recently, some critical theorists have argued that scientists are remiss ethically for not addressing value arguments more explicitly—and some see this silence as acquiescence or complicity in inequity. I respond to these critiques at length elsewhere (Charney, 1996, 1997), arguing that scientists use other forums than research articles to address moral and ethical questions, that qualitative methods that seem to discuss ethical issues more explicitly do not necessarily avoid the problems, and that experimental methods should not be dismissed wholesale on ideological grounds.

5. Cook and Campbell point out that Mill drew a sharp distinction between correlation and causation—and so do experimentalists today. Correlational arguments describe the frequency of co-occurrence, such as the presence of fire engines at fires. Causal arguments require evidence of a direct connection between factors and outcomes, such as the presence of oxygen for fire to occur. For these reasons, in their discussion of Mill, Cook and Campbell combine concomitant variation and elimination.

6. Reder's (1982) studies compared two treatment groups, a summary group and a full-text group. In Reder's case, a control group might have been used in the early stages of the research to check on the difficulty of the passages and the test questions. A group of students might have been asked to read a passage on a different topic than the experimental passage but of equivalent length and difficulty and then asked to take the tests on the main ideas from the experimental passage that they had not read. If the control group's scores were high, then the test questions or the passages themselves might have been too easy. For a lively (if not brash) discussion of control groups and artificiality, see Stanovich (2001).

REFERENCES

Abelson, R. (1995). *Statistics as principled argument*. Mahwah, NJ: Lawrence Erlbaum Associates.

Allwood, C.M., Wikstrom, T., & Reder, L.M. (1982). Effects of presentation format on reading retention: Superiority of summaries in free recall. *Poetics, 11*, 145–153.

Bazerman, C. (1988). *Shaping Written Knowledge*. Madison: University of Wisconsin.

Bereiter, C., & Scardamalia, M. (1987). *The psychology of written composition*. Hillsdale, NJ: Lawrence Erlbaum Associates.

Charney, D. (1996). Empiricism is not a four-letter word. *College Composition and Communication, 47*, 567–593.

Charney, D. (1997). Paradigm and punish (response to Marilyn Cooper). *College Composition and Communication, 48*, 562–565.

Charney, D., Rayman, J., & Ferreira-Buckley, L. (1992). How writing quality influences readers' judgments of résumés in business and engineering. *Journal of Business and Technical Communication, 6*, 38–74.

Charney, D., Reder, L., & Wells, G. (1988). Studies in elaboration in instructional texts. In Steven Doheny-Farina (Ed.), *Effective documentation: What we have learned from research* (pp. 47–72). Cambridge, MA: MIT Press.

Cohen, M., & Riel, M. (1989). The effect of distant audiences on students' writing. *American Educational Research Journal, 26*, 143–159.

Cook, T., & Campbell, D. (1979). *Quasi-experimentation: Design and analysis issues for field settings*. Boston, MA: Houghton Mifflin.

Cook, T., & Shadish, W. (1994). Social experiments: Some developments over the past fifteen years. *Annual Review of Psychology, 45*, 545–578.

Fahnestock, J. (1986). Accommodating science: The rhetorical life of scientific facts. *Written Communication, 3*, 275–296.

Fahnestock, J., & Secor, M. (1988). The stases in scientific and literary argument. *Written Communication, 5*, 427–443.

Fahnestock, J., & Secor, M. (1990). *A rhetoric of argument* (2d ed.). New York: McGraw Hill.

Flower, L. (1989). Cognition, context, and theory building. *College Composition and Communication, 40*, 282–311.

Galegher, J., & Kraut, R. (1994). Computer-mediated communication for intellectual teamwork: An experiment in group writing. *Information Systems Research, 5*, 110–138.

Gutfeld, R. (1987, February 17). Sad returns of W-4: One bureaucrat's "spirit" becomes another's "parody." *Wall Street Journal*, p. 26.

Hartley, J., & Sydes, M. (1997). Are structured abstracts easier to read than traditional ones? *Journal of Research in Reading, 20*, 122–136.

Hillocks, G. (1986). *Research on written composition: New directions for teaching*. Urbana, IL: National Council of Research in English.

Kuhn, D., Amsel, E., & O'Loughlin, M. (1988). *The development of scientific thinking skills*. San Diego, CA: Academic Press.

Lunsford, A., & Ruszkiewicz, J. (1999). *Everything's an argument*. Boston: Bedford/St. Martin's.

Mill, J.S. (1843; 1930). *A system of logic, ratiocinative and inductive: Being a connected view of the principles of evidence and the methods of scientific investigation*. London/New York: Longmans, Green.

Neuwirth, C., Chandhok, R., Charney, D., Wojahn, P., & Kim, L. (1994). Distributed collaborative writing: A comparison of spoken and written modalities for reviewing and revising documents. In *Proceedings of the Computer-Human Interaction '94 Conference*, April 24–28, 1994, Boston, MA (pp. 51–57). New York: Association for Computing Machinery.

Prelli, L. (1989). *A rhetoric of science: Inventing scientific discourse*. Columbia: University of South Carolina Press.

Ramage, J., Bean, J., & Johnson, J. (2000). *Writing arguments* (5th ed.). Boston: Allyn & Bacon.

Reder, L.M. (1982). Elaborations: When do they help and when do they hurt? *Text, 2*, 211–224.

Reder, L.M., & Anderson, J.R. (1980). A comparison of texts and their summaries: Memorial consequences. *Journal of Verbal Learning and Verbal Behavior, 19*, 121–134.

Reder, L.M., & Anderson, J.R. (1982). Effects of spacing and embellishment on memory for the main points of a text. *Memory & Cognition, 10*, 97–102.

Shaughnessy, J.J., Zechmeister, E.B., & Zechmeister, J.S. (2000). *Research methods in psychology* (5th ed.). Boston, MA: McGraw-Hill.

Slavin, R. (1992). *Research methods in education* (2d ed.). Boston: Allyn & Bacon.

Stanovich, K. (2001). *How to think straight about psychology* (6th ed.). New York: Longman.

Swales, J. (1990). *Genre analysis: English in academic and research settings*. Cambridge, UK: Cambridge University Press.

Thompson, D. (1993). Arguing for experimental facts in science: A study of research article results sections in biochemistry. *Written Communication, 10*, 106–130.

CHAPTER

Identifying and Accommodating Audiences for Technical and Professional Communication Research

Jo Allen and Sherry Southard

Since the early 1980s, technical communication literature is replete with calls for more research (see, for instance, Moran & Journet, 1985; Rubens, 1982; and Flatley, 1994), for better research (see, e.g., Goubil-Gambrell, 1992), and for more applicable research (see, for example, Carliner, 1994). Other critics ask for a better clarification of the roles, sites, and purposes of research and its attending concepts: theory and practice (see Debs, 1993; Doheny-Farina, 1993; Sullivan & Porter, 1993; and, especially, Gross, 1994). And arguments over the methods and methodologies of technical communication research reveal our angst over definitions, clarifications, and applications—especially as they insinuate particular philosophical stances toward knowledge making and interpretation (see Blyler, 1995; Charney, 1996; Herndl, 1993; and Lay, 1991).

One source of confusion seems to be over terminology, especially regarding what qualifies as "research." We define *research* to mean an ideally systematic, though fluid process for uncovering or generating knowledge that should hold meaning for a particular audience. As such, investigations may constitute either established research or formal research, terms we have appropriated to differentiate between rather passive and active forms of information seeking and knowledge building. *Established research*, which is a prerequisite for formal research (as well as scholarship and theory-building[1]), is the search for information in already available, usually published or online, forms—the uncovering of existing knowledge.

Most professional communicators would associate established research with library (both corporate and academic libraries) research, although it may also entail searches through data files, corporate records, or unpublished manuscripts.

Formal (or *empirical*) *research*, on the other hand, is typically described as a more active pursuit to generate new knowledge—knowledge that does not currently exist in published or accessible forms. Encompassing both qualitative and quantitative methods, formal research seeks to provide answers to questions that have not been resolved or whose resolutions are dubious or, possibly, outdated. Once formal research is published, it remains a work employing formal research methods, but it now serves as established research.

In this chapter, we address what we see as a major flaw in formal research publications: the omission of considerations for audience in theoretical and ideological discussions of and, moreover, in the practical carrying out of technical communication research. By "audiences" we mean not so much the reading audience, for our editorial boards, book editors, and general reviewers are charged with accepting works that will attract the appropriate readership for our publications. Instead, we are more concerned with the actual readers/users of research—those who might ponder and use the findings of any given study in any multitude of ways. Ironically, readers who read to remain current in their field, as well as readers who read to be able to apply what they have read, may be equally dismayed by what they read, feeling abandoned by the author/researcher who embarks on a research discovery that holds little value for the readers' needs or describes the conclusions of the research without explaining what to make of those conclusions (see Rainey & Kelly, 1992).

Thus, we seek to clarify the role that audience plays in technical communication research. Following a brief review of literature that more pointedly identifies the omission of an extended examination of audience, we analyze the role-based audience classification, developed by S. Doheny-Farina (1993), in which he describes five research audiences and appropriately cautions against their motivations that can skew the ethical considerations in technical communication research. First, we extend that classification by acknowledging the equally valid and more admirable alternative sides of the five role-based research audiences. Cautioning that even the expanded role-based classification may lead to monolithic constructs, we offer suggestions for accommodating any audience for technical communication research.

THE OMISSION OF AUDIENCE FROM RESEARCH IN TECHNICAL COMMUNICATION

In their work *Composition Research: Empirical Designs*, J.M. Lauer & J.W. Asher (1988) write that the results of a good research question "must make a contribution to the field, falling within the realm of those problems deemed significant and unresolved" (p. 9). Unfortunately, the agent of that determination is undefined, creating a dilemma in discussions about technical communication research. *Who* is supposed to deem a problem "significant and unresolved"? The researcher? The researcher's boss? Editors and reviewers of publications? The reading audience? Practicing communicators? Funding sources? Teachers? Students? Other researchers? Clearly, a number of decisions about the significance and resolution of research questions does fall to these groups. But we seem to have done little to investigate the kinds and uses of power these groups have in directing the research our discipline pursues. In short, and although no one seems to dispute that significance and resolution are key factors in quality research, no one seems to have expressed much thought about whose decisions (and the motivations for and consequences of their decisions) we are relying on. As Nancy Blyler (1995) writes, "We have largely avoided discussing the tough questions concerning ideology: questions such as whose interests are advanced by our research and what kinds of social and institutional contexts are reproduced" (p. 287).

Although they may identify their own immediate reading audiences, authors of recent books and book-length collections on research in technical communication also fail to address audience as an integral part of the research process. Three popular textbooks on the topic—L.R. Porter & W. Coggin's *Research Strategies in Technical Communication* (1995), D.E. Zimmerman and M.L. Muraski's *The Elements of Information Gathering: A Guide for Technical Communicators, Scientists, and Engineers* (1995), and M.S. MacNealy's *Strategies for Empirical Research in Writing* (1999)—do not address audiences for research as a special consideration in the research/development process. More scholarly publications (e.g., J.M. Lauer & J.W. Asher's *Composition Research: Empirical Designs* [1988] and J.R. Hayes, R. E. Young, M. L. Matchett, M. McCaffrey, C. Cochran, and T. Hajduk's *Reading Empirical Research Studies: The Rhetoric of Research* [1992], borrowed from our composition/rhetoric colleagues) also ignore audience's effects on the research process.

Works that relay the results of explorations and reconsiderations of the research process, such as R. Spilka's *Writing in the Workplace: New Research*

Perspectives (1993), again offer no insights on research audiences—with the exception of S. Doheny-Farina's classification of audiences whose needs might skew the ethics of a research project, which we discuss and expand at length in the next section. In that same collection of essays, T. Bouldin and L. Odell (1993) claim that in evaluating research in workplace writing, we need "to consider two basic questions: What has been accomplished thus far? And how does one build on past accomplishments in planning future work?" These are, no doubt, important beginnings, but their conclusion—that "research is an ongoing transaction among researcher, prior conclusions, and new data"—again ignores audience and, consequently, disengages matters of relevance, purpose, and usefulness from the process (p. 281).

As a very telling means of addressing audience, J.D. Beard, D.L. Williams, and S. Doheny-Farina (1989) present a useful study of nonacademic technical communicators' attitudes toward research in technical communication. Even though the authors readily announce that their respondents are self-selected based on their attendance at a particular session of a particular professional conference, the respondents reflect a favorable overall view of research in technical communication. Unfortunately, their experiences are based on three-year reading periods in which they need identify only one useful research-reading experience. Further, the work offers no direction, other than topical, for researchers; it should, we believe, admonish researchers to consider the needs of an audience (whether nonacademic practitioners or some other audience) as at least a potential raison d'être for any research project.

J.D. Beard and D.L. Williams's follow-up in 1992 reveals many of the same attitudes toward research—primarily that it is important although, tellingly, respondents admit not reading the research journals. Perhaps in an effort to encourage more research reading, the authors recommend that researchers incorporate an "Implications for the Practitioner" segment, an idea to which we return and expand later.

IN PLACE OF AUDIENCE ...

As a discipline that, by and large, agrees on the social constructionist's view of communication and meaning-making, technical communication's failure to attend fully to audiences for its research is a critical weakness. For if, as social constructionists argue, audiences are a significant part of communications, wouldn't they also have to be part of our research? And, as part of our research, wouldn't they have to be intrinsic to our research method, methodology, theory, practice, and reporting? If not, are we not back to square one: with audiences being the passive, indiscriminate consumers of whatever the initiators of communication (in this case, researchers) may deign to feed them? Should we be surprised if readers stop reading our research altogether? On the other hand, if audiences are, indeed, intrinsic to our research, why are they so often invisible *in* it?

What does garner attention in discussions of technical communication research—often, ironically, at the exclusion of audience—is ethics. Rather than including matters of audience, several of these works on research seem to promote the researcher's exclusive self-absorption within his or her own ethical enterprise. We would contend that the researcher's concerns for his or her own ethics and motivations, without any consideration for audience, is missing the point. Of course, all works on research and ethics do not promote such self-absorption (see, e.g., the chapters by L.K. Breuch, A.M. Olson, and A.B. Frantz and by L.J. Gurak and C.M. Silker in this collection that show the kinds of practical implications that desperately need to be expanded in our disciplinary dialogue about research and ethics), but those that do seem to do so at the exclusion of any consideration for audience.

As just one example of this kind of soul-searching, M.B. Debs's chapter in R. Spilka's (1993) collection of essays on various aspects of research admirably describes six methods from extramural disciplines that might inform the quality and breadth of topics and approaches in technical communication research. Her work provides a valuable heuristic for research design, and she concludes her chapter by admonishing that researchers "must ... turn [their] study back on [their] own practice as well—that is, to examine [their] research as a rhetorical act and to recognize the consequences of that act" (p. 252). Although we certainly agree that researchers should investigate their motives and the consequences of their research, surely one of the consequences of research should be that it ethically affects some reader or group of readers.

As valuable as Debs's focus on the researcher is, without a reference to audience, it results in a skewed configuration for the exploratory nature of research. She writes: "For the individual researcher, this [research] process begins with questions addressed not to a problem, but to oneself" (p. 252). Then she encourages researchers to ask,

> What is my view of knowledge at this time, in this project? What claims can be made in research? Do I see through a lens of metaphor? If I change that metaphor, how do I see differently and what does that say to me? Is the primary focus of my study the individual? My understanding? Our interaction? Of the intersection of these with configurations offered by others in this field? Can I employ more than one method in my inquiry? To what advantage or

disadvantage? What have people said in other fields that relates to my study? How would I enter that conversation?

... [By] helping to create tensions in our work, these questions represent the type of reflection and articulation needed to inform our choices, and uses, of method and to ensure that our inquiry is well conceived. (p. 252)

The nature—and problem—with this litany of questions (excellent though they are) is the exclusion of any consideration whatsoever for the *reader* of the research. And if we do not relate the researcher-based concerns to those for the research audience, then the result is incontrovertible: the emperor has no clothes. If no one cares what a particular research venture uncovers, if it is not somehow meaningful to someone, then are we not a bit silly to fawn over the role, methods, methodology, rhetoric, motivations, and ideology of research in technical communication? We suggest adding the following questions to those Debs proposes:

1. Who, besides me, cares what answer I find?
2. How can the answer(s) contribute to our knowledge and/or serve a specific audience or group of audiences?
3. How can I write the research report to clarify the work's significance for a particular audience?

The incorporation of audience concerns, clearly at the heart of these questions, moves the researcher beyond self and toward "other," and the value of research now becomes more clearly focused on someone's need for information.

The result of ignoring an authentic, tangible research audience is profound. We contend that one of the reasons that technical communication research is so muddled, as several authors claim (see Carliner, 1994; Moran & Journet, 1985), is that the audience for technical communication research is often very poorly defined. The very pointed question, "Who wants to know the answer to the question the researcher has posed?" seems at once obvious, overlooked, and irrelevant.

The argument can be made, of course, that one researcher's wanting to know the answer to the question establishes a fundamentally sound basis for conducting (and later publishing the results of) the research. We think not. Mere ponderings and supposings are not—or should not be, we contend— the stuff of respectable research. Research is desperately needed; it is expensive and time-consuming. Thus, although we are fundamentally committed to knowledge for the sake of knowledge, and we applaud anyone who sets out on any quest for more knowledge, regardless of how arcane that knowledge—or quest—might be, we still contend that *published* formal research should be held to more rigorous accountability than mere ponderings. And the most significant fulcrum of that accountability must be audience.

So must an audience specifically ask a question and call for research in order to make the research worth pursuing? Of course not. To believe so would cripple the proactive initiatives of our discipline and limit our research to a reactive pathology. And as many would point out, one of the researcher's primary responsibilities is to anticipate the direction and concomitant needs of a discipline. In other words, given today's situation in our discipline, what is likely to be the next confounding factor? Can we anticipate the kinds of issues surrounding that factor? What do we need to know about it and its effects on our work, on communication in general, and on human relationships and well-being? We would simply argue that these questions be asked in the context of a specific group's need for that information. As such, any kind of research and questioning may be valid; and our attempt here is not to limit the research or its validity. What we do seek, however, is to encourage attention to the audience's needs and uses for the information, whether for practical application or theory building or anything in between. The variety of our professional and scholarly publications, along with their distinctive niches, clarifies a place for each of these pursuits.

CURRENT ACKNOWLEDGMENTS OF AUDIENCES FOR TECHNICAL COMMUNICATION RESEARCH

As described earlier, the primary references to audiences for technical and professional communication's research are brief mentions for the sake of ethical considerations. Unfortunately, this concern most often extends only to the audience of sponsoring agencies, with the relationship between the researcher and the audience often characterized as an entanglement (see Blyler, 1995; Herndl, 1993). And there is little doubt that such relationships can, indeed, be controversial and even damaging—although the kinds of questions most researchers take into the sponsor's environment are not so likely to create such symbiotic chaos.

Only one discussion that we can find describes the concrete role of audience(s) in technical communication research beyond the ideological, political realm of entanglement and patronage in which all roads lead to evil management (à la Dilbert) or to positivism. Again focusing on ethical considerations of research, S. Doheny-Farina (1993) briefly identifies five salient audiences for research: "the actual participants in the study," "our disciplinary colleagues," "the gatekeepers," "the nonnative practitioners," and "our bosses" (pp. 266–267).

As challengers to researchers' ethics, these five audiences for research garner a rather cynical disdain, intimating that they are somehow unworthy of our efforts. And, in the invasive role in which the author casts them, that disdain is certainly warranted. For instance, the actual participants in the study are described as those concerned primarily with anonymity; our disciplinary colleagues represent an entrance into an exclusive discourse community; and gatekeepers monitor the "uniqueness in our research" (p. 266). The nonnative practitioners/nonacademic technical communicators[2] are the recognized workplace writers, managers, and editors who intend to use the research's findings to "improve the ways that they do their jobs," typically requiring, Doheny-Farina claims, reduction of "certain aspects of a study to some practical suggestions" (p. 267). Finally, the bosses to whom he refers include only academic bosses—department chairs, deans, and personnel committees who evaluate researchers for tenure, promotion, and merit. The message that research becomes the stick with which these bosses either measure or beat the researcher is embedded, but unmistakable. Thus, although these categories of audiences may be illuminating, the descriptors are skewed because of the essentialism—and negative determinism—they reveal. No mention is made, for instance, of these audiences' opportunities for ensuring the quality and rigor of ethical research; nor is the possibility proffered that the audience members are well-informed, savvy, well-intentioned users of research who are knowledgeable about the dangers of affixing an inappropriate level of reality or decisiveness to what they read. We'll discuss this interpretation of our audience later.

For now, we must acknowledge that we have taken the descriptors out of context. Doheny-Farina's classification of audiences for research is not the gist of his chapter, which seeks, instead, to clarify the rhetorical nature of reporting research, emphasizing the ethical responsibilities of that nature. And clarifying the potential dangers of these audiences and their motives serves his purpose of discussing the ethical ramifications of research; after all, he says, "Our interpretations of these forces [predispositions and motivations] affect the ways that we construct our research arguments" (p. 267). We hope to expand his point: that how researchers respond to these forces should be identified "to themselves" (i.e., to the researchers), thus setting the foundation for ethical research into an acknowledgment that these forces should also be identified to the *audience*—a point well argued in discussions of feminist methodologies.

Clearly, the description of audiences for technical communication research is limited by the scope and purpose of Doheny-Farina's work, but the classification does not acknowledge the complexity of audiences and their potential for using research-generated knowledge in some admirable fashion.

AUDIENCES FOR RESEARCH: EXPANDING THE DISCUSSION

As we have explained and in spite of its problems, the role-based five-audience classification offers a useful starting point for thinking about audiences for technical communication's formal research. In this segment, we hope to expand those five classifications by describing their positive contributions to research, moving beyond surface description and into richer contextual sites for these audiences, while also warning against monolithic constructs of these five audiences.

Participants

Although Doheny-Farina accurately notes that some participants are most concerned with the presentation of themselves (as good writers, good colleagues, or even as anonymous participants) in the study, there are other reasons that participants in a study might want to read the resulting research report. Even more relevant for our purposes is a modification of that concern, that is, why the readers would find the report *useful*.

Because research discussions necessarily (even if tentatively) evaluate findings, participants might use the information provided in the research report to reconsider their behaviors or responses (e.g., strategies, organizational goals, responsibilities, and assessments—to name just a very few possible illuminations). Participants who learn that their organization's goals raise serious ethical problems have new ways to think about their role and their work within that organization. If they learn that their responsibilities as communicators might be better served taking alternate routes of information gathering, collaborating, or revising, they can make those strategic changes.

On the other hand, the participants might use the study's findings as a basis for more extensive, internal investigations of the same or similar issues. Learning that the procedures for collaborative processes contradict the standard document flow, the participants may take a closer look at, say, the editorial contributions to the collaboration and their potential disruptions in the document flow. They may investigate the reasons the document flow is prescribed in a certain fashion, or they may study the collaborative process to see if it can be reorganized to parallel the document flow.

Participants may also use the research report to verify the particulars of the research findings. Indeed, some research studies have been challenged because participants themselves stepped forward to contest the researchers' claims for methods, procedures, statements, observations, or conclusions.

In short, participants do have a great deal at stake in many research situations, but their abiding concern for anonymity, when that concern exists, may be only a small part of that stake.

Our Disciplinary Colleagues

Agreeing with Doheny-Farina's opening statement that "[o]ne of our primary goals is to shape the complex and largely indeterminate events that we witness in the field so that those events speak to current disciplinary issues," we applaud his view of what our colleague audiences seek in technical communication research. Unfortunately, that description (along with the agreement and applause) is quickly undermined by the follow-up sentence: "To paraphrase a concern noted earlier, we go into an organization looking for writing and we damn well better find it!" (p. 266). The clear suggestion that research exists as the professional equivalent of "everyone else is doing it" and, thus, as a means of entry into enviable conversation circles within our profession—requiring a suitably distant nod to pedagogy—constitutes the worst form of professional social climbing.

For some, as Doheny-Farina suggests, research may indeed be an entrance into an exclusive discourse community. On the whole, however, we would argue—purely from our own observations and experiences—that our disciplinary colleagues in technical communication are not nearly as contentious or hierarchically encumbered as those in some other disciplines and are more than willing to admit colleagues to conversations, regardless of what the colleague can contribute. As technical communicators, and by virtue of our discipline, we are instilled with a "teaching" mission—explaining, demonstrating, illustrating, exploring, questioning, revising, and reshaping our explanations. Our behaviors at professional conferences—inclusive of the student, the uninitiated, the well seasoned, and the retired—attest to that spirit of collegiality. Quality research is respected, not as an admit-one pass into a select society, but as what it is—a contribution to an ongoing discussion. And, fortunately, one does not have to contribute every time the collection plate is passed; unrequited taking is allowed.

Gatekeepers

In the truest sense, all of the audiences Doheny-Farina describes are gatekeepers. The participants want to ensure their protection, the disciplinary colleagues want to protect the discussion, and so on. Is gatekeeping a worthwhile activity? Certainly, for respectable research demands ongoing assessments of its respectability, and gatekeepers (such as editorial review boards, for instance) offer that assessment.

Although Doheny-Farina states that the currency and "uniqueness" of the research is the gatekeeper's mission (p. 266), the gatekeeper's mission is also the respectability of the research. That there are systematic procedures for conducting certain kinds of research is well known. That there are innumerable defensible research strategies is increasingly clear, and that some of those procedures can be modified (and announced as modifications in the published report) is equally well known. That researchers do not, however, have the option of changing any or all features of a procedure and still contend that the result is respectable research seems not so well known by some (perhaps novice) researchers. Editors and reviewers will certainly attest to the existence of unstable research submitted to our professional journals and presses. That so little of this unstable research actually finds its way into print is laudable; that any of it *does* get printed, however, is embarrassing. Gatekeepers must maintain a constant vigil over the respectability of the research and must challenge methods that seem unsound.

Further, we ask that the gatekeeper represent the audiences' interests and represent them without patronization. By asking, "Who would want to know this information?" reviewers of all sorts of research submissions can perform an invaluable service to our profession. Some studies, without further elucidation, mean little: for instance, that 37 percent of a random sampling of *Fortune 500* companies accept faxed résumés or that most managers communicate by memos rather than by e-mail. More important, even with that additional elucidation, many of our research studies still seem to have no audience that would find the information useful.

In these examples, for instance, a researcher may conclude that because most managers communicate by memos, we need to investigate the wisdom of that selection, the means for making those memos more effective, or the elements of organizational culture that engender a preference for memos. But, again, who wants to know the answer to these explorations— and why? *Communications consultants* might investigate the wisdom of selecting memos versus e-mail as the medium for communicating in a particular organization *because they can learn how to steer their future clients toward useful media choices. Teachers* might want to know how to make memos more effective *because they feel a responsibility to teach this information to the next generation of communicators,* and *sociologists and sociological communicators* might want to know how preferences are formed regarding communication media *so they can solidify characterizations of workers, organizations, and communication media.* There: we now have an authentic research audience. We have a *reason* for the research audience to *read* and a *means* by which they can *use* what they read.

We ask the disciplinary gatekeepers—reviewers, editors, and other readers (teachers, practitioners, theorists, other researchers, students, responders, all of us)—to react appropriately when no recognizable audience for a research message exists: to reject submissions, to write responses to the publications, and to resist trying to interpret meaning of the research for our own purposes and, thus, endanger the research's actual message. Gatekeepers, in short, can and often do serve a valiant role in our profession. But they should demand more than *uniqueness*; they should demand *meaning* in the most profoundly ontological sense of the word.

The Nonnative Practitioners/Nonacademic Technical Communicators

Perhaps most distressing in the role-based classification of audiences is the treatment of nonacademic technical communicators: the managers, writers, editors, and other workplace practitioners of technical communication. Their inroad to compromising the integrity of research (and researchers) is that they want something applicable from the research they read and that their profession supposedly values. Unfortunately, responding to this request seems somehow beneath the dignity of some researchers/writers. Indeed, Doheny-Farina writes that "in addition to shaping our interpretations to satisfy the demands of our other audiences, we often try to reduce certain aspects of a study to some practical suggestions" (p. 267). The meaning is rather clear: nonacademic practitioners have no right to muddy the research publication with calls for usefulness. Reducing the research findings to "practical suggestions" is, at best, distasteful—at worst, demeaning. The assignment of such calls for practicality to functionalism or positivism further distorts the call for usefulness. For, although usefulness may be an embedded characterization of these ideologies, the mere valuing of usefulness does not make the expectation or call functionalist or positivist—a very important distinction that seems to elude many writers and theorists. For one can certainly hope for something useful from research without expecting the kind of definitive reality these ideologies proclaim. Further, given human nature's propensity for making meaning, it is most likely that readers/users will make something useful of the research—even if it's wrong. Far better to guide the uses of information toward at least a generally appropriate use than to leave readers to their own interpretations, a point to which we return in a moment.

Finally, if we acknowledge, which we do rather consistently in our profession, that practitioners need researchers who need theorists who need practitioners and back and forth and so on, then why is it disdainful that potential users of research findings cannot be accommodated or can be accommodated only as a gesture of haughty acquiescence? There is clearly, however, no reason to view the nonacademic technical communicator's use of research findings as necessarily less elegant than any other audience's use. Thus, the implication that these readers cannot understand our research is erroneous; that they cannot use it, however, may be more to the point.

Ironically, the solution is uncannily simple: If researchers' findings should not be the basis for practical application, they need only say so—and explain why not. A realistic example of such a practice comes from popularized medical science, for instance, which reported a 1997 scientific study showing that vitamin E, taken in massive doses, may delay the onset of Alzheimer's disease. That does not mean that vitamin E can be used as a preventative for Alzheimer's, nor does it mean that vitamin E lessens the severity of cognitive shortcomings, nor does it mean that the consequences of such massive doses have necessarily been tested. The presentation of the research report clearly explained and warned against these potential misinterpretations.

Researchers in technical communication should be equally concerned with how their own results might be misinterpreted or misapplied. Thus, in addition to explaining the findings and interpreting their significance, detailed implications for application should be a standard part of the research report—not as a reduction to some practical applications, but as a recognition of a real audience's realistic use of research.

Bosses

In the description of bosses as only academic bosses, the role-based classification obviously misses a huge segment of technical communication's managerial population: bosses in the traditional technical communication workplace. These bosses are certainly not absorbed with matters of tenure per se, although they are concerned with hirings, firings, promotions, and merit pay raises. But to classify the function of both groups of bosses as purely committed to (gatekeepers for) personnel and economic matters gives short shrift to the common role they play as ensurers of quality control. And just as we acknowledge that this role is crucial to every organization—from the scientific laboratory to the waste disposal plant to the World Series championship team—most of us feel the importance of technical communication and its mission (whether inside the academy or in organizations) necessitates unrelenting vigilance over quality. Managers/bosses who can neither make such determinations nor delegate those determinations to those with appropriate expertise are useless to those of us who depend on quality communications.

Nonacademic bosses value research for purposes other than personnel and economic ones. On a cynical note, some organizations (even academic ones) promote research primarily for increasing the publicity and/or improving the image of that organization to a community of colleagues or users. For instance, it certainly does not harm a software developer to be able to claim in its literature that it spends over $1 million per year on improvements in communication and documentation strategies.

More charitably, the nonacademic boss in some organizations will just as often promote research as an ongoing quest for improvements with true humanitarian benefits. Finding the results of the research illuminating, he or she may encourage the researcher to publish the findings and may even provide support for that publication. That a number of organizations reward their in-house researchers for research publications should not be disparaged because we all can benefit from the results of that research—provided it is written with an appropriate audience in mind.

RECOMMENDATIONS FOR ACCOMMODATING AUDIENCES

In an effort to remedy much of the listlessness we sense about research in technical communication, we offer the following specifics and cautions for research writers who want to be more attentive to the audiences who read and use the results of their research:

- Select questions and topics for research whose "answers" are valuable to a particular group of readers.
- Specify that group of readers in the introduction to the research article.
- Identify one's ideological, political, or theoretical stance toward the research project, the question/hypotheses formed, and the anticipated use of the research's conclusions.
- Explain why the group of readers should value the research in terms of specific understandings or potential applications.
- Clarify the selection of methods, with careful description that points out exclusions and inclusions, as well as justifications for the selection.
- Discuss fully the statistical results of the research within the text of the "Results" segment of the article in terms the uninitiated reader will comprehend.

- Anticipate the audience's potential applications of the findings, offering encouragement, caution, and/or parameters for particular applications and strategies when used in specified environments.

- Conclude with calls for additional research (specifying how and why any element of the study should be pursued) whenever necessary.

With these audience-based considerations in mind throughout the development, analysis, and writing of the research project, technical communicators can accommodate the audience while practicing ethical and substantive decision making.

BENEFITS OF CHARACTERISTICS-BASED AUDIENCE ANALYSIS FOR TECHNICAL COMMUNICATION RESEARCH

An audience's uses for and experiences with published research suggest that researchers must be more attentive to various audience's needs if we are to improve the quality and respectability of research in technical communication. Other characteristics of a research audience prevent monolithic categories of audiences and should also be considered as touchstones for anticipating how research might be interpreted, applied, or otherwise used by technical communicators: the audience's own environment; their experiences in circumstances similar to the respondents' situations; the vocabulary level and terminology of the publication; the effects of age, race, class, and gender on various questions and answers in technical communication research; and the likelihood of the audience's experiences or interpretations conflicting with those found in the research. In short, static checklists for ascertaining the qualities of any given audience are neither feasible nor desirable; careful, in-depth consideration of that audience, however, is.

We may well ask at this point how technical communication research might look if it were more finely attuned to audience and what the benefits of that sort of calibration might be. We have no doubt that the research would increase exponentially in depth, as well as in its value to the profession. Asked to consider who else would want an answer to any given research question, the researcher would at least be encouraged to move beyond the solipsistic and into the "other" to determine the value—in terms of time, energy, and money—of investing in this particular question. Asked "why" the audience would care about this inquiry, the researcher could begin to assemble an understanding of the variety of uses for research and could, we hope, move toward an appropriate research agenda (or series of agendas) for our discipline. Asked to consider how audiences might use any given bit of information, authors could then address their own—as well as their audience's—theoretical, ideological, political, and environmental platforms that inform their research, interpretations, and applications. Such perspectives on actual audiences and uses for research should move us safely beyond the temptation to research merely "what will sell" to some group because of its esoteric nature. Making our research valuable means forgoing the tendency toward "sexy" research (lots of glitz, little substance) and investing in the real issues facing our discipline.

Audiences should, therefore, have at least a moderating effect on our research. Without the power to control research—which may lead to some of the very dangers that Doheny-Farina (1993), Blyler (1995), Herndl (1993), and others suspect—audiences and their needs should, nevertheless, have some say in the research agenda of technical communication. The result, we predict, would be a more useful enterprise that is more defensible in the realm of every audience's concerns and more valuable in clarifying a research agenda. The neglect, we predict, will lead to more research that affects no one, engenders no response, and leaves the reader to shrug and lament, once more, the status of research in technical communication.

NOTES

1. We distinguish research—the active pursuit of knowledge—from scholarship and theory building, two equally critical activities in our profession. To our minds, scholarship is the arrangement or rearrangement of various ideas (most often from published works) that offers a new perspective on those already existing ideas (e.g., investigations into the textual history of technical and professional communication, along with related disciplines, has uncovered the significant roles that women have played in technical and professional communication's evolution). Theory building, on the other hand, is an attempt to construct new frameworks for our thinking about scholarship, research, and practice (e.g., social constructionism or postmodernism as frameworks for technical communication). As such, it does not result in immediate applications but often does foster scholarship, research, and practice that might "fill the rooms" of the theoretical construct. The result of those efforts often helps refine, refute, or solidify the theory and its tenets.

2. At this point, we are altering the terminology from Doheny-Farina's "nonnative practitioner" to "nonacademic technical communicator." We do so on the basis of our own confusion over Doheny-Farina's term, which we initially read to mean "nonnative" in the sense of non-English speaking or English as a Second Language. Because of the implications for language and cultural barriers, and so

on, associated with the term "nonnative"—concepts that extend far beyond the context in which we are talking here—we use the term "nonacademic technical communicator" throughout the remainder of this chapter except where we quote Doheny-Farina's text.

REFERENCES

Beard, J.D., & Williams, D.L. (1992). A survey of practitioners' attitudes toward research in technical communication. *Technical Communication*, 39: 571–581.

Beard, J.D., Williams, D.L., & Doheny-Farina, S. (1989). Directions and issues in technical communication research. *Technical Communication*, 36: 188–193.

Blyler, N.R. (1995). Research as ideology in professional communication. *Technical Communication Quarterly*, 3, 285–313.

Bouldin, T., & Odell, L. (1993). A systems theory perspective on research on writing in the workplace. In R. Spilka (Ed.), *Writing in the workplace: New research perspectives* (pp. 268–281). Carbondale: Southern Illinois University Press.

Carliner, S. (1994). A call to research. *Technical Communication*, 41, 615–619.

Charney, D. (1996). Empiricism is not a four-letter word. *College Composition and Communication*, 47, 567–593.

Debs, M.B. (1993). Considering research methods from writing-related fields. In R. Spilka (Ed.), *Writing in the workplace: New research perspectives* (pp. 238–252). Carbondale: Southern Illinois University Press.

Doheny-Farina, S. (1993). Research as rhetoric: Confronting the methodological and ethical problems of research on writing in nonacademic settings. In R. Spilka (Ed.), *Writing in the workplace: New research perspectives* (pp. 253–267). Carbondale: Southern Illinois University Press.

Flatley, M.E. (1994). Thoughts on research. *Bulletin of the ABC*, 57(2), 62–63.

Goubil-Gambrell, P. (1992). A practitioner's guide to research methods. *Technical Communication*, 39, 582–592.

Gross, A.G. (1994). Review: Theory, method, practice. *College English*, 56, 828–840.

Hayes, J.R., Young, R.E., Matchett, M.L., McCaffery, M., Cochran, C., & Hajduk, T. (1992). *Reading empirical studies: The rhetoric of research*. Hillsdale, NJ: Lawrence Erlbaum Associates.

Herndl, C.G. (1993). Teaching discourse and reproducing culture: A critique of research and pedagogy in professional and non-academic writing. *College Composition and Communication*, 44, 349–363.

Lauer, J., & Asher, W.J. (1988). *Composition research: Empirical designs*. New York: Oxford University Press.

Lay, M.M. (1991). Feminist theory and the redefinition of technical communication. *Journal of Business and Technical Communication*, 5, 348–370.

MacNealy, M.S. (1999). *Strategies for empirical research in writing*. Needham Heights, MA: Allyn & Bacon.

Moran, M.G., & Journet, D. (Eds.). (1985). Preface. *Research in technical communication: A bibliographic sourcebook*. Westport, CT: Greenwood Press.

Porter, L.R., & Coggin, W. (1995). *Research strategies in technical communication*. New York: John Wiley.

Rainey, K.R., & Kelly, R.S. (1992). Doctoral research in technical communication, 1965–1990. *Technical Communication, 39*, 552–570.

Rubens, P.M. (1982). Needed research in technical communication: A report from the front. In *Proceedings of the 29th ITCC* (pp. E100–E102). Washington, DC: Society for Technical Communication.

Spilka, R. (Ed.) (1993). *Writing in the workplace: New research perspectives*. Carbondale: Southern Illinois University Press.

Sullivan, P., & Porter, J. (1993). On theory, practice, and method: Toward a heuristic research methodology for professional writing. In R. Spilka (Ed.), *Writing in the workplace: New research perspectives* (pp. 220–237). Carbondale: Southern Illinois University Press.

Zimmerman, D.E., & Muraski, M.L. (1995). *The elements of information gathering: A guide for technical communicators, scientists, and engineers*. Phoenix, AZ: Oryx.

CHAPTER

Evaluating the Complete User Experience: Dimensions of Usability

Roger A. Grice

"Is it accurate?" "Is it complete?" Maybe even "Is it clear and understandable?"

Much of the focus on usability and ease of use has centered around these questions, and certainly they are important ones—if people do not have access to accurate, complete information that they can understand, they will not be happy. But is there more to usability than that? There is, and those concerned with providing information—through printed and online documents, through training, and through interactive interfaces between people and computers—have broadened their understanding of all that usability encompasses. To accompany this broadening of understanding, we must also broaden our views of how we test and evaluate usability.

In this chapter, I discuss several dimensions, or aspects, of usability and how they come into play when evaluating users' experiences and satisfaction with using products. I then take a look at how we might define tests and evaluations to obtain a more complete assessment of usability and develop plans for improving usability than we might otherwise have done.

TWO STORIES

Here are two stories that involve my own reactions to computers and computer programs.

The first is about my first desktop computer. I received the computer at work and was very excited and eager to start using it. In those days, the software diskettes were shipped with the manuals, and both were packaged in a cardboard slip case surrounded by a stiff, glossy paper band that identified the product. In my eagerness to get started, I put my finger through the plastic wrap that covered the package and ripped it off with one big sweeping motion. Unfortunately, my finger ran against the edge of the stiff, glossy paper, and I got a very deep paper cut. The cut was painful, and the software package got smeared with blood. Every time I used the software, the memory of the incident and the pain in my finger came back. The computer was a good one; the software was very usable. But I was never comfortable using it—the memory of the pain got in the way.

The second is about the first software package I ever used to make slides. Again, I was excited and eager to use it. The software was preinstalled, so I clicked on its icon to activate it. A sample slide appeared—done up in full, rich colors (coincidentally, with a background that was my favorite color) with a very attractive design. I was impressed and wanted to jump right in and produce slides of my own that looked like that.

The moral of these stories? Both incidents made a strong impression on me and affected my perception, and subsequent use of the products to a very large degree. Yet neither story reflects the types of issues we typically look for when evaluating usability. Usability as a wider scope than the mere sum of its component parts.

THE COMPLETE USER EXPERIENCE

Much of the work that has been done on assessing usability of products and documentation has focused on determining how well users can perform selected, key tasks. We measure accuracy, success, and attitude toward the product and the tasks that were performed. Although this is certainly important—critical to success and acceptance of products—it only tells part of the story.

A more realistic assessment of how usable a product is must take into account all the aspects of users' involvement with the product, that is, their complete experience. This assessment must take into account the ways that users first become aware of the product, their motivations and decision to purchase or use it, their actual use of the product, and then their satisfaction and acceptance as people associated with the product and identified with its use.

Although this assessment is wide ranging and complex, it can more easily be defined and measured by looking at certain key aspects—or dimensions—of the product and its use.

DIMENSIONS OF USABILITY

For purposes of this discussion, I identify six dimensions of usability that can be used to characterize people's involvement with a product and assessment of their satisfaction. These dimensions are

- Task dimension
- Motivation or goal dimension
- Product dimension
- Cognitive dimension
- Interactivity dimension
- Comfort dimension

Although some of these dimensions may overlap with others, they are independent enough to give us a handle on assessing usability. I discuss the elements that constitute each dimension and then move on to exploring techniques for assessing each.

Task Dimension

The task dimension measures people's comfort and satisfaction with using the product to perform meaningful tasks. This dimension is concerned with how people do tasks, how happy they are doing them, and their sense of closure for completing the task. Some measures of the task dimension are:

- Comfort with task itself. At the core of assessing the task dimension is how comfortable people are with performing the task itself. They may feel comfortable with the task because it is one with which they are familiar, because it is one that is presented and structured in a clear, logical manner, or because it is one for which the product provides clear indications of successful progress for each step of the way. If people are not satisfied at this level, if they are uncomfortable going through each step of the task, it is not likely that the product will be considered usable, no matter how many other good and positive features the product possesses.

- Complexity of task. Tasks that are overly complex place high cognitive demands on users. If people are continually being forced to make complex decisions, to work through involved sets of prerequisite and corequisite conditions, they will (rightly) perceive the task as complex. If the complexity is compounded by inadequate or confusing directions, prompts, and feedback, any complexity inherent in the task will be compounded.

- Frustration level inherent in task. Some tasks are inherently frustrating, making it unlikely that a product will score very highly in the task dimension. For example, I do enjoy filling out and filing my tax forms. Some of the software packages that have been developed simplify the task greatly and do a very good job of removing some of the frustration, but the work involved in locating, collecting, and sorting the tax records still makes the task very frustrating for me. The tax-preparation packages seemed to be designed with an awareness of the inherent frustration level, and help to work through it. However, if the designers were not aware of the inherent frustration, or did not address it well, working with tax-preparation products could increase the frustration level already associated with the task, compounding the problem.

- Rewards for completing the task. Some tasks have rewards associated with them. When we write a memo or other document, for example, we can print it out and get a tangible measure of success: We get to hold the printed document in our hands. When we order products over the Internet, we get the products that we ordered. Rewards such as these can increase our satisfaction with the task we performed. However, if the task has no associated reward, or an award we do not value highly (such as, in most cases, cleaning up the hard drives on our computers), we may not receive much sense of satisfaction. Similarly, if we do receive some payback but are not clearly made aware that we are receiving it, we may not get a great sense of satisfaction.

Motivation or Goal Dimension

The degree to which people are motivated—or unmotivated—to use a product to perform their work will also affect the satisfaction with the product. If product designers and information designers are aware of the potential level of motivation, they can design the product and its interface to take advantage of this factor. Level of motivation can affect:

- Willingness to overcome obstacles. People who are highly motivated to use a product will work through obstacles placed in front of them: a poorly designed interface, poor information, or lack of sufficient and meaningful feedback, for example. Designers working to this audience may have a relatively easier job because the users will ignore deficiencies or, at least, not place too much weight on them. However, people who are not motivated to use the product will see obstacles and defects as a reason to stop using the product or to complain about its design and functioning. They will not have a pleasant or rewarding experience with the product.

- Rewards and penalties. People who are highly motivated to use the product to achieve their goals may be less dependent on rewards—complimentary messages, for example—for their satisfaction; achieving their goals may be enough. They may not be overly concerned by penalties such as error messages or the need to reenter small amount of data. They will most likely not be happy with the penalties, and their experience will be less pleasant and rewarding than it might otherwise be, but they will be less daunted than less-motivated users might be.

- Immediacy of reward. The lower the user's motivation, the more important it is to provide rewards, confirmation of success, and status of work in a very timely manner. Delays in providing this information will be tolerated less well by users with low motivation than by users with high motivation.

- Mental attitude. Highly motivated users will have a more positive mental attitude towards a product, its interface, and its performance than will users with less motivation. Designers can take advantage of any advance knowledge of mental attitude by helping those with a negative attitude to overcome that attitude, if possible.

Product Dimension

Some products are lucky enough to have a base of customers who truly appreciate them, who will sing their praises to the world, and who enjoy the time they spend using them. A high rating on the product dimension will certainly enhance the complete user experience. In some instances, users are so enthralled with a product that they will not only overlook flaws and obstacles, but they also may remain unaware that they exist at all. Some factors contributing to the product dimension are:

- Opinion of product. People may form their opinion of a product based on their own experience and judgment or based on the experience and judgment of those whose opinion they respect. In general, the higher their opinion of the product, the more positive is the complete user experience—provided that the product lives up to expectations. If the product, or use of the product, does not live up to expectations, however, users may well be more frustrated and unhappy than they would have been had there been no prior expectation.

- Perceived status of product. If a product is perceived as being a high-status product, users may achieve an additional degree of satisfaction: the satisfaction of being seen with, or associated with, a winner. (This may be why people often drive around aimlessly, just to be seen, when they get a new car.)

- Prior experience with product. People's prior experiences with a product carry over, in some form, to their current use of the product—the "halo effect." If their prior experiences have been pleasant and productive, they will anticipate a similar experience during their current use. However, if their experiences have not been pleasant, they will approach their current use of the product with apprehension and low expectations. Although there is generally little opportunity to change this attitude during the current version of a product, shows of good faith and concrete promises of improvement can eliminate some of the negatives. And certainly steps should be taken in subsequent releases to dim the bad memories—by ensuring that the offending characteristics are fixed and that the improvements are highlighted.

- Experience with similar products. Just as prior experiences with a product have their effect on current use, so too can experiences with similar products leave an impression on the current use of a product. If it is known that users may have had unfavorable prior experiences with a similar product, highlighting the differences and positive characteristics can help.

Cognitive Dimension

The amount of thinking and recall of facts affects user satisfaction with a product. Although it is usually necessary to do some thinking and to recall information stored in people's memories, the demands are sometimes higher than they need be. Asking users to enter a piece of information more than once is wasteful and annoying. People assume—quite rightly—that if they have entered information (e.g., their name or address), the information should be stored somewhere and available for use. They have the right to feel imposed upon if they are asked to enter the same information a second, or third, time. Some other factors that place an unnecessary cognitive load on people are:

- Demands on long-term and short-term memory. The process of retrieving information from long-term memory is not the same as the process of retrieving information from short-term memory. But people are often asked to mix the two processes during their interaction with a computer system. This can be both tiring and confusing. A more user-centered approach would be to group the requests for information into long term and short term. For example, mixing questions about the current time, date, and transaction number with questions about date of birth, how long at the current address, and year graduated from school can be taxing. But if the requests are booked by type, the cognitive demand may be less.

- Analytic versus spatial thinking. Similarly, asking people to provide information in such a way that they are required to mix analytic thinking (often referred to as "left brain") with spatial or relational thinking (often called "right brain") can increase the cognitive load and cause confusion.

Again, grouping the information requests by type of information requested can be helpful in making the user's experience less stressful and more pleasant and productive.

- Amount of tedium. Just as requiring too much thinking can make product use unpleasant, so too can requiring people to go through tedious, almost mindless actions for an extended period of time result in decreased satisfaction and productivity and, possibly, an increase in errors due to lack of attention and interest.

Interactivity Dimension

The amount of interaction that people have with a product, the amount of control that they have—or appear to have—over the interaction, and the clarity and comfort of that interaction play a large role in determining how satisfied people are with the use of a product. Some items that shape the interactivity dimension are:

- Control of dialogue. Dialogues between people and computers can be structured in one of two basic modes: the person can appear to be in charge, or the computer can appear to be. If people are in control, they issue commands or make requests of the computer and receive responses to those commands or requests. If the computer is in control of the dialogue, users are asked questions or are asked to supply information, which can be accepted or not, depending on the way the program is designed to accept responses. In many, but not all, cases, people are happier if they feel they are in control.

- Clarity of dialogue structure and requirements. Dialogues with computers, like dialogues with people, can be clear, logical, and meaningful, or they can be otherwise. And people are generally happier with the former than with the latter. Although many factors contribute to the clarity of a dialogue and the requirements that dialogues place on people, people can generally make an overall assessment of how satisfied they are with the dialogue. Although they may not be able to express their assessment in quantifiable terms, they can usually be quite clear, and expressive, in their overall assessment.

- Amount and pace of interaction. Again, as with dialogues with people, dialogues with computers can vary widely in the amount and pace of interaction. If people are required to deal with too much interaction, they may find it tiresome or redundant; if there is too little, they may lose interest or find the interaction to be not satisfying. Interaction that is too slow may become boring, and people will lose interest; interaction that is too fast paced may be stressful, making people feel that they must respond more rapidly than they would like to.

- Tone of interaction. The tone of the interaction is a reflection of the perceived "personality" of the computer and real personality of the user. If the computer is perceived as rude, condescending, inaccurate, or irrelevant, most users will not consider the dialogue to be a success.

Comfort Dimension

The final dimension of usability to be discussed is comfort—how comfortable, relaxed, and "at home" users feel while working with a computer or computer application. Two aspects of comfort are mental comfort and physical comfort.

- Mental comfort. Mental comfort can be measured as the extent to which people feel familiar with what they are doing and the degree of confidence or certainty they have in their actions. If the actions that people must take to use a program are familiar to them—because they are like actions they would take in the noncomputer world or because they are like actions they would take when using other computer programs—people will feel comfortable because they do not need to make stressful decisions about what actions to take or how to interpret responses. If the choices they must make are clear and if the feedback and responses they receive indicate clearly what has happened or what they must do, users will feel confident in interpreting them and acting upon them.

- Physical comfort. Physical comfort can be measured by observing how people must move and act physically to use a computer or a computer application. Factors to be considered include how well, or poorly, the screen displays are designed to prevent eyestrain, the complexity of key strokes or mouse clicks required to do the work, and the likelihood of repetitive motion injuries. And even though this aspect of use is often outside the realm of many interactivity design sessions, it can be absolutely important to people who are faced with physical discomfort while trying to perform computer-based tasks.

COLLECTING DATA ABOUT THE COMPLETE USER EXPERIENCE—TRADITIONS WE CAN DRAW FROM

Often when we think of testing or evaluating the usability of information and products, we think of one evaluation method—often the one we are most familiar with, or the one that we have been told is "the one to use." And even though tried-and-true methods can be useful and effective, we might do well to widen our repertoire and consider a variety of traditions from which to draw. For example, we might consider:

- Cognitive psychology
- Anthropology/ethnography
- Software engineering
- Market research
- Language and literature
- Technical communication

Each of these traditions stresses a viewpoint, or set of related viewpoints, and lends itself most readily to a set of evaluation methods. Some of the traditions are, in fact, at odds with each other. The skillful and conscientious usability evaluator will select from among the methods suggested by these traditions to obtain as full and accurate an assessment of usability as possible.

Drawing on the Tradition of Cognitive Psychology

Much of the work of cognitive psychologists is clinical, based on experiments conducted in a research laboratory. Great attention is paid to experimental design, so that experiments are "clean" and worth reporting to peer groups. Repeatability of experiments is of high priority, so that the experiments can be duplicated or extended to verify or extend the results obtained. Results are generally analyzed using statistical methods, and achieving statistically significant results is a major goal.

Drawing on this tradition, usability evaluators could conduct highly structured usability evaluations in usability laboratories, carefully measuring and recording how people perform specified scenarios of typical applications of product use.

Drawing on the Tradition of Anthropology/Ethnography

Work done in these traditions involves making neutral observations of people in their own environments; care must be given to causing as little disruption as possible to the way that work is done. Anthropologists and ethnographers work to observe actions in natural, or "normal," settings and place importance on observing and recording subjects' methodology and terminology.

Drawing on this tradition, evaluators could visit users at their place of work and observe them as unobtrusively as possible performing the tasks that they usually perform in the manner and sequence in which they usually perform them.

Drawing on the Tradition of Software Engineering

Software engineers have worked to make the processes used to design, develop, and test software as efficient and effective as possible. Taking a cue from them, usability evaluators can work to ensure that usability activities are integrated with other development activities so that the results obtained from usability evaluation can be incorporated in a timely manner into the product being evaluated. There is an emphasis on engineering methodology and practice and on the timing of usability-evaluation activities and application of results.

Drawing on this tradition, evaluators would make sure that their evaluation activities are done early enough so that the results obtained can be applied to the product while it is under development, rather than needing to hold them until the next version of the product is being worked on. This tradition also implies that the most efficient and effective methods for each type of evaluation will be used appropriately.

Drawing on the Tradition of Market Research

Specialists in marketing products have concern for adoption and use products by a target audience. Their focus is on ensuring that the products conform to the requirements that have been set for them, usually by discussing with potential users their needs and requirements. The major emphasis of this orientation is feedback from users and improvement of a product by use of that feedback.

Drawing on this tradition, evaluators would make sure that they understand fully the needs of their target audience and would then make sure that whatever is designed and developed truly meets those needs. Strong emphasis would be placed on having continuous communication with users and a high level of user participation in design and evaluation of the product.

Drawing on the Tradition of Language and Literature

Those who focus on the study of language and literature have developed skills and techniques for analyzing language and meaning—ways of expressing thoughts, ways of understanding texts. They focus on the structure and presentation of information and how structure and presentation can affect meaning and perception of quality, usability, and validity. They have developed numerous techniques for achieving clarity of expression and ways of providing the proper notion of clarity for a wide range of audience and environment.

Drawing on this tradition, usability evaluators could focus on clarity of expression and analytic techniques for structuring information presentation.

Drawing on the Tradition of Technical Communication

Those who practice or understand the theories and practice of technical communication focus heavily on understanding of, and concern for, audience. They have developed techniques for producing clear, effective communication and for infusing clarity into information that is convoluted or obscure. Technical communication is focused on audience and helping the audience perform their required tasks.

Drawing on this tradition, usability evaluators can work to ensure that all information is presented clearly and is structured and developed towards its stated purpose.

PULLING IT ALL TOGETHER—MAKING A WIDE-RANGING ASSESSMENT TO EVALUATE THE COMPLETE USER EXPERIENCE

Using the dimensions of usability as a structure for performing a usability evaluation, we can draw on the range of usability techniques suggested by the various traditions just discussed to put together a comprehensive evaluation plan, a plan to make a wide-ranging assessment of the complete user experience rather than a more narrowly focused assessment of selected key tasks. This section brings the two previous sections together by following the analysis of the slide-making software package mentioned at the beginning of this article. The analysis covers the purchase, installation, and use of the package.

Although a specific product is not to be used as the example, the analysis includes uses of the methods of the various traditions just described to measure and evaluate the factors that make up the dimensions of usability described at the beginning of this chapter.

A thorough analysis of the case needs to include the time before users come into contact with (or ownership of) the application package. For example, in the case of my personal introduction to a slide-making program, for some time before I purchased the package, I had admired the slides that others used at conferences and wished that I could do the same.

A complete evaluation of my experience with the product would start with my first awareness of the product and the way I could use it, my decision to buy, installation of the product, initial use, and subsequent use as a more experienced user. We could do a similar analysis of other users whom we intended to study.

DETERMINING WHAT TO MEASURE
AND HOW TO MEASURE

Measuring across the Task Dimension

For this dimension, we consider comfort with task itself, complexity of task, frustration level inherent in task, and reward for completing the task. We can measure this dimension by asking questions such as:

- How easy is it to install the product and get started with it?
- How complex is it to develop individual slides and put the slides together into presentations?
- How frustrating is it to develop slides and presentations?

To assess usability across the task dimension, we can use a mixture of quantitative and qualitative methods. For example, to assess how easy it is to install the product and get started, we can collect data on time to install, time to bring up the first screen, and time to start filling in information. We can count the number of errors made, the number of times that the manual or help system was consulted, or the number of times people redid work that was already completed because they were uncertain. We could make quantitative assessments of complexity and frustration by measuring indirect indicators of complexity and frustration (references to manuals or help systems, number of times users closed the application and restarted it rather than determining a cause of error).

We could also measure complexity and frustration qualitatively by observing users' looks of anger, frustration, and bewilderment. We could record or write down comments they make that indicate their feelings towards using the product. We could give them a posttask survey or questionnaire asking them to describe their satisfaction with the way the application program worked for them.

And depending on what types of information we were looking for or needed to report, we could take quantitative measures using a Likert scale ("on a scale of 1 to 7, how satisfied ... ") or qualitative measures ("describe what you thought when ... "). Methods such as these are familiar to cognitive or behavioral scientists working in laboratories and to anthropologists and ethnographers working in the field. Increasingly, these are becoming familiar to technical communicators and usability engineers.

Measuring across the Motivation or Goal Dimension

For this dimension, we consider willingness to overcome obstacles, rewards and penalties, immediacy of reward, and mental attitude. We can measure this dimension by asking questions such as:

- Did the prospect of having a slide presentation for their own use make the effort worthwhile?
- How quickly could users see the finished product or drafts of it?
- Did users feel that they were reaching their goal as they developed the presentation?

Assessments across this dimension encompass users' wants and feelings before they purchase or start to use a product, as well as their feelings and observations while using the product. For example, if someone had observed others using well-made, effective slides at conferences and meetings and wanted to be able to do the same, they would be highly motivated to obtain the slide-making program and learn to use it well. They would equate their ability to use the program with their ability to make effective presentations and appear as a true professional in front of a group. Market researchers and advertising specialists have honed their skills at making products seem appealing to potential audiences and at measuring the effectiveness of advertising and publicity campaigns. They often supply the motivation for people to want products, and, to some extent, sales or licensing are one measure of motivation.

Measuring across the Product Dimension

For this dimension, we consider users' opinion of the product, perceived status of the product, users' prior experience with the product, and users' experience with similar products. We can measure this dimension by asking questions such as:

- What did users think about the product and what it could do for them?
- What did users think about other people who were users of the product?
- Have they watched others use the product to develop slide presentations?
- How had they developed slide presentations in the past?

Much of the information used to measure this dimension is qualitative data obtained by methods familiar to anthropologists and ethnographers. Methods of contextual inquiry are gaining in popularity as people become more familiar with techniques and applications (see, e.g., Beyer and Holtzblatt, 1997).

The importance of users' perception of the product or application they are using cannot be overemphasized—it can color their whole experience. If the product is perceived to be "a winner," then those who use it are often given the same status. Measures for this dimension tend to be subjective— perceptions of status, expectations for improved performance and recognition, and a sense of belonging are key. Information can be obtained through surveys, focus groups, and observations.

Measuring across the Cognitive Dimension

For this dimension, we consider demands on long-term and short-term memory, spatial versus analytic thinking required, and amount of tedium involved. We can measure this dimension by asking questions such as:

- Did users have to remember a lot of procedural and content information to develop slides?
- Could they separate the tasks of content development and formatting? Or did they need to do both simultaneously?
- Did slide development become boring?

Measures across this dimension can be quantitative or qualitative. By observing users in action, we could observe quantitative measures such as: how often they needed to refer to reference information rather than being able to recall it from memory, how often they needed to refer back to the same information, or how often they appeared lost, even though they had been exposed to the information they needed. We can obtain qualitative measures of cognitive load—perhaps more useful for assessing usability— by asking them to explain their thought processes and how easy or diffi- cult those processes seemed to be.

Measuring across the Interactivity Dimension

For this dimension, we consider user control of dialogue, clarity of di- alogue structure and requirements, amount and pace of interaction, and tone of interaction. We can measure this dimension by asking questions such as:

- Did users feel like they were in charge of dialogues and activities?
- Did they usually know what they had to do next? If not, could they find out easily?
- Were they made to feel that they had done something dumb or wrong when slides did not look the way they had planned?

Few factors promote—or detract from—a product's usability as does the feeling users have that they are in control of their interaction with an application or that the application is in control. This sense is subjective, and a structure that may make some users feel in control may well make others feel that they are being controlled, perhaps even manipulated. There is little about this dimension that can be measured quantitatively, short of analysis of dialogue structure, but that measure only examines formal structure of a dialogue; it does not measure users' sense of it.

The most useful measurements for this dimension are subjective and are obtained by talking with users—either directly or through focus groups and surveys.

Measuring across the Comfort Dimension

For this dimension, we consider mental comfort and physical comfort. We can measure this dimension by asking questions such as:

- Were users anxious, concerned, or confused?
- Did they develop hand or eye strain while developing the slides?

Physical comfort can often be measured by applying what we have learned from ergonomics—by measuring distances between eyes and computer screen, position of head and hands, and so on. But, once again, the true measures of this dimension are subjective and individual. Do people *feel* comfortable? Did they *feel* anxious or confused? This information is best obtained by talking with people, often coaxing them to reveal sources of anxiety or discomfort that they might otherwise gloss over.

COMBINING FINDINGS INTO A UNIFIED SET

Other dimensions of usability might well be defined. I find the set described in this chapter to be useful. The dimensions identified cover a sufficiently wide range of usability concerns to make a total assessment possible. On the other hand, the set is small enough to be manageable when trying to make an assessment of a product's usability that encompasses more than just the performance of major tasks. Using this set of dimensions, we can explore users' total experience with a product—from the time they first become aware of a product or a need for the product, through learning and use of that product.

The range of needed findings requires a range of methods. It is generally not sufficient to pick a favorite technique or two and rely only on them, to the exclusion of all other methods. The wise usability evaluator picks and chooses from available tools and techniques to learn the most about a user's complete experience as it is possible to learn.

CONCLUSIONS

Evaluating usability of products, interfaces, and documents involves more than applying a few simple rules; it is not an activity that can be done thoroughly, as if by following a cookbook. There are a variety of evaluation methods available—some simple and inexpensive, others more elaborate and time consuming. Each has its place in an overall evaluation process; each can be used to advantage to increase usability.

The skillful usability evaluator will chose wisely from the methods available, not limiting the evaluation process to a narrow subset of what is available. By using the methods in combination and to best advantage, evaluators can improve not only selected aspects of usability, but the users' complete experience, from start to finish.

REFERENCES

Barker, T. T. (1998). *Writing software documentation: A task-oriented approach*. Needham Heights, MA: Allyn & Bacon.

Beyer, H., & Holtzblatt, K. (1997). *Contextual design: A customer-centered approach to systems design*. San Francisco, CA: Morgan Kaufmann Publishers.

Carroll, J.M. (Ed.). (1998). *Minimalism beyond the Nurnberg funnel*. Cambridge, MA: MIT Press.

Dumas, J.S., & Redish, J.C. (1994). *A practical guide to usability testing*. Norwood, NJ: Ablex Publishing Corp.

Hackos, J.T., & Redish, J.C. (1998). *User and task analysis for interface design*. New York: John Wiley & Sons, Inc.

Hargis, G., Hernandez, A.K., Hughes, P., Ramaker, J., Rouiller, S., & Wilde, E. (1998). *Developing quality technical information*. Upper Saddle River, NJ: Prentice-Hall.

Nielsen, J., & Mack, R.L. (Eds.). (1994). *Usability inspection methods*. New York: John Wiley & Sons, Inc.

Rubin, J. (1994). *Handbook of usability testing*. New York: John Wiley & Sons, Inc.

CHAPTER 9

Feminist Criticism and Technical Communication Research

Mary M. Lay

Because of the cross-disciplinary nature of feminist scholarship, feminism is usually defined as a perspective on research rather than as a research method.[1] For example, Shulamit Reinharz (1992) defines feminism as "a perspective on an existing method in a given field of inquiry or a perspective that can be used to develop an innovative method" (p. 241). Therefore, feminist researchers may adapt traditional methods of gathering and interpreting evidence, or they may develop new ones. Certainly feminist researchers foreground the behavior of women at any given research site, listening carefully to their feedback and concerns. Some feminist researchers would also be critical of perspectives offered by male researchers and/or male research participants. These researchers would begin their research projects "by listening more skeptically to what men say and more sympathetically to what women say; they observe both men and women with new critical awareness; they ask different questions of history" (Harding 1987b, p. 23). Regardless of the approach, feminist perspectives are based on an epistemology or theory of knowledge that "generates its problematics from the perspective of women's experiences" (Harding, 1987b, p. 7; see also Harding, 1993; Hekman, 1997; Scott, 1991; Smith, 1990).

Straightforward as this basis of feminist research might seem, however, these perspectives are problematized by diverse and sometimes competing constructions of woman and gender and by the activist stance of feminist research. Thus, at the same time feminist scholars attempt to capture the voices of women, these scholars recognize that not all women are the same.

Although feminist scholars include the voices and experiences of women and listen to and observe women sympathetically, they attempt to resist essentializing women—they must decide how research can define, describe, or understand women but avoid collapsing all women into the category of "woman" (see, for example, Hawkesworth, 1997, pp. 650–651; see also Alcoff, 1988, p. 407; Lather, 1991, p. 5). This recognition of diversity makes one goal of feminist research—improving the private and public lives of women—difficult, given the many and sometimes competing needs and values of women. Reinharz describes this goal of feminist research as "[m]aking the invisible visible, bringing the margin to the center, rendering the trivial important, putting the spotlight on women as competent actors, understanding women as subjects in their own right rather than objects for men" (1992, pp. 248–249). And, because the gender roles to which women are assigned are socially constructed rather than "naturally" linked to biological sex, women differ in the extent to which they find comfort in these roles or seek liberation from them. Thus, the feminist research perspective might suggest new and different ways to gather and interpret data in recognizing the voices, needs, and interests of diverse women. In contributing this new knowledge, feminist research might liberate women from gender roles and the hierarchies in which these roles are constructed.

COMMON FEATURES OF FEMINIST RESEARCH

In attempting to achieve the dual goals of contributing new understanding of women's voices, needs, and interests, and of questioning gender structures to provide liberation from them, feminist scholars have identified some common traits within their work. For example, Reinharz (1992) identifies ten features of feminist research:

- Feminism is a perspective, rather than a method.
- Feminist researchers use a "multiplicity" of research methods.
- Feminist research "involves an ongoing criticism of nonfeminist scholarship."
- Feminist research is guided by feminist theory.
- Feminist research is often "transdisciplinary."
- Feminist researchers identify social change as one goal.
- Feminism "strives to represent human diversity."
- Feminist researchers acknowledge their personal traits and the impact of those traits on their research.

- Feminist researchers may "develop special relations" with the people they study.

- Feminist researchers may establish or define special relationships with their readers (p. 240).

To this list, Hawkesworth (1997) would add that gender, however variously defined, becomes as an analytical tool or heuristic research device that "illuminates an area of inquiry, framing a set of questions for investigation" (p. 655). The feminist researcher must always ask, "But what about women?"

Additionally, Mary Margaret Fonow and Judith Cook (1991) identify four common features of feminist research as "reflexivity; an action orientation; attention to the affective components of the research; and use of the situation-at-hand" (p. 2). Reflexivity includes critical examination of the researcher's and her participants' assumptions about gender that might inform the research process.[2] For example, consciousness raising may result from reflexivity, and use of research techniques such as role-playing, psychodrama, and collaboration may result in reflexivity on the part of both researcher and participant (pp. 3–5). Action orientation, Fonow and Cook say, includes emancipation as the result of documenting past struggles of women and formulation of future social policy about violence, pornography, poverty, health, education, work, and so on (pp. 6–7). Finally, feminist research, say Fonow and Cook, not only focuses on the details of daily life that sustain gender inequity but also acknowledges the emotional intimacy that might evolve between the researcher and her participants (pp. 10–11; see also Cook & Fonow, 1990; Kirsch, 1992; Mascia-Lees, Sharpe, & Ballerion Cohen, 1989; Miller, 1986).

Moreover, feminists almost uniformly are suspicious of claims of objectivity in research. As Maria Mies (1983) puts it: "The postulate of *value free research*, of neutrality and indifference towards the research objects, has to be replaced by *conscious partiality*, which is achieved though partial identification with the research objects [or participants]" (p. 122; emphasis in original). Hierarchical relationships between the researcher and those who participate in her study are replaced by mutual identification and active involvement in women's emancipation. Similarly, Dawn Currie and Hamida Kazi (1987) suggest that feminist researchers can competently use traditional social science research methods but also should adopt a "participatory model" that "requires that the research question be of concern and of interest to the subjects" (p. 81). The result of such a model is "a non-hierarchical, non-authoritarian, non-manipulative, humble relationship" with the participant (Currie & Kazi, 1987, pp. 81–82; see also

Alcoff, 1988; Reay, 1996; Wolf, 1992). Such a subjective stance, Sandra Harding (1987a) suggests, actually increases the objectivity of the research because the researcher reveals information to her readers that she might conceal in a more traditional distanced and neutral stance (p. 9). The researcher places herself in the same critical plane as her research participant and becomes, as described by Harding (1987a), a "real, historical individual with concrete, specific desires and interests—and ones that are sometimes in tension with each other" (p. 32). In doing so, the researcher achieves, suggest some scholars, a more ethical stance and therefore greater credibility (see Doheny-Farina, 1993, for an example of this redefined *ethos* as applied to technical communication).

In defining these features of feminist research perspectives, scholars have also considered whether feminist methodology is equally suited for qualitative and quantitative studies. For example, Anne Opie (1992) suggests that feminist qualitative research, such as that based on unstructured interviews, best empowers participants because

> [t]he researcher, in the analysis and writing of her text, is engaged in a fluid process of identifying and questioning ideology (her own, not merely the other's), her location within the literature, the nature of her textual practice and the personal and political implications of methodology for the participants in the study. (p. 57)

The feminist qualitative researcher can focus on the marginal, the different, the "quantifiably insignificant," and avoid essentializing (Opie, p. 59).

On the other hand, Toby Jayartne and Abigail Stewart (1991) suggest that the feminist researcher can apply feminist perspectives equally well to quantitative research. But the feminist quantitative researcher should always ask, "*what different interpretations, always consistent with the findings, might imply for change in women's lives,*" and the research most likely would also offer a political analysis of her findings (p. 103; emphasis in original). Different questions might be asked, and different interpretations might be offered within the guidelines of traditional quantitative research.

Therefore, when initiating a research study from the feminist perspective, the researcher would

- Include gender as the major variable or heuristic
- Critique or revise traditional research methodology to accommodate the needs and interests of women
- Focus on the particular experiences of women's lives—those lives that are often defined as "other" or "abnormal" in traditional research studies
- Make visible those lives and audible those voices that might be neglected in traditional research studies

- Acknowledge and honor the reciprocal relationship with research participants and with readers by collapsing the hierarchy that might separate and by shortening the distance that might alienate or create misunderstanding in order to share the power that knowledge brings to both researcher and research participant[3]

- Conclude the research study with appropriate calls for social action or public policy, and, if possible, participate in these

When assessing feminist perspectives across disciplines and within the methods of gathering and interpreting research frequently used by technical communication researchers, such as case study, textual analysis, interviewing, and ethnography, this compilation of features challenges or extends our traditional research designs, as seen in the next section of this chapter.

FEMINIST METHODOLOGY AND TECHNICAL COMMUNICATION RESEARCH METHODOLOGIES

The case study frequently informs our knowledge of workplace writing and technical communication practices and offers a fully developed description of an organization, person, group, or community. For example, case studies in technical communication research, such as Dorothy Winsor's (1996) study of novice engineers' understanding of rhetoric, and Jamie MacKinnon's (1993) study of entry-level economists' and financial analysts' understanding of genre, add to our understanding of the pervasiveness of rhetorical strategies in workplace writing.

However, case studies conducted with a feminist perspective often illustrate that a generalization about gender or women is invalid by offering an exception to that generalization. Therefore, case studies, according to Reinharz (1992), "rectify research tainted by gynopia, misogyny, and male-dominated theorizing" (p. 168).[4] Moreover, case studies of women illustrate the relationship between individual lives and social structure (p. 170). Therefore, feminist case studies may refute or correct theory or expand upon theory by the exceptional case. Taking gender as the essential variable, feminist case studies often use practice to limit theory or to place theory and practice in dialectical tension. Patricia Sullivan and James Porter (1993) recommend that technical communication researchers consider methodology a way to achieve praxis or to elevate practice to the level of theory (see also Lather, 1991). Such recommendations bring traditional case study methods well in line with feminist methodology.

Textual studies within technical communication illustrate rhetorical links between text and context and therefore assume the social construction of knowledge. For example, Greg Myers (1991) analyzed how writers of scientific review articles shape the story of that field's literature, and Charles Bazerman (1993) studied how the intertext against which new texts are placed become sites of contention. Therefore, researchers conducting textual analyses look at particular features of written (and sometimes oral) discourse and assume, as Bazerman and James Paradis (1991) state, that "written discourse is produced by a complex of social, cognitive, material, and rhetorical activities; in return, written texts dialectically precipitate the various contexts and actions that constitute the professions" (p. 4; see also Berkenkotter in this volume). In other words, discourse both reflects and contributes to social contexts, in particular, professional activities and relationships.

Within feminist perspectives, scholars employing textual analysis may focus on gender-power relationships as they examine the contexts within which texts have been generated. To discover these power relationships, the feminist researcher might examine texts that have been neglected in other more traditional studies, such as journals, diaries, memories, letters, and such—frequently ignored or discounted by scholars more interested in public or organizational documents (see, for example, Cott, 1977; Hampsten, 1982). Or the feminist researcher might examine the effect or consequence of the text on silenced or neglected members of a discourse community. For example, Sullivan (1992) sums up such feminist methodologies in composition research as follows:

> Feminist scholarship ... focuses on received knowledge—on the existing studies, canons, discourses, theories, assumptions, and practices of our discipline—and rexamines [sic] them in light of feminist theory to uncover male bias and androcentrism; and it recuperates and constitutes distinctly feminine modes of thinking and expression by taking gender, and in particular women's experiences, perceptions, and meanings, as the starting point of inquiry or as the key datum for analysis. (pp. 40–41)

Therefore, textual analysis as informed by feminist perspectives examines women's texts or the contexts that produce or silence women (see, for example, Tebeaux, 1993; Tebeaux & Lay, 1992; Tebeaux & Lay, 1995).

Technical communication research often employs interviews and talk-aloud protocols to understand research participants' attitudes toward workplace writing. For example, within their workplace interviews, Andrea Lunsford and Lisa Ede (1990) discovered what might be a gender preference for collaborative workplace writing. Using talk-aloud protocols, Davida Charney (1993) reveals how the tendency of scientists to skim texts might defeat even the most carefully constructed arguments meant to be read linearly.

Using feminist perspectives, scholars recognize that standard interview categories and questions might exclude what is important to women. As Marjorie Devault (1990) says, researchers need to "create space for respondents to provide accounts rooted in the realities of their lives" (p. 99). Language might be inadequate to express these realities, so the interviewer must adopt a different kind of listening skill, such as attention to hesitations and in-drawn breath (pp. 102, 108). Moreover, when presenting the results of an interview, the researcher must be aware how, according to Devault, "[s]tandard practice that smoothes [sic] out respondents' talk is one way that women's words are distorted; it is often a way of discounting and ignoring those parts of women's experience that are not easily expressed" (p. 107). And, the feminist researcher should be aware of the ethics of asking women to reveal private information that will be published in the public sphere (Patai, 1991, p. 142).

To capture the words of women, feminist researchers often turn to oral history, extending beyond the traditional interview, to shift the focus from asking the right questions to interacting with the participant, in what Kathryn Anderson and Dana Jack (1991) call a "dynamic unfolding of the subject's view point" (p. 23). Moreover, the feminist researcher might find it more fruitful to depart from the usual format of the researcher asking questions and one participant offering answers to instead gathering women to converse together. As Kristina Minister (1991) has found, "Women talking with women use a unique dialectical choice of words coordinated with a unique nonverbal system for the purpose of exploring and naming issues unique to women. Women engage in the process of self and gender construction, and they do so protected and sustained within their own sociocommunication system" (p. 34; see also Etter-Lewis, 1991; Geiger, 1990). Therefore, feminist researchers using interviews and oral histories are aware of how the method itself and the nature of language might limit their findings. Although technical communication researchers might look for aspects of gender within their interviews, surveys, and talk-aloud protocols, they must also question the limits of the method itself.

Finally, ethnographic studies of organizations and the creation of their documents are quite valuable in technical communication research (e.g., Doheny-Farina's 1986 study of the negotiations around a business plan; see also Doheny-Farina & Odell, 1985). Such extended observations provide the researcher and reader with rich detail about the organization and its processes. Feminist researchers embrace the nonpositivist assumptions possible in ethnography as they make women's lives visible and observe women's behavior in a social context. As Judith Stacey (1988) says:

> Like a good deal of feminism, ethnography emphasizes the experiential. Its approach to knowledge is contextual and interpersonal, attentive like most women, therefore, to the concrete realm of everyday reality and human agency. Moreover, because in ethnographic studies the researcher herself is the primary medium, the "instrument" of research, this method draws on those resources of empathy, connection and concern that many feminists consider to be women's special strengths and which they argue should be germinal in feminist research. (pp. 22–23; see also Stacey 1994)

The participant/observer stance challenges feminist ethnographers to emphasize closeness, to eliminate hierarchical relationships, and to focus not only on understanding but also on possible action. Such total immersion in the world the researcher is studying, says Reinharz (1992), "comes about when the researcher begins to share the fate of those she is studying" (p. 69). Ideally the feminist ethnographer is open to transformation of her own values, and she is careful not to measure her participants against her own standards.

As close a fit as ethnography and feminism might seem, feminist scholars have begun to refine that fit. Stacey (1988) wonders whether the ethnographic approach has potential for exploitation, because ethnographic research "depends upon human relationship, engagement, and attachment, it places research subjects at grave risk of manipulation and betrayal by the ethnographer," and the written ethnography necessarily seems to offer the researcher's interpretations, to fit the researcher's purposes (pp. 22–23; see also Abu-Lughod, 1990). Stacey proposes that the ethnographer acknowledge the limits of her process and claims, to engage her participants as collaborators, and to acknowledge the intrusive nature of her work (p. 25; see also Stacey, 1994). And, Elizabeth Enslin (1994) cautions that if feminist ethnographers want to counter women's oppression rather than just describe it, they must recognize that some people cannot read English, and because many people cannot understand academic jargon, they cannot be empowered by ethnographic work (pp. 551–552).

Moreover, Anne Balsamo (1990) proposes another term—the feminist imagination—to express the methodology of the feminist ethnographer (see also Wheatley, 1994a; Wheatley, 1994b, p. 412). Feminist imagination is "theoretical practice that is both a theory of practice—ethnography, and a practice of theory—a history of the present" (p. 47). Acknowledging that all interpretations are partial and political, the ethnographer uses her feminist imagination to conduct two theoretical moves, according to Balsamo

(1990): "one to study everyday life as it is simultaneously a site of individual experience and of social and cultural determinations, and another to start with the contemporary movement, the here and now, to work with women's biographies, their personal stories as they continually unfold over, in, and against time" (p. 49). Balsamo herself engaged her research participants in collective memory work in which each contributed a written account to Balsamo's ethnography.

FEMINIST STUDIES IN TECHNICAL COMMUNICATION

The work of those technical communication scholars who use feminist perspectives generally makes visible previously ignored female rhetors, suggests how the field will benefit from adapting feminist perspectives, asks how the gender of communicator might affect preferred rhetorical strategies, or demonstrates how language and knowledge making are gendered.

For example, Kathryn Neeley's (1992) study of women writers in the eighteenth and nineteenth centuries revealed the role of the woman mediatrix who clarified scientific knowledge for general audiences. Additionally, Elizabeth Tebeaux and I suggested that, during the Renaissance, women were more engaged in technical writing than previously thought (Tebeaux, 1993; Tebeaux & Lay, 1992; Tebeaux & Lay, 1995). Moreover, by calling attention to the connections between feminism and technical communication research, scholars ask different questions. For example, Allen (1991) asked: "That women are entering the technical communication profession in increasing numbers may be good news, but how steadily and how quickly are they moving up in the industry?" (p. 376); and "If women are better communicators than men, and communication skill is the primary asset for management positions, then why are so few women in managerial positions?" (p. 385). And so, in one essay, Deborah Bosley (1992) proposed that a feminist theory of design would eliminate the hierarchy of visuals and text. In other essays, Laura Gurak and Nancy Bayer (1994) and Amy Koerber (2000) illustrated what technical communication scholars could learn from feminist critiques of technology (see also LaDuc & Goldrick-Jones, 1994; Lay, 1991; Lay, 1993; Lay, 1994).

Technical communication scholars who attempt to determine what difference gender makes in communication situations often study men and women in workplace or classroom settings and trace how their responses, experiences, and successes might differ. Some studies reveal few differences. For example, Carolyn Boiarsky and her collaborators (1995) found that both women and men in scientific and technical communities seemed to use an androgynous style, which included tentative language and collaborative approaches (see also Lay, 1992). In a study of four proposal developers at Southwestern Bell Telephone, Kathryn Raign and Brenda Sims (1993) found that the discourse and persuasive techniques used by men and women did not parallel so-called gendered communication style. And when Bosley (1994) discovered little difference between genders when undertaking a specific communication task, she refuted previous researchers' assumptions that women were better at audience analysis, an assumption based on Belenky and her colleagues' (1986) description of women's connected knowing (see also Smeltzer & Werbel, 1986; Sterkel, 1988).

On the other hand, other scholars have found that men and women do have different communication styles and preferences and have different experiences in such activities as collaborative writing. For example, in an early piece, Tebeaux (1990) demonstrated that women brought more tact and sensitivity to the task of telling bad news, whereas men preferred more directness, but, after work experience, both men's and women's preferences were more closely aligned. Meg Morgan (1994) studied different perceptions of styles of leadership in small writing groups, and I found that men and women perceived conflict in different ways during the collaborative process (Lay, 1989). Duane Roen and Donna Johnson (1992) studied the ways men and women used compliment intensifiers differently in written discourse. Recently technical communication scholars have investigated how men and women might experience communication over the Internet differently (see, for example, Gurak, 1997).

Some scholars have gone beyond explorations of gender difference but have asked instead in what ways women are disadvantaged, silenced, or degraded by exclusive language or organizational hierarchies. For example, Steve Bernhardt (1992) displayed examples of sexism in army maintenance manuals (see also Rifkind & Harper, 1992). Sam Dragga (1993) asked what happens when women dominate a profession, such as technical communication, looking in particular at wages and prestige (see also Allen, 1994; Baker & Goubil-Gambrell, 1991; Dell, 1992; Griffeth, Carson, Carson, Ragan, & Wan-Huggins, 1994; Halterman, Dutkiewicz, & Halterman, 1991). Elizabeth Flynn and her cowriters (1991) predicted that women were oppressively silenced in collaborative writing groups of engineers. In a study relating feminist research to technical communication, Rebecca Burnett and Helen Ewald (1994) offer an exercise in self-reflexivity as they suggest how feminist critiques of research methodology can signal areas of conflict within collaborative research groups.

Other research using feminist perspectives to study technical communication asks how knowledge structures themselves are gendered or limited by the patriarchal structures and contexts. For example, Susan Mallon Ross

(1994) offered a case study of a Mohawk community on the border of Canada and northern New York in conflict with the Environmental Protection Agency. She showed how a feminist perspective could reform the communication practices in policy making. Mary Rosner and Georgia Rhoades's (1993) explication of Gould and Lewontin's "The Spandrels of San Marco" asks whether a communication act supports or questions the gendered nature of science. I have explored how women's embodied or experiential knowledge might differ from other knowledge systems (Lay, 2000; see also Bleier, 1986; Harding, 1986, 1991; Keller, 1985; Lather, 1991; Latour and Woolgar, 1986; Rose, 1994).

ONE CASE STUDY

Finally, a closer look at one case study, Beverly Sauer's (1993) investigation of mining postaccident reports, demonstrates how a feminist perspective informs

> (a) how the conventions of public discourse privilege the rational (male) objective voice and silence human suffering, (b) how the notion of expertise excludes women's experiential knowledge, (c) how the conventions of public discourse sanction the exclusion of alternative voices and thus perpetuate salient and silent power structures, and (d) how interpretative strategies that fail to consider unstated assumptions about gender, power, authority, and expertise seriously compromise the health, safety, and lives of miners—and in a broader sense—all of those who are dependent on technology for their personal safety. (p. 63)

Because Sauer employs the feminist research perspective to illuminate the context and texts of the Mine Safety and Health Administration postaccident investigation reports, her article can serve as a model for beginning feminist technical communication researchers. She examines not only what is contained within the accident report genre but also what is missing—the other, the abnormal, the supposedly nonimportant. She looks for the silences and the gaps, and, in finding them, she identifies a way to improve the lives of miners and their families.

In general, Sauer finds that the focus of the postaccident investigation report and its organization and style negate the human concerns of the miners and their families. Moreover, the postaccident report genre does not accommodate information that would help ensure the safety of the miners. In perhaps the most memorable part of Sauer's analysis, she includes domestic evidence that "represents truth" for the miners' wives: "'Dillard [Ashley] would come home filthy from the mines, and his work clothes always required two or three wash cycles to get all the coal dust out of them.... And had the mines been properly rock dusted the explosion would never have happened'" (p. 74). Dillard Ashley's wife, Annis, had certain knowledge about the dangers within the mines that was negated because it was domestic, women's knowledge. The genre of the investigation report and technical analysis of the accident could not accommodate her evidence, as she is able to reveal it in the oversight hearings. Thus, Sauer includes gender as a heuristic in her investigation—What were women's experiences: What would their knowledge reveal? Was there a place for it in the postaccident investigation? She discovers answers to these questions by focusing on the particular experience of women's lives— such as their difficulty in cleaning the miners' work clothes. Sauer then makes visible those experiences (see also Sauer 1992).

Sauer concludes that women's voices were not heard in postaccident reports because they had not learned the language of "agreement addition— the unarticulated code beneath the carefully categorized data in the inspection reports—a code that intentionally or unintentionally operates to maintain power structures within mining communities" (p. 76). Women are also excluded because of their lack of expertise from the conventions of discourse and the power structures that control the discourse within mining communities. Thus, Sauer reveals the gender structure within this community and the hierarchy that maintains it. Finally, Sauer speculates that the women had "internalized the silent power structures of the mining community" and so depreciated the value of their own experience and knowledge—they had agreed to the silence imposed upon them. However, as Sauer reveals, listening to and appreciating women's voices and experiences would lead to greater safety for the miners—certainly a feminist call for action. Listening to the women's evidence and knowledge constituted a call for a change in policy.

Feminist research contains some common traits and directives:

- Gender is the primary variable.
- Traditional research methods are critiqued or modified.
- Multiplicity of voice and discipline is embraced.
- Women's experiences form the research site.
- Researchers reflect upon their relationships with their participants and lessen the distance between them.
- Researcher and disciplinary objectivity are questioned.
- Empowerment of women and new knowledge about women and their role in society are dual goals.

These traits and directives are somewhat complicated as feminists wrestle with postmodernism and the emphasis on social construction of the self and the possibility of agency. These complications appear in feminist researchers' applications of the case study, textual analysis, interviewing, or ethnographic method as a means of gathering and interpreting information useful in technical communication research.

Surveying technical communication research that claims to use feminist methodology reveals four general categories of research, often representing a chronology of research attempts as feminism develops within a field: those scholars who make visible previously ignored female rhetors; those who invoke the field to use feminist methodology and theory; those who study whether the gender of the communicator makes any difference in communication choices and successes; and those who reveal how knowledge, discourse, and power are gendered.

As with Sauer's work on the genre of accident reports, feminist researchers must start by asking what voices are missing or silenced within the text and context examined—and what differences would occur if they were included. As Sauer found, the conventions of the genre, the text, might not accommodate those silenced voices, but they might be recovered from other sources, such as the oversight hearings. So discovering these voices causes the researcher to reframe definitions of truth and knowledge and to discover how her research might not only increase understanding of the research subject but might also improve the lives of her research participants.

NOTES

1. In preparing this essay, I benefited greatly from the assistance of my research assistant, Amy Koerber, who located and gathered a wealth of writing about feminist methodology for me to study. Thus, I read widely about feminist methodology across the disciplines and the tensions surrounding its use within the disciplines, probably getting a shortened version of the education that Amy has received in taking her two required seminars in feminist theory and methodology as she completed her graduate minor in feminist studies at the University of Minnesota. Then, Amy and I surveyed broadly articles in composition and technical communication journals that claimed feminist methodology and gender as a major variable. However, that survey is by no means exhaustive; I essentially wanted to capture an impression of what kinds of topics and questions technical communication researchers were attempting to answer through feminist methodology.

2. Feminist scholars deliberately avoid the use of the word "subject" to describe those whom the research might observe and study, as these subjects too often are

objectified in some traditional research studies. I use instead "participant" to capture the reciprocal relationship between researcher and person interviewed or observed.

3. Postmodernist and feminist researchers in such disciplines as anthropology, archaeology, and geography have theorized not only about gender but also about space and physical materials. For example, Gupta and Ferguson (1992) note that representatives of space are often "remarkably dependent on images of break, rupture, and disjunction" and a presumption that the spaces and the cultures that inhabit them are autonomous (p. 6). Such assumptions hide what Gupta and Ferguson call the topography of power. However, if researchers begin instead with the premise that spaces are hierarchically interconnected, not naturally disconnected, then social change is "not a matter of cultural contact and articulation but one of rethinking difference through connection" (p. 8). Such rethinking leads researchers to study such issues as immigration problems as matters of disempowerment rather than maintenance of the natural order (p. 17). Similarly, Janet Spector (1993) revealed how such physical objects as an awl in a nineteenth-century Sioux village reflected gendered-based differences in power.

4. Gynopia is the inability to see women or to see them in other than distorted ways; misogyny is hatred of women; and male-dominated theories defend or propose male superiority (Reinharz, 1992, p. 168).

REFERENCES

Abu-Lughod, L. (1990). Can there be a feminist ethnography? *Women & Performance: A Journal of Feminist Theory, 5*, 7–27.

Alcoff, L. (1988). Cultural feminism versus post-structuralism: The identity crisis in feminist theory. *Signs, 13*, 405–436.

Allen, J. (1991). Gender issues in technical communication studies: An overview of the implications for the profession, research, and pedagogy. *Journal of Business and Technical Communication, 5*, 371–392.

Allen, J. (1994). Women and authority in business/technical communication scholarship: An analysis of writing features, methods, and strategies. *Technical Communication Quarterly, 3*, 271–292.

Anderson, K., & Jack, D.C. (1991). Learning to listen: Interview techniques and analyses. In S.B. Gluck & D. Patai (Eds.), *Women's words: The feminist practice of oral history* (pp. 11–26). New York: Routledge.

Baker, M.A., & Goubil-Gambrell, P. (1991). Scholarly writing: The myth of gender and performance. *Journal of Business and Technical Communication, 5*, 412–443.

Balsamo, A. (1990). Rethinking ethnography: A work for the feminist imagination. *Studies in Symbolic Interaction, 11*, 45–57.

Bazerman, C. (1993). Intertextual self-fashioning: Gould and Lewontin's representations of the literature. In J. Selzer (Ed.), *Understanding scientific prose* (pp. 20–41). Madison: University of Wisconsin Press.

Bazerman, C., & Paradis, J. (1991). Introduction. In C. Bazerman & J. Paradis (Eds.), *Textual dynamics of the professions: Historical and contemporary studies of writing in professional communities* (pp. 3–10). Madison: University of Wisconsin Press.

Belenky, M.F., Clinchy, B.M., Goldberg, N.R., & Tarkle, J.M. (1986). *Women's ways of knowing: The development of self, voice, and mind.* New York: Basic Books.

Bernhardt, S.A. (1992). The design of sexism: The case of an Army maintenance manual. *IEEE Transactions on Professional Communication, 35,* 217–221.

Bleier, R. (Ed.). (1986). *Feminist approaches to science.* New York: Pergamon Press.

Boiarsky, C., Northrop, B., Grove, L., Phillips, M., Myers, L., & Earnest, P. (1995). Men's and women's oral communication in technical/scientific fields: Results of a study. *Technical Communication, 42 (3),* 45–59.

Bosley, D.S. (1992). Gender and visual communication: Toward a feminist theory of design. *IEEE Transactions on Professional Communication, 35,* 222–229.

Bosley, D.S. (1994). Feminist theory, audience analysis, and verbal and visual representation in a technical communication writing task. *Technical Communication Quarterly, 3,* 293–307.

Burnett, R., & Ewald, H.R. (1994). Rabbit trails, ephemera, and other stories: Feminist methodology and collaborative research. *Journal of Advanced Composition, 14 (1),* 21–51.

Charney, D. (1993). A study of rhetorical reading: How evolutionists read "The spandrels of San Marco." In J. Selzer (Ed.), *Understanding scientific prose* (pp. 203–231). Madison: University of Wisconsin Press.

Cook, J.A., & Fonow, M.M. (1990). Knowledge and women's interests: Issues of epistemology and methodology in feminist sociological research. In J.M. Nielsen (Ed.), *Feminist research methods: Exemplary readings in the social sciences* (pp. 69–93). Boulder, CO: Westview Press.

Cott, N. (1977). *The bonds of womanhood: "Woman's sphere" in New England, 1780–1835.* New Haven: Yale University Press.

Currie, D., & Kazi, H. (1987, March). Academic feminism and the process of de-radicalization: Re-examining the issues. *Feminist Review, 25,* 77–98.

Dell, S. (1992). A communication-based theory of the glass ceiling: Rhetorical sensitivity and upward mobility within the technical organization. *IEEE Transactions on Professional Communication, 35,* 230–235.

Devault, M.L. (1990, February). Talking and listening from women's standpoint: Feminist strategies for interviewing and analysis. *Social Problems, 37,* 96–116.

Doheny-Farina, S. (1986, April). Writing in an emerging organization: An ethnographic study. *Written Communication, 3,* 158–185.

Doheny-Farina, S. (1993). Research as rhetoric: Confronting the methodological and ethical problems of research on writing in nonacademic settings. In R. Spilka (Ed.), *Writing in the workplace: New research perspectives* (pp. 253–267). Carbondale: Southern Illinois Press.

Doheny-Farina, S., & Odell, L. (1985). Ethnographic research on writing: Assumptions and methods. In L. Odell & D. Goswami (Eds.), *Writing in nonacademic settings* (pp. 503–535). New York: Guilford Press.

Dragga, S. (1993). Women and the profession of technical writing: Social and economic influences and implications. *Journal of Business and Technical Communication, 7,* 312–321.

Enslin, E. (1994). Beyond writing: Feminist practice and the limitations of ethnography. *Cultural Anthropology, 9*, 537–568.

Etter-Lewis, G. (1991). Black women's life stories: Reclaiming self in narrative texts. In S.B. Gluck & D. Patai (Eds.), *Women's words: The feminist practice of oral history* (pp. 43–58). New York: Routledge.

Flynn, E.,. Savage, G., Penti, M., Brown, C., & Watke, S. (1991). Gender and modes of collaboration in a chemical engineering design course. *Journal of Business and Technical Communication, 5*, 444–462.

Fonow, M.M., & Cook, J.A. (1991). Back to the future: A look at the second wave of feminist epistemology and methodology. In M.M. Fonow & J.A. Cook (Eds.), *Beyond methodology: Feminist scholarship as lived research* (pp. 1–15). Bloomington: Indiana University Press.

Geiger, S. (1990, Spring). What's so feminist about women's oral history? *Journal of Women's History, 2*, 169–182.

Griffeth, R.W., Carson, K.D., Carson, P.P., Ragan, J, & Wan-Huggins, V. (1994). The effects of gender and employee classification level on communication-related outcomes: A test of structuralist and socialization hypotheses. *Journal of Business and Technical Communication, 8*, 299–318.

Gupta, A., & Ferguson, J. (1992, February). Beyond "culture": Space, identity, and the politics of difference. *Cultural Anthropology, 7*, 6–23.

Gurak, L.J. (1997). *Persuasion and privacy in cyberspace: The online protest over lotus marketplace and the clipper chip.* New Haven: Yale University Press.

Gurak, L.J., & Bayer, N.L. (1994). Making gender visible: Extending feminist critiques of technology to technical communication. *Technical Communication Quarterly, 3*, 257–270.

Halterman, C., Dutkiewicz, J., & Halterman, E. (1991). Men and women on the job: Gender bias in work teams. *Journal of Business and Technical Communication, 5*, 469–481.

Hampsten, E. (1982). *Read this only to yourself: The private writings of midwestern women, 1800–1910.* Bloomington: Indiana University Press.

Harding, S. (1986). *The science question in feminism.* Ithaca, NY: Cornell University Press.

Harding, S. (1987a). Introduction: Is there a feminist method? In Harding, S. (Ed.), *Feminism & methodology* (pp. 1–14). Bloomington: Indiana University Press.

Harding, S. (1987b, Fall). The method question. *Hypatia, 2*, 19–35.

Harding, S. (1991). *Whose science? Whose knowledge? Thinking from women's lives.* Ithaca, NY: Cornell University Press.

Harding, S. (1993). Rethinking standpoint theory: What is "strong objectivity"? In L. Alcoff and E. Potter (Eds.), *Feminist epistomologies* (pp. 49–82). New York: Routledge.

Hawkesworth, M. (1997). Confounding gender. *Signs, 22*, 649–685.

Hekman, S. (1997). Truth and method: Feminist standpoint theory revisited. *Signs, 22*, 341–365.

Jayartne, T.E., & Stewart, A.J. (1991). Quantitative and qualitative methods in the social sciences: Current feminist issues and practical strategies. In M.M. Fonow & J.A. Cook (Eds.), *Beyond methodology: Feminist scholarship as lived research* (pp. 83–106). Bloomington: Indiana University Press.

Keller, E.F. (1985). *Reflections on gender and science.* New Haven: Yale University Press.

Kirsch, G. (1992). Methodological pluralism: Epistemological issues. In G. Kirsch & P. Sullivan (Eds.), *Methods and methodology in composition research* (pp. 247–269). Carbondale: Southern Illinois University Press.

Koerber, A. (2000). Toward a feminist rhetoric of technology. *Journal of Business and Technical Communication, 14,* 58–73.

LaDuc, L., & Goldrick-Jones, A. (1994). The critical eye, the gendered lens, and "situated" insights—feminist contributions to professional communication. *Technical Communication Quarterly, 3,* 245–256.

Lather, P. (1991). *Getting smart: Feminist research and pedagogy with/in the postmodern.* New York: Routledge.

Latour, B., & Woolgar, S. (1986). *Laboratory life: The construction of scientific facts.* Princeton, NJ: Princeton University Press.

Lay, M. (1994). The value of gender studies to professional communication research. *Journal of Business and Technical Communication, 8 (1),* 58–90.

Lay, M.M. (1989). Interpersonal conflict in collaborative writing: What we can learn from gender studies. *Journal of Business and Technical Communication, 3,* 5–28.

Lay, M. M. (1991). Feminist theory and the redefinition of technical communication. *Journal of Business and Technical Communication, 5,* 348–370.

Lay, M.M. (1992). The androgynous collaborator: The impact of feminism on collaboration. In J. Forman (Ed.), *New visions of collaborative writing* (pp. 82–104). Portsmouth, NH: Boynton/Cook-Heinemann, 1992.

Lay, M.M. (1993). Gender studies: Implications for the professional communication classroom. In N.R. Blyler & C. Thralls (Eds.), *Professional communication: The social perspective* (pp. 215–229). Newbury Park, CA: Sage.

Lay, M.M. (2000). *The rhetoric of midwifery: Gender, knowledge, and power.* New Brunswick, NJ: Rutgers University Press.

Lunsford, A., & Ede, L. (1990). *Singular texts/plural authors: Perspectives on collaborative writing.* Carbondale: Southern Illinois Press.

MacKinnon, J. (1993). Becoming a rhetor: Developing writing ability in a mature, writing-intensive organization. In R. Spilka (Ed.), *Writing in the workplace: New research perspectives* (pp. 41–55). Carbondale: Southern Illinois University Press.

Mascia-Lees, F.E., Sharpe, P., & Ballerion Cohen, C. (1989). The postmodernist turn in anthropology: Cautions from a feminist perspective. *Signs, 15,* 7–33.

Mies, M. (1983). Towards a methodology for feminist research. In G. Bowles & R. D. Klein (Eds.) *Theories of women's studies* (pp. 117–139). London: Routledge.

Miller, N.K. (1986). Changing the subject: Authorship, writing, and the reader. In T. de Laurentis (Ed.), *Feminist studies: Critical studies* (pp. 102–120). Bloomington: Indiana University Press.

Minister, K. (1991). A feminist frame for the oral history interview. In S.B. Gluck & D. Patai (Eds.), *Women's words: The feminist practice of oral history* (pp. 27–41). New York: Routledge.

Morgan, M. (1994). Women as emergent leaders in student collaborative writing groups. *Journal of Advanced Composition, 14,* 203–219.

Myers, G. (1991). Stories and styles in two molecular biology review articles. In C. Bazerman & J. Paradis (Eds.), *Textual dynamics of the professions: Historical and contemporary studies of writing in professional communities* (pp. 45–75). Madison: University of Wisconsin Press.

Neeley, K.A. (1992). Woman as mediatrix: Women as writers on science and technology in the eighteenth and nineteenth century. *IEEE Transactions on Professional Communication, 35,* 208–216.

Opie, A. (1992, Spring). Qualitative research, appropriation of the "other" and empowerment. *Feminist review 40,* 52–69.

Patai, D. (1991). U.S. academics and third world women: Is ethical research possible? In S. B. Gluck & D. Patai (Eds.), *Women's words: The feminist practice of oral history* (pp. 137–153). New York: Routledge.

Raign, K., & Sims, B. (1993). Gender, persuasion techniques, and collaboration. *Technical Communication Quarterly, 2,* 89–104.

Reay, D. (1996, Summer). Insider perspectives or stealing the words out of women's mouths: Interpretation in the research process. *Feminist review, 53,* 57–73.

Reinharz, S. (1992). *Feminist methods in social research.* New York: Oxford University Press.

Roen, D., & Johnson, D. (1992). Perceiving the effectiveness of written discourse through gender lenses: The contribution of complimenting. *Written Communication, 9,* 435–464.

Rose, H. (1994). *Love, power and knowledge: Towards a feminist transformation of the sciences.* Bloomington: Indiana University Press.

Rosner, M., & Rhoades, G. (1993). Science, gender, and "The spandrels of San Marco and the Panglossian paradigm." In J. Selzer (Ed.), *Understanding scientific prose* (pp. 83–105). Madison: University of Wisconsin Press.

Ross, S.M. (1994). A feminist perspective on technical communication action: Exploring how alternative worldviews affect environmental remediation efforts. *Technical Communication Quarterly, 3,* 325–342.

Sauer, B.A. (1992). The engineer as rational man: The problem of imminent danger in a non-rational environment. *IEEE Transactions on Professional Communication, 35,* 242–249.

Sauer, B.A. (1993). Sense and sensibility in technical documentation: How feminist interpretation strategies can save lives in the nation's mines. *Journal of Business and Technical Communication, 7 (1),* 63–83.

Scott, J.W. (1991, Summer). The evidence of experience. *Critical Inquiry, 17,* 773–797.

Smeltzer, L.R., & Werbel, J.D. (1986). Gender differences in managerial communication: Fact or folk-linguistics? *Journal of Business Communication, 23 (2),* 41–50.

Smith, D.E. (1990). *The conceptual practices of power: A feminist sociology of knowledge.* Boston, MA: Northeastern University Press.

Spector, J.D. (1993). *What this awl means: Feminist archaeology at a Wahpeton Dakota village.* St. Paul: Minnesota Historical Society Press.

Stacey, J. (1988). Can there be a feminist ethnography? *Women's Studies International Forum, 11,* 21–27.

Stacey, J. (1994). Imagining feminist ethnography. A response to Elizabeth E. Wheatley. *Women's Studies International Forum, 17,* 417–419.

Sterkel, K.S. (1988). The relationship between gender and writing style in business communication. *Journal of Business Communication, 25 (4),* 17–38.

Sullivan, P. (1992). Feminism and methodology in composition studies. In G. Kirsch & P. Sullivan (Eds.), *Methods and methodology in composition research* (pp. 37–61). Carbondale: Southern Illinois University Press.

Sullivan, P., & Porter, J. (1993). On theory, practice, and method: Toward a heuristic research methodology for professional writing. In R. Spilka (Ed.), *Writing in the work-*

place: New research perspectives (pp. 220–237). Carbondale: Southern Illinois University Press.

Tebeaux, E. (1990). Toward an understanding of gender differences in written business communications: A suggested perspective for future research. *Journal of Business and Technical Communication, 4 (1)*, 25–43.

Tebeaux, E. (1993). Technical writing for women of the English Renaissance: Technology, literacy, and the emergence of a genre. *Written Communication, 10 (2)*, 164–199.

Tebeaux, E., & Lay, M. (1995). The emergence of the feminine voice, 1526–1640: The earliest published books by English Renaissance women. *Journal of Advanced Composition, 15 (1)*, 53–81.

Tebeaux, E., & Lay, M. (1992). Images of women in technical books from the English Renaissance. *IEEE Transactions on Professional Communication, 35*, 196–207.

Wheatley, E.E. (1994a). Dances with feminists. Truths, dares, and ethnographic stares. *Women's Studies International Forum, 17*, 421–423.

Wheatley, E.E. (1994b). How can we engender ethnography with a feminist imagination? A rejoinder to Judith Stacey. *Women's Studies International Forum, 17*, 403–416.

Winsor, D. (1996). *Writing like an engineer: A rhetorical education*. Mahwah, NJ: Erlbaum.

Wolf, M. (1992). *A thrice-told tale. Feminism, postmodernism, and ethnographic responsibility*. Stanford, CA: Stanford University Press.

CHAPTER 10

Cultural Studies: An Orientation for Research in Professional Communication

Charlotte Thralls and Nancy Blyler

Scholars in professional communication (e.g., Blyler, 1995, pp. 286–287; Herndl, 1996, p. 455; Longo, 1998, pp. 58–59; Thralls & Blyler, 1993, p. 33) have begun to call for increased attention to the political, in relation to the methods, contexts, and subjects of research. Accompanying this move toward the political has been a growing interest in cultural studies as a research orientation.

An examination of the work produced under a cultural studies banner over the past forty years suggests several shared concerns or broad themes around which the movement loosely coheres. Chief among these is a concern with political effects of social practices and modes of representation. Committed to the idea that these practices and representations organize cultural power and knowledge, cultural studies researchers typically focus on the relationships between the knowledge a society produces and the material conditions and ideological structures through which that knowledge is produced.

A second common thread is the belief that culture—its objects and practices—is complex. Driven by the notion that the specialized knowledge of disciplines downplay this complexity—fragmenting knowledge and discouraging alternative understandings—cultural studies researchers typically advocate a highly interdisciplinary approach to the study of culture.

A third shared concern is with the social practices and social discourses of everyday life. In an effort to break the association of culture with merely the high or literary arts, cultural studies research is bound by an interest in broadening research agendas to include the ordinary and mundane as primary sites in the production and circulation of cultural power and knowledge.

A final common concern of cultural studies is with agency and social action: how people can intervene to change social and discursive practices. Here, cultural studies typically looks not just at the historical conditions that shape human identities and social activities but also at the historical processes that enable new meanings for practices and roles to emerge. Of special concern is how the researcher, through analyses of institutions, disciplines, and discursive practices, can facilitate human agency and resistance to patterns of cultural domination.

Emphasizing only these concerns that run throughout cultural studies, however, can produce a distorted picture of the movement and its research. Even a cursory glance at the extensive body of scholarship identified with cultural studies reveals considerable disagreement about how the term should be defined and affiliated research carried out (see, e.g., Grossberg, 1995; Johnson, 1986/87). We begin then with some additional background on cultural studies in order to acknowledge its diversity as a research orientation and, at the same time, to narrow the field, identifying a version of cultural studies we believe to be particularly fruitful for research in professional communication.

BACKGROUND ON CULTURAL STUDIES

In his historical account of cultural studies formation, Grossberg (1993) points out that cultural studies developed in different forms over the course of a half century in response to a wide variety of local or national conditions and in tandem with the rise and fall of various theoretical paradigms in the humanities and social sciences. As a formal movement or project, for example, cultural studies began in the late 1950s and early 1960s with the founding of the *New Left Review* and the Centre for Contemporary Cultural Studies in Birmingham. Motivated by immediate problems in both the academy and British society, early leaders saw cultural studies as an interdisciplinary perspective for addressing class issues in postwar Britain, the growth and effects of electronic media and mass culture, elitism in the humanities (especially literary studies), and limitations in traditional interpretations of Marxism.

Since that time, as interest in cultural studies has spread throughout the globe, the movement has been influenced by quite different local and national conditions, adapting itself to a variety of research methods and topics as well as theoretical paradigms. In terms of research methods, for example, cultural studies has employed both qualitative and quantitative approaches. Its research topics have ranged from technology, gender and sexuality, race and ethnicity, popular culture and audiences, pedagogy, the politics of disciplinarity, workplace and educational institutions, science and ecology, and nationhood and national identity (see, e.g., Ferguson and Golding, 1997, p. xiii). Cultural studies theoretical paradigms, too, have been quite diverse. Described by Bratlinger as a "sort of magnet gathering" of various theories (1990, p.10), cultural studies has employed a range of hybridized positions, including structuralism, poststructuralism, psychoanalysis, feminism, new historicism, Marxism, and postcolonialism.

This diversity underscores the dangers of characterizing cultural studies as a clearly demarcated orientation for research. Rather than a tightly coherent, unified perspective—with consensus about what constitutes a cultural study or how a study should be done—cultural studies is a plurality of positions. Bound by a set of loosely configured concerns, cultural studies may best be understood as a range of debates and engagements that have played out in different formulations for research.

One such formulation, or version, of cultural studies, which we describe in the remainder of this chapter, reflects a line of development in current cultural studies informed by feminist and poststructuralist perspectives. What distinguishes this recent version of cultural studies from other instantiations is a rejection of essentialist and reductionist conceptions of culture and an interest in widening cultural studies political agenda.

A poststructuralist-oriented cultural studies research agenda, for example, rejects essentialism—the idea that the meanings or political effects of an object or practice are intrinsic to it and thus can be generalized or known in advance. A poststructuralist cultural studies approach would thus not accept that the meaning and conditions attributed to a term—for example, the term intellectual property—is in any way permanently fixed or built into it. A poststructuralist cultural studies approach would similarly reject reductionism—the notion that a condition producing an effect in one set of circumstances will automatically produce the same effect in a different set of circumstances. From a poststructuralist perspective, models of culture and communication grounded in essentialist and reductionist assumptions create a static and an ahistorical conception of human identities and social practices.

Insisting that no intrinsic criteria govern cultural and communication practices and that no effects can be guaranteed prior to their enactment in specific historical conditions, a poststructuralist orientation toward cultural studies offers a more radically contingent conception of culture, locating cultural practices and their effects on human experience in the connections that can—but need not necessarily—be forged under specific historical conditions.

Although poststructuralist theory has served as an impetus for cultural studies to theorize a more dynamic, historical, and contingent conception of culture, feminist theory has prompted current scholars to broaden cultural studies understanding of the political, including the objects and practices suitable for research. Building on the long-standing belief in cultural studies that the political cannot be extracted from cultural analysis, feminist scholars are credited (Hall, 1992, p. 282) with bringing attention to exclusionary practices endemic to earlier culturalist and structuralist versions of cultural studies, in which patriarchal and gendered practices remained largely unexamined. Radical feminists, such as Gubar (1981), for example, have argued that gender and patriarchy are historical and cultural constructions that have excluded and misrepresented women as objects, "texts," and "blank pages" (pp. 244–245) authored by men, thus denying women the opportunity and authority to represent themselves.

Informed by these critiques, a poststructuralist and feminist cultural studies assumes a broad and inclusive research agenda, targeting issues of representation and paying special attention to those individuals and groups that have been misrepresented or, more important, excluded from participation in the process of constructing meaning.

In the following sections, we further characterize this version of cultural studies in order (1) to describe its focus and purpose for research, and (2) to discuss its implications, including some of the benefits and challenges for research in professional communication.

THE FOCUS OF CULTURAL STUDIES RESEARCH

Cultural studies research, as informed by poststructuralist and feminist theory, analyzes discourses and practices in order to account for the processes whereby meanings and values are socially produced, represented, and circulated. Rather than focusing on social practices as discrete or autonomous entities, however, researchers examine practices in their contingent relationships to other practices, reconstructing connections across practices, including the relations of terms, texts, and practices to a wider network of historical institutions, discourses, and social structures.

This emphasis on relational elements stems from the cultural studies-belief that meaning—how people experience the conditions of social existence—is a product of the way texts or practices connect up with other texts and practices within concrete historical conditions. Hall (Grossberg,1986) refers to these relationships as articulations: "the form of a connection that *can* make a unity of two different elements under certain conditions" (p. 53; italics in original). According to Hall (1981), the articulation, or linkage, of a practice with a particular set of connotations or uses is never fixed; how people interpret and deploy a practice depends instead on the "social field into which it [a cultural symbol] is incorporated, the practices with which it articulates and is made to resonate. What matters," in cultural studies research, Hall explains, "is *not* the intrinsic or historically fixed objects of culture, but the state of play in cultural relations" (p. 235; italics in original).

The work of cultural studies research is to unpack this "play of cultural relations," identifying the linkages that, under particular historical conditions, allow certain ideas, habits, and interpretive frames to emerge in social life. In identifying and then tracking these linkages, researchers are especially concerned with three areas of analysis: the organization of linkages into structures, the relationships among multiple networks of linkages, and the instability of linkages.

ORGANIZATION OF LINKAGES

Examining linkages between elements is part of an analytic process designed to discover how these linkages are organized into structures that provide maps of reality—to discover how, as Grossberg (1992) explains, "articulation links this practice to that effect, this text to that meaning, this meaning to that reality, this experience to those politics" and then how "these links are themselves articulated into larger structures" (p. 54).

In tracing networks of linked elements, researchers pay particular attention to the hierarchical organization of elements within a discursive structure. Their focus on hierarchies is driven by the assumption that not all linkages of terms, events, and practices within a discourse system count equally; rather, elements are weighted with different values accorded to elements at a given time. This weighting organizes elements, so that within a discursive system some practices, Grossberg (1992) explains, "are dominant, others are tolerated, and still others excluded if not rendered radically unimaginable" (p. 57).

In examining linkages that produce this hierarchical effect, researchers emphasize the importance of situating discourses and practices within multiple networks of linkages.

MULTIPLE NETWORKS OF LINKAGES

Studying what an object represents culturally, researchers analyze discourses and practices not as singular entities but as interconnected assemblages or groupings. As Hall (Grossberg, 1986) explains, it is not the "individual elements of a discourse that have political or ideological connotations ... it is the way these elements" (p. 55) operate in discursive chains, semantic fields, and discursive formations. In other words, researchers view cultural representations as emerging from interconnected discourses that, in Lidchi's (1997) words, "construct a specific object/topic of analysis in a particular way," limiting "ways in which that topic/object might be constituted" (p. 191).

This emphasis on tracking multiple and interconnected linkages is illustrated through a recent analysis of the Sony Walkman by Du Gay, Hall, Janes, Mackey, and Negus (1997). These coauthors argue that understanding the "full range of meanings, connotations, and associations that the Walkman has acquired over time in our culture" requires tracking the multiple linkages or "semantic networks" (p. 15) that "have gone into constructing it meaningfully" (p. 17). According to Du Gay et al., the popular discourse that constitutes a public identity for the Walkman derives from the way the object has been brought into relationship with a combination of several discourses—for example, the "high-tech" (as opposed to "low-tech") discourse of technology, the discourse of "Japanese-ness" (a stereotype connoting "high quality, precision consumer commodities"), the discourse of youth and popular music, and the discourse of entertainment connected to the "world of leisure and pleasure" (p. 16).

Because researchers see all cultural representations (discourses and practices) as constituted through such plural linkages, they emphasize the importance of situating cultural representations in connection with larger social and cultural relations. As the Walkman analysis suggests, then, it is not enough for the researcher to track networks of relationships *within* an organization, company, discipline, profession, institution, or industry; researchers must also track linkages with discourses and practices outside these domains. From a cultural studies perspective, these latter relationships are important because discourses and practices never exist in a vacuum, separate from larger social and cultural relations; rather, the practices and discourses of an industry, discipline, or profession emerge and take shape within what Johnson (1986/87) describes as the "whole ensemble of discourses and social relations'" preexisting articulatory activity (p. 65).

According to Johnson (1986/87), any historically produced construction, as in the case of the Sony Walkman, derives its identify from the way, at any given historical moment and site, the discourse is brought into a relationship with the "stock of already existing cultural elements drawn from the reservoirs of lived culture or from the already public fields of discourse" (p. 55).

This emphasis on the relationship of a discourse or practice to the wider cultural and historical structures reflects cultural studies researchers' interest in expanding and challenging notions of context. According to Murdock (1997), for example, researchers have too often tended to study practices "of sense making, interpretation, and expression" as embedded in and sustained by the immediate contexts of action "with little or no reference to more general forces." Situating practices only in their immediate social contexts," Murdock argues, provides "no account of how localized situations are themselves shaped in fundamental ways, by broader, underlying, social and economic dynamics" (p. 90) that "sustain and organize everyday activity and expression." Examining cultural practices and discourses on multiple levels and planes will produce, Murdock concludes, "a more comprehensive and symmetrical analysis" (p. 91).

Yet another concern is the instability of linkages within any discourse system.

INSTABILITY OF LINKAGES

A concern with instability springs from the assumption that the historical and cultural contexts that enable practices to emerge and become meaningful are always fluid. Because there is no underlying structure or intrinsic essence that requires a practice to be linked to a fixed web of connotations or effects, the same term or practice, Hall (1981) argues, can carry quite different connotations and political effects depending on how it is employed under specific conditions: "This year's radical symbol or slogan will be neutralized into next year's fashion; the year after, it will be the object of a profound cultural nostalgia" (p. 235). In short, "all symbolic patterns are seen as provisional, open to dispute" (Murdock, 1997, p. 89).

Instability also arises through the multiple and contradictory forces at play in any social structure. Cultural studies researchers believe that built into all situations, contexts, and historical moments is a certain antagonism, a struggle over how social life will be represented and carried out. The "domain of cultural forms and activities," Hall (1981) maintains, is a "constantly changing field" (p. 235): discourses and practices are continually acting upon and adjusting to other practices, discourses, and contexts.

Given this conception of historical discourses as fluid and changeable, researchers explore those circumstances that enable discourses and practices to emerge and change. For example, in tracking how a discourse or practice is intertextually linked within a historical structure of discourses, practices, and relations, cultural studies researchers explore the process whereby practices, by pulling in fragments of other already existing practices, create new combinations and arrangements. In tracing evolutionary connections between new and preexisting forms, and in noting the hierarchical organization of values the new forms produce, cultural studies researchers also target possibilities for effecting change in disciplines, professions, institutions, and workplaces.

This interest in change relates to the purpose of cultural studies research.

THE PURPOSE OF CULTURAL STUDIES RESEARCH

Researchers examine linkages or articulations, not only to describe and explain how groupings of practices are accorded different values and thus linked hierarchically within social formations, but also to use that information in order to intervene in existing relations of domination and subordination (Grossberg, 1993, p. 22). Hall (1992) notes that there is "something *at stake* in cultural studies" (p. 278; italics in original) and hence, say Blundell, Shepherd, and Taylor (1993), its "constant" sense of "critical political involvement" and its desire to alter "structures of dominance" (p. 3).

Guided by the assumption that a just society is a worthy goal, cultural studies researchers oppose the "instrumental reduction" of human beings to tools (Slack & Whitt, 1992, p. 573), wanting instead to critique and change oppressive cultural and social practices and formations (p. 572). Researchers thus view themselves as "politically engaged participants" (Nelson, Treichler, & Grossberg, 1992, p. 5), who serve as a "voice for those individuals and groups who are variously seen as subjugated, silenced, repressed, oppressed, and discriminated against" (Slack & Whitt, 1992, p. 573; see Lay in this collection for a discussion of political engagement in the context of feminist research).

As politically engaged participants, cultural studies researchers are particularly concerned with power.

POWER

In cultural studies, power is seen as a productive force that, says Grossberg (1987), "operates at every level of our lives" (p. 95). It "shapes relationships, structures differences, draws boundaries, delimits complexity, reduces contradictions to claims of unity, coherence and homogeneity, and organizes the multiplicity of concrete practices and effects into predefined identities, unities, hierarchical categories, and apparently necessary relationships" (p. 92).

By "draw[ing] and redraw[ing] lines of articulation," power "works to *fix meanings*, that which empowers some possibilities and disempowers others" (Slack, Miller, & Doak, 1993, p. 28; italics in original). Hence, says Grossberg (1987), power is "the conditions of possibility that enable a particular practice or statement to exist in a specific context, and that enable people to live their lives in different ways" (p. 95).

As this productive and enabling force, power is always situated—never an abstraction, a universal that can be reproduced, or a "reified set of presupposed structures" (Grossberg, 1987, p. 95). Neither, however, is power inherent in concrete social practices—textual or otherwise—groups, or individuals. Contrary to our popular belief, "people do not possess power" (McLaren, 1991, p. 153) because of anything that is inherently theirs.

Rather, power results from positioning in relation to other individuals or social practices, as well as from the effects of such positioning. Positioning, effects, and power itself are thus relational. Regarding positioning, for example, Grossberg (1987) claims that "whether someone has power over someone else depends upon where you and they stand" (p. 95). And regarding effects, because they result from struggles to link practices to specific outcomes, they are never determined in advance (Grossberg, 1987, p. 93) and cannot be guaranteed. As Grossberg and Slack (1985) maintain:

> The struggle is always—on the one side—to articulate meanings and practices by creating or constructing those "unities" which favor a particular disposition of power; and—on the other hand—to disrupt or "disarticulate" those constructed unities and to construct in their place alternative points of condensation between practice and experience which enable alternative dispositions of power and resistance to emerge and be empowered. (p. 90)

In enabling alternative dispositions of power or constructed unities to emerge—even though at times with great struggle—power is related to empowerment, a second issue that concerns cultural studies researchers.

EMPOWERMENT

Because power is relational—arising from a "changing network" (Grossberg, 1987, p. 95) of articulations—empowerment is relational as well. As Grossberg claims, "Whether a particular group is empowered or disempowered, whether a particular practice empowers or disempowers its subjects, is never a simple matter; it depends on where one positions those subjects ... within the social field" (p. 95).[1]

Additionally, empowerment is never identical for all subjects. Because "a social event or practice ... may have multiple and contradictory effects" (Grossberg, 1987, p. 96), the same social practice may empower some individuals while disempowering others. Similarly, the same individual may be both empowered and disempowered by a particular effect. Grossberg explains:

> One can gain power in the economic domain, while losing power over one's emotional life. One can be empowered through cultural consumption, even while still disempowered productively.... Thus, not only can't we be sure whether any practice is empowering or disempowering, but the question makes no sense apart from concrete contexts and concrete political struggles. (p. 96)

Regardless, however, of how disempowered an individual might be at a particular moment and site, cultural studies researchers believe that change and empowerment are always possible. Says Hall (Grossberg, 1986), "The question is not the unfolding of some inevitable law but rather the *linkages* which, although they can be made, need not necessarily be" (p. 96; italics in original). People "remain open to be positioned and situated in different ways, at different moments throughout [their] existence" (p. 106). As Slack and Whitt (1992) claim, therefore, "people are never entirely subordinated; there are always ways in which their practice is enabling, creative—opening up possibilities" (p. 573). And as Grossberg (1987) asserts, "people are actively appropriating what they are given in unpredictable ways, constantly attempting to bend what they have had no control over to their advantage, to win a bit of purchase on their situation" (p. 94).

Although this active appropriation—in other words, change and empowerment—can occur at any time, cultural studies researchers nonetheless recognize that "limits and constraints" exist on the degree to which people can be empowered. "The field" is not "entirely open," and "our possibilities for struggle" are not "unlimited" (Grossberg, 1987, p. 93). Rather, some articulations are stronger than others—articulations "vary," Slack, Miller, and Doak (1993) claim, "in their tenacity" (p. 26)—and these more tenacious linkages are "more difficult to disarticulate/rearticulate than others" (p. 27).

Cultural studies researchers thus focus on articulations, in order to intervene in existing relations of domination and subordination and to empower. (Lay in this collection also discusses empowerment, within the context of feminist research.) This orientation then has direct implications for the way cultural studies research in professional communication would be conducted.

CULTURAL STUDIES: IMPLICATIONS FOR RESEARCH IN PROFESSIONAL COMMUNICATION

If scholars in professional communication choose to conduct cultural studies research, they must recognize that—as Grossberg (1987) suggests—research practices (e.g., research methodologies, the uses to which research results are put [academic advancement, assistance to research sponsors], or the formulaic structure of research articles) are neither "innocent and benign" nor self-apparent: They do not "appear 'in themselves.'" Instead, like all practices, these are "always already articulated into larger political/theoretical frameworks." The task, therefore, is to "struggle to rearticulate" or relink those research practices with which they are already familiar, "construct[ing] them within a different set of relations" (p. 87)—one that would be informed by a cultural studies focus and purpose.

If rearticulation of this kind is their goal, scholars in professional communication should consider three important implications for their research: They would have to (1) complicate and more rigorously contextualize what they examine; (2) view the researcher as always already positioned; and (3) endorse empowerment as the goal of the research. In the following discussion, we illustrate these three points as they are being carried out in professional communication research. Although our reference to a single, extended example would be consistent with the strategy employed in many chapters of this collection, we are compelled instead to offer multiple, abbreviated examples. One reason is our reluctance to hold up a single example as an ideal instantiation of cultural studies research. Cultural studies research can legitimately employ a variety of methods and rhetorical frameworks to realize the overarching research implications we outline here. For example, as we illustrate below in our discussion of empowerment as a research goal, researchers in professional communication target different audiences to empower through their research, resulting in divergent models of cultural studies research.

Our second reason for employing multiple examples is our observation that scholarship in professional communication, despite an intensified focus on the political, has only partially explored the rich potential of a cultural studies perspective, with most existing studies embodying one or two but not all three of the above implications. By citing several of these studies, we thus attempt to ferret out from a range of examples how each implication of a cultural studies perspective might look in actual research practice.

COMPLICATING AND CONTEXTUALIZING RESEARCH

Because—as Grossberg (1987) suggests—"the cornerstone" of cultural studies is "its committed opposition to any reductionism, its recognition that concrete reality is always more complex and contradictory than our intellectual schemes can represent," scholars in professional communication who wish to do work informed by cultural studies must "[learn] to live with this complexity" (p. 89). In their research, that is, they will be faced with situating the practices under study within "a complex array of signifying practices, intertextual connotations, historical contexts, social relations, and modes of production, distribution, and consumption" (p. 91). The challenge, therefore, is to remain true to the complexity of this approach to reality by more deeply contextualizing practices—examining them as existing in complex and hierarchical assemblages or discursive systems.

This reconsideration of what it means to contextualize is illustrated by Zachry's (1999) analysis of management discourse and Slack, Miller, and Doak's (1993) analysis of the technical communicator as author.

Zachry's (1999) analysis is instructive for scholars in professional communication because it points up that more rigorous methods of contextualizing—as advocated within cultural studies—can allow researchers to explain how workplace discourses are formed and why large-scale discourses, such as total quality management (TQM) systems, can vary and change. As Zachry points out, scholars have been frustrated in their efforts "to pin TQM down" (p. 112) citing its "ambiguous and insubstantial nature." The problem, he argues, is that these scholars have attempted to "systematically study TQM" (p. 111) as a definable set of practices, universally instantiated across organizational contexts. What this conventional, and reductive, approach fails to recognize, Zachry says, is that—rather than a fixed and stable discourse—total quality programs actually "depend on underarticulated definitions of key terms" (p. 112) so that "every instantiation of TQM is (re)formed by the culture in which it exists."

Zachry offers an alternative framework, emphasizing the "network of social activities" (p. 114) that surround and shape instantiations of TQM at specific sites. Consistent with cultural studies emphasis on the multiple networks and multiple linkages that form practices, Zachry urges researchers in professional communication to view TQM—not as a single narrative—but as "a shifting collection of narratives" (p. 112) or an "assemblage of narratives" (p. 109) that link and combine in various permutations, thus determining the shape that total quality discourse and practices take in different organizational settings.

Tracking this complex narrative interplay, Zachry (1999) argues, requires that researchers focus contextual analysis on the relationships among stories circulating within an organization, but even more important, on the linkages between these internal stories and external ones circulating in the broader culture. For example, as his analysis illustrates, local instantiations of TQM entail the appropriation and transformation of narratives from wider social settings—for example, academic and popular management literature, as well as cultural metaphors drawing on the large-scale institutional discourses of religion, sports, and science. Tracking the interplay of TQM's assemblage of narratives, Zachry further demonstrates, also requires that researchers examine the relationship between stories and concrete communication practices. As he points out, the "variety of tools and practices upon which participants may draw" (p. 114)—for example, collaborating or brainstorming which are not especially innovative in themselves—only become meaningful, or seem revolutionary, when situated in the context of TQM stories about progress and quality.

Equally significant as an example of contextualizing is Slack, Miller, and Doak's (1993) analysis of the technical communicator. Interested, like Zachry, in tracking the complex interplay of contextual factors that render concepts undefinable in absolute terms, these authors examine three communication models in professional communication—transmission, translation, and articulation—to show how elements (social, economic, and historical) differently construct the identity of the technical communicator. The Slack, Miller, and Doak study is especially instructive, in terms of cultural studies and context, because they focus their contextual analysis on the relations of power at play in each communication model, with "different arrangements mak[ing] different possibilities and practices" (p. 27). They point out, for example, that in the transmission model, the technical communicator is rendered a disempowered entity (a conduit) because he or she is linked to a conception of language as transparent. In contrast, the articulation model links the communicator with a more open-ended notion of language, constructing technical authors as active creators of meaning. By making power relations central to their analysis of the status of technical communicators and technical discourse, Slack, Miller, and Doak foreground the political agenda that typically informs cultural studies research. In their case, they wish to foreground the agency implicit in the technical communicator's work—even if masked in some communication models—and thus to rearticulate readers' understanding of the technical communicator as author.

In modeling what contextualizing means within a cultural studies framework, the studies of Zachry (1999) and of Slack, Miller, and Doak (1993) demonstrate the challenges that contextual analysis can pose for researchers in professional communication. Chief among these is the impossibility of the researcher tracking all the relevant linkages for a practice and thus the origins and significance of a term or practice within an organization. Given the multiple and unstable nature of these linkages, scholars must recognize that—despite the admittedly practical cast of professional communication as a discipline and its desire for research results that will translate into pedagogical practice (Spilka, 1993, pp. 214–216)—researchers' knowledge of practices under study will be incomplete and provisional, never yielding the kind of certainty that the discipline has desired but instead providing a glimpse taken at a particular moment.

Scholars in professional communication who wish to do work informed by cultural studies face other challenges as well, as they further recognize that they are themselves positioned within complex and contradictory sets of relations.

POSITIONED RESEARCHER

Scholars in professional communication must understand that they too occupy subject positions: They are "structured as subjects or social agents" and "constructed by the discourses [they] embody and the metaphors [they] enact" (McLaren, 1991, pp. 151–152). Researchers' work, therefore, is directed by their own particular life experiences, values, and interests, and—far from neutral, as scholars in professional communication might have been indoctrinated to believe (Herndl, 1993, p. 349)—their research results are interested as well.

Given the interested nature of their work, scholars in professional communication employing a cultural studies perspective must realize that their research practices will affect the situations under study. In their research designs and reporting techniques, researchers must thus openly interrogate their choices and commitments. Researchers should, for example, clarify, upfront, the nature of the experiences and values that have shaped their research, including conditions of production and reception and the researcher's own involvement in the topic.

They should also be intensely self-reflexive, recognizing, as Grossberg has pointed out, that as academics they inhabit a complex and paradoxical situation, "existing in the heart of the beast, so to speak, in one of the most powerful and complex ideological institutions" (1987, p. 89), yet at the same time committed to bringing what is left off the agenda to the fore. Reflection on this paradoxical positioning and the dominance it may grant would entail researchers to disclose ways their research practices are connected to what McLaren terms "larger structures of power and privilege" (1991, p. 150): "Whose interests are being served by our research efforts? Where do we stand ethically and politically on matters of social justice? What principles should we choose from in structuring and navigating our relations in the field?" (p. 150).

As an end result of this self-reflexivity, scholars in professional communication may hope to achieve what McLaren (1991) terms "theoretical decolonization": "unlearning accepted ways of thinking" and "refusing to analyze in the mode of the dominator" (p. 152; see also Lay in this collection). When researchers question their dominance in the research process, it becomes, says McLaren, a "hermeneutical journey of self-discovery" (p. 158) where researchers themselves—along with the audiences of or the participants in the research—learn and are changed. To envision research in this way "is but a first step to the larger goal of transforming our field relations within the context of a politics of difference and a vision of social justice" (p. 152).

Clark's dissertation (2001), an ethnographic study of communication practices in a small, but growing, software company, demonstrates the interrogation of—and self-disclosure about—researcher positioning that a cultural studies perspective would encourage in professional communication. Clark's study, designed to benefit scholars, teachers, and practitioners in his field, examines how a technical/nontechnical split within the company structured (and was structured by) power relations and a division of labor that marginalized written communication and the work of the technical writer. His study is especially relevant to researchers in professional communication because it highlights the complex positioning that researchers may experience at workplace sites—for example, when researchers are also employees within the organizations they study and when the research involves potentially negative information about participants or a negative critique of the organization, disclosure of which might embarrass participants but enrich readers' (academic audiences') understanding of the researcher's topic. Such a research dynamic—embodying tensions among the researcher's, participants,' and readers' interests—can create great difficulties for the researcher wanting to behave ethically toward participants—avoiding simply analyzing in the mode of the dominator—while, at the same time, wanting to produce knowledge about ideological and cultural practices that will benefit the discipline.

Rather than masking these conflicts, Clark (2001) openly discusses them in the methodology section of his study. What's instructive about his discussion, as an example of a cultural studies emphasis on researcher positioning, is Clark's effort to "problematize" (p. 23) his methodology through "self-reflection," illustrating how such reflection led him to interrogate his ethical relationships with participants and thus eventually to develop a new understanding of the researcher's responsibilities.

In Clark's (2001) case, for example, he reveals how reflection on his dual role—a researcher and outsider when he began his research but then later an employee when he was hired by the company as a technical writer— sharpened his awareness of the impact his own positioning had on the research dynamic. Being a "participant in the very structuring of the company that I now chose as my research subject, the technical/non-technical split" (p.30) made "me," he reports "fully complicit" (p. 34) in the very structuring he was critiquing. Understanding this complicity, he explains, made him question "any easy conclusions I might have reached about [their] participants' political agendas and commitments" and made him realize it would be "hypocritical for me to then excoriate my participants for their participation" (p. 34).

Reflections on his positioning also forced him to develop a more complex understanding of openness and trust. In terms of openness, the evolving nature of his work as ethnography, coupled with changes in the company itself, meant that "at the beginning of, and indeed throughout, my project, I knew very little myself about the potential negative impact of my work ... making it difficult to represent to my current and new participants the serious nature of my work" (p. 42). Participant trust, he came to understand, further complicated his efforts to be open. He points out, for example, that despite his efforts to share his research impressions with participants, the trust he gained as an insider/colleague made "it difficult for current and new participants to imagine my work as having a negative impact on their interests" (p. 42).

The intense self-reflection that Clark (2001) exhibits does not, of course, resolve or diminish researchers' conflicts about their positioning. His reflection does, however, enable a journey of self-discovery—the learning of new ways of thinking that cultural studies value. In Clark's case, self-reflection led to a deeper understanding of ethics in professional communication research and responsibilities to participants. At the outset of his study, he reports, he had considered ethics "far less important when researching workplaces" than "composition contexts," in part because so much corporate research "is conducted at a distance, often through textual analysis, making it easier for us to be negative without raising too many ethical questions" (p. 32).

The end of his research process finds his views significantly changed: Noting that "the trust of and relationships with the members of the organization" made it increasingly difficult to "have the sort of critical take to which I was accustomed, despite my difficulties with SecureCom's corporate structure and politics" (2001, p. 43), Clark says,

> Part of that was good—through my ethnographic process I'd been forced to greatly complicate the simple belief in corporate evil I'd had when I entered. I'd found myself engaged with corporate people who, despite their very overt and honest focus on money making, were complex and interesting and, above all else, with whom I'd built trust and who might, given the right subject, feel upset, betrayed, and alienated by my critiques of their work, regardless of how early in the process I presented them. The easy answer is not to care, and nothing in our current ethical frameworks or from our review boards would stop me. But not caring is difficult after spending a year with people rather than just being surrounded by a mound of primary texts. (p. 43)

As Clark's (2001) comments suggest, researchers attempting to employ a cultural studies perspective can, through intense self-reflection, gain—and help readers gain—insight into the complexities of researcher positioning. Some of these complexities, as we shall now see, are connected up with the ultimate goal of cultural studies research—empowerment—and the decisions researchers make in formulating that goal.

RESEARCH GOAL AS EMPOWERMENT

In understanding their goal to be empowerment, scholars in professional communication must focus on what has been marginalized—for example, on disempowered people or excluded discourse practices—"actively seek[ing] out that which, for whatever reasons, is being kept off the agenda (including [their] own), whatever is being silenced in the production, not only of social reality, but of social knowledge as well" (Grossberg, 1987, p. 89).[2]

Scholars in professional communication can support this effort toward empowerment in at least two ways: (1) through analyses—written largely for academic audiences—of relations of power and (2) through participatory research, where the researcher and the participants collaborate as co-investigators in the research process.

Analyses for Academic Audiences

Situated analyses of relations of power, directed largely to academic audiences, have been the most common form of cultural studies employed by professional communication researchers. Examples include Barton and Barton's (1993) article on the ideology of the map, Slack, Miller, and Doak's

(1993) aforementioned study of authorship, Herndl's (1996) study of resistance in military report writing, and, to some extent, Clark's (2001) study of the technical/nontechnical split in a corporation, to name just a few. In studies of this type, researchers typically critique texts or organizational processes to show how dominant forces or elements delimit representation and human action. In directing these insights toward academic audiences, the researcher's goal is to provide knowledge—often including strategies of intervention and resistance—that will empower teachers and researchers in our discipline.

Herndl's (1996) study serves as a case in point. Interested in the military's "powerful discursive strategies for both producing and disciplining knowledge" (p. 462) on environmental policy, Herndl examines the "resistant activities" (p. 456) of a military field biologist, who "intervenes in and, to a limited degree, alters the activities of the institution within which he works" (p. 456). Viewing his research as a corrective to our discipline's narrow understanding of resistance and the "cultural dynamics of writing," Herndl sees his analysis as a way to provide academic audiences with greater insight into the "many ways in which writers often work at cross purposes to the dominant position legitimized by discourse" (p. 456).

Analyses of the kind Herndl conducts will, he believes, empower those in our discipline in specific ways. Such research will, for example, help to alleviate "a number of problems" with "the way we think about and teach nonacademic writing," enabling us and our students to envision specific means for effecting "organizational and cultural change" (p. 456). This type of research will also allow us to see that resistance—far from being embodied solely in "large scale action and public confrontations" (p. 457)—can be found in the "ongoing, mundane activity" of organizational life. In this way, we can escape a "problematic narrative legacy" that "displaces resistance, locating it outside the normal process of institutional and cultural activity of which it is a part" (p. 468). Finally, by helping us "think beyond the classroom," this type of research will enable us to heal an "all too common schism between the way many teachers talk about learning in writing classrooms and the way we represent the writing that occurs outside the academy" (p. 456).

Despite this interest in empowering academic audiences, an important caveat is in order about this type of cultural studies research. Scholars in professional communication should recognize that this goal may not necessarily be compatible with the beliefs and aims of the entities, organizational or otherwise, that they study. Herndl (1996), for example, clearly understands that his study of resistance in many ways ran counter to the "dominant interests" (p. 468) of the commanders at the military base where he did his work. Despite the challenges that a lack of fit such as this may pose—for example, to gaining access (see Herndl, p. 469) or securing funding—cultural studies emphasis on empowerment urges scholars to wrestle, as Clark (2001) did in conducting his study, with ways of existing within the constraints of their positioning.

Although analyses such as Herndl's are one possible avenue for scholars in professional communication who wish to do cultural studies research, another less commonly employed option exists. This option, frequently labeled participatory research, aims to empower participants by positioning them as co-investigators in the research process (see also Lay in this collection).

Participatory Research

Scholars who engage in participatory research address directly an important issue in empowerment: ownership of the research knowledge. In participatory research, the researcher is not, according to Mumby (1993), "the sole arbiter of what counts as knowledge" (p. 20). Rather, asserts Gaventa (1991), "the distinction between the researchers and the researched and the subjects and objects of knowledge production" is broken down "through the participation of the people-for-themselves in the attainment and creation of knowledge" (p. 121). In this way, says Mumby, researchers who engage in participatory research try to "overcome the continued marginalization of those whom we study" (p. 21).

In participatory research, the researcher and the participants together define the problem that the research will address, the way knowledge will be gathered, and the uses for that knowledge, of which the participants continue to be the owners (see, e.g., Fals-Borda, 1991b, p. 9; Gaventa, 1991, p. 124; Mumby, 1993, p. 20 for a discussion of participants' ownership of research results). As Fals-Borda (1991a) claims, the participants engage in the research process

> from the very beginning, that is, from the moment it is decided what the subject of research will be. And they remain involved at every step of the process until the results (of which they continue to be rightful owners) have been published and the information has been returned in various ways to the people. (p. 149; see also Whyte, Greenwood, & Lazes, 1991, p. 20)

By involving the participants in this way, participatory researchers believe that they are—as Fals-Borda (1991a) claims—"doing research with and for the people, and not on them" (p. 148; see also McLaren, 1991, pp. 154, 162), for the "mutual goal of advancing knowledge in search of greater justice" (p. 152).

To date, participatory research has been relatively scarce in professional communication, although a few examples are emerging, such as Grabill's analysis of HIV/AIDS policy making (2000). (See also Lay in this collection for a discussion of participatory research in connection with women.) Interested in how research in technical communication can help shape public policy in ways that will "solve problems and/or change local practices with those most affected by them" (Grabil, p. 34; see also Holter & Schwartz-Barcott, 1993, p. 299), Grabill describes a research project he conducted in collaboration with members of a federally funded HIV/AIDS planning council in Atlanta, the mission of which is to establish local policies for supporting AIDS clients, helping "alleviate the effect of the disease" (p. 29) in the area.

The project was designed to address a problem of participant involvement on the council. Although technically the council met federal guidelines requiring that a percentage of the council "be made up of individuals affected by the disease" (Grabill, 2000, p. 30), certain barriers in the institutional structuring of the council kept many HIV/AIDS—women, the poor, and people of color—from participating, thus "limiting the voices influencing public policy." By conducting research (via a questionnaire and interviews with these excluded groups) designed to identify and document these barriers to involvement, Grabill demonstrates how technical communication research can act as an intervention, serving the interests of research participants—in this case, members of the council, who wanted to effect broader involvement, and those currently disenfranchised from participation.

As an example of participatory research, Grabill's (2000) work demonstrates a number of strategies consistent with cultural studies principles and values for this type of research. The research process was guided by the principle of reciprocity so that participants benefited from the "processes of research just as much as the researcher." As Grabill points out, he gained by being able to conduct research relevant to his field, but his interests did not dominate the process. Rather, he was invited by council members "to work with them and to understand and solve problems" (p. 34) they had identified as important and which would, in turn, benefit disenfranchised participants, His research was also guided, he explains, by "mutual knowledge construction" so that participants had an "opportunity to participate in analysis, reflection, and meaning making."

Participatory research, Grabill (2000) argues, can be a powerful tool for empowering others. In his case, documenting barriers to participation led to changes in institutional processes within the council—the establishment of an official Client Involvement Committee, as well as changes in council meeting times and procedures to better accommodate involvement of participants previously excluded. Grabill also argues for greater adoption of participatory research within professional and technical communication. Because rhetoric is fundamental to institutional processes, Grabill maintains, researchers in technical communication are well positioned to use their knowledge—not just to critique institutional injustices from afar—but also to help actually influence public policy.

Although participatory research may not be suitable or feasible for many research projects in professional communication, as Grabill's project suggests, participatory research—rather than being a departure—can be compatible with the practical bent of professional communication and can further impulses already present—for example, the desire to assist research sponsors—in ways that respond to an emancipatory goal, if those sponsors are open to a goal of this kind. Indeed, as traditional hierarchies within the workplace are flattened and organizations bring their workers more fully into the decision-making process, participatory research that aims at empowerment can offer a viable means for balancing the needs and desires of the researcher, the research sponsor, and the research participants.

Choosing to follow a cultural studies orientation has a number of important implications that affect profoundly the way scholars in professional communication complicate and contextualize the entities they study, their view of themselves as positioned researchers, and the goal of their work. These implications also present scholars with both benefits and challenges.

BENEFITS AND CHALLENGES
OF A CULTURAL STUDIES ORIENTATION

We believe that research informed by cultural studies has a number of benefits to offer professional communication. First, by urging scholars to complicate and contextualize more deeply what it is they study, cultural studies research enables them to view these entities in a richer and more complex way, thereby increasing their understanding of the world. Second, by mandating more recognition of the interested nature of academic work and the researcher's positioning, cultural studies research furthers initiatives already underway in professional communication—allowing scholars, for example, to further explore the critique of objectivism that recently has come to the fore (Blyler, 1995; Flynn, 1997) and to respond to the call within professional communication for greater self-reflexivity and a greater attention to the ethics of research (Doheny-Farina, 1993, pp. 254, 266–267).

Third, by taking emancipation as its goal, cultural studies research also extends the work currently being done on the social nature of discourse, focusing attention not solely on describing discourse practices and sites but also on the hierarchical nature of linked practices and thus on dominance and marginalization—what Herndl (1996) calls "the ideologically coercive effects of institutional and professional discourse" (p. 455). By extending socially oriented work in this way, cultural studies research expands the options available to scholars in professional communication who wish to investigate discourse practices but who also wish to incorporate the political into their research agendas.

These benefits are significant but with them come a number of challenges. In terms of the focus of research, for example, cultural studies belief in the instability of truth problematizes any easy connection between research results and the desires of research sponsors to obtain concrete and lasting answers to their problems or the demands of pedagogy for effective, tried-and-true teaching practices. Further, this belief in instability also means that scholars in professional communication must constantly rehistoricize or relink the practices they examine, as the significance of these practices will change over time and in relation to the contexts in which the practices are embedded.

In terms of the purpose of research, cultural studies commitment to empowerment may complicate both access to research sites and funding for research initiatives, requiring scholars in professional communication to search for sites (e.g., alternative organizations such as the former Ben and Jerry's) and sources amenable to cultural studies emancipatory impulses. Additionally, despite cultural studies call for self-reflexivity, academic colonization of the objects of and participants in research projects remains a challenge. In response, scholars must explore alternatives to, for example, the traditional employment of research results solely for academic advancement or organizational use and the standard form of the academic article as a means of writing about and disseminating research results. With this mandate as well comes the challenge of educating both journal editors and tenure and promotion committees at all institutional levels about the value of these alternate uses of research results and modes of writing and dissemination.

Despite challenges, however, we believe that professional communication will be well served by the increased understanding of the world and attention to the political that a cultural studies orientation offers.

NOTES

1. According to Slack and Whitt (1992), disempowerment occurs when people are "subordinat[ed] in hierarchical relations" and "den[ied] the inherent ability to construct alternative practices, structures, and spaces" (p. 573). Along these

lines, we have discussed disempowerment as the exclusion from participation in constructing representations.

2. This desire of cultural studies researchers to focus on the marginalized and excluded is far more complex and contradictory than, because of space limitations, we have been able to represent here. The perception, for example, of what constitutes a marginalized or excluded individual or practice of course results from the positioning—the values, beliefs, knowledge, and so forth—of the researcher. An individual or practice that appears to be marginalized to one researcher, therefore, may not necessarily appear to be so to another. Further, cultural studies researchers must struggle constantly against the possibility for elitism that accompanies this identification of the marginalized.

REFERENCES

Barton, B.F., & Barton, M.S. (1993). Ideology and the map: Toward a postmodern visual design practice. In N. Blyler & C. Thralls (Eds.), *Professional communication: The social perspective* (pp. 49–78). Newbury Park, CA: Sage Press.

Blundell, V., Shepherd, J., & Taylor, I. (1993). Introduction. In V. Blundell, J. Shepherd, & I. Taylor (Eds.), *Relocating cultural studies: Developments in theory and research* (pp. 1–17). London: Routledge.

Blyler, N.R. (1995). Research as ideology in professional communication. *Technical Communication Quarterly, 4,* 285–313.

Bratlinger, P. (1990). *Crusoe's footprints: Cultural studies in Britain and America.* London and New York: Routledge.

Clark, D.P. (2001). *The rhetoric of boundaries: Living and working along a technical/non-technical split.* Unpublished doctoral dissertation, Iowa State University.

Doheny-Farina, S. (1993). Research as rhetoric: Confronting the methodological and ethical problems of research on writing in nonacademic settings. In Spilka, R. (Ed.), *Writing in the workplace: New research perspectives* (pp. 253–267). Carbondale: Southern Illinois University Press.

Du Gay, P., Hall, S., Janes, L., Mackay, H., & Negus, K. (1997). *Doing cultural studies: The story of the Sony Walkman.* London: Sage.

Fals-Borda, O. (1991a). Remaking knowledge. In O. Fals-Borda & M.A. Rahman (Eds.), *Action and knowledge: Breaking the monopoly with participatory-action research* (pp. 146–164). New York: Apex.

Fals-Borda, O. (1991b). Some basic ingredients. In O. Fals-Borda & M.A. Rahman (Eds.), *Action and knowledge: Breaking the monopoly with participatory-action research* (pp. 3–12). New York: Apex.

Ferguson, M., & Golding, P. (1997). *Cultural studies in question.* Thousand Oaks, CA: Sage.

Flynn, E.A. (1997). Rescuing postmodernism. *College Composition and Communication, 48,* 540–555.

Gaventa, J. (1991). Toward a knowledge democracy: Viewpoints on participatory research in North America. In O. Fals-Borda & M.A. Rahman (Eds.), *Action and knowledge: Breaking the monopoly with participatory-action research* (pp. 121–131). New York: Apex.

Grabill, J. T. (2000). Shaping local HIV/AIDS services policy through activist research: The problem of client involvement. *Technical Communication Quarterly, 9,* 29–50.

Grossberg, L. (1986). On postmodernism and articulation: An interview with Stuart Hall. *Journal of Communication Inquiry, 10* (2), 45–60.

Grossberg, L. (1987). Critical theory and the politics of empirical research. In M. Gurevitch & M.R. Levy (Eds.), *Mass communication review yearbook* (Vol. 6) (pp. 86–106). Newbury Park, CA: Sage.

Grossberg, L. (1992). *We gotta get out of this place: Popular conservatism and postmodern culture.* London: Routledge.

Grossberg, L. (1993). The formations of cultural studies: An American in Birmingham. In V. Blundell, J. Shepherd, & I. Taylor (Eds.), *Relocating cultural studies: Developments in theory and research* (pp. 21–66). London: Routledge.

Grossberg, L. (1995). "Cultural studies: What's in a name? *Taboo, 1,* 1–37.

Grossberg, L., & Slack, J.D. (1985). An introduction to Stuart Hall's essay. *Critical Studies in Mass Communication, 2,* 87–90.

Gubar, S. (1981). "The blank page" and the issues of female creativity. *Critical Inquiry, 8* (2), 243–263.

Hall, S. (1981). Notes on deconstructing the popular. In R. Samuel (Ed.), *People's history and socialist theory* (pp. 227–240). Boston: Routledge and Kegan Paul.

Hall, S. (1992). Cultural studies and its theoretical legacies. In L. Grossberg, C. Nelson, & P. Treichler (Eds.), *Cultural studies* (pp. 277–294). New York: Routledge.

Herndl, C.G. (1993). Teaching discourse and reproducing culture: A critique of research and pedagogy in professional and nonacademic writing. *College Composition and Communication, 44,* 349–364.

Herndl, C.G. (1996). Tactics and the quotidian: Resistance and professional discourse. *Journal of Advanced Composition, 16,* 455–470.

Holter, I.M., & Schwartz-Barcott, D. (1993). Action research; What is it? How has it been used and how can it be used in nursing? *Journal of Advanced Nursing, 19,* 298–304.

Johnson, R. (1986/87). What is cultural studies anyway? *Social Text, 16,* 38–80.

Lidchi, H. (1997). The poetics and the politics of exhibiting other cultures. In S. Hall (Ed.), *Representation: Cultural representations and signifying practices* (pp. 151–208). London: Sage.

Longo, B. (1998). An approach for applying cultural study theory to technical writing research. *Technical Communication Quarterly, 7,* 53–74.

McLaren, P. (1991). Field relations and the discourse of the other: Collaboration in our own ruin. In W.B. Shaffir & R.A. Stebbins (Eds.), *Experiencing fieldwork: An inside view of qualitative research* (pp. 149–163). Newbury Park, CA: Sage.

Mumby, D.K. (1993). Critical organizational communication studies: The next 10 years. *Communication Monographs, 60,* 18–25.

Murdock. G. (1997). Base notes: The conditions of cultural practice. In M. Ferguson & P. Golding (Eds.), *Cultural studies in question* (pp.86–101). Thousand Oaks, CA: Sage.

Nelson, C., Treichler, P.A., & Grossberg, L. (1992). Cultural studies: An introduction. In L. Grossberg, C. Nelson, & P A. Treichler (Eds.), *Cultural studies* (pp. 1–22). London: Routledge.

Slack, J.D., Miller, D.J., & Doak, J. (1993). The technical communicator as author: Meaning, power, authority. *Journal of Business and Technical Communication, 7,* 12–36.

Slack, J.D., & Whitt, L.A. (1992). Ethics and cultural studies. In L. Grossberg, C. Nelson, & P. A. Treichler (Eds.), *Cultural studies* (pp. 571–592). London: Routledge.

Spilka, R. (1993). Influencing workplace practice: A challenge for professional writing specialists in academia. In R. Splika (Ed.), *Writing in the workplace: New research perspectives* (pp. 207–219). Carbondale: Southern Illinois University Press.

Thralls, C., & Blyler, N. (1993). The social perspective and professional communication:
Diversity and directions in research. In N. Blyler & C. Thralls (Eds.), *Professional
communication: The social perspective* (pp. 3–34). Newbury Park: Sage Publications.

Whyte, W.F., Greenwood, D.J., & Lazes, P. (1991). Participatory action research: Through
practice to science in social research. In W.F. Whyte (Ed.), *Participatory action research* (pp. 19–55). Newbury Park, CA: Sage.

Zachry, M. (1999). Management discourse and popular narratives: The myriad plots of total
quality management. In J. Perkins & N. Blyler (Eds.), *Narrative and professional communication* (pp. 107–120). Stamford, CT: Ablex.

CHAPTER 11

Science and Technology Studies as a Research Method: Toward a Practical Ethics for Technical Writing

John Monberg

The title of Carolyn R. Miller's essay in the 1989 volume *Technical Writing Theory and Practice* poses the question, "What's practical about technical writing?" Miller identifies a central paradox in the field of technical writing as an academic discipline. If technical writing simply draws on the best work done in industry as a guide for technical writing, then work models are authoritative, and the intellectual space available to the discipline of technical writing for knowledge production is empty. If technical writing is to be more than merely an instrumental means to a predetermined (by others) end, then what technical writing requires, Miller argues, is a set of criteria that can be used to determine whether a practice is good or bad instead of merely asking whether a practice is common or rare. Historically, technical writing instruction has tended to emphasize clarity, organization, and effective presentation (Herndl, 1996, p.23). When good practice is determined by how well information is presented, many other concerns are foreclosed. The ethical guidelines developed by the Society for Technical Communicators highlight the values of legality, honesty, confidentiality, quality, fairness, and professionalism. These values help to ensure that work performed by technical writers fulfills the terms and obligations of the work contracted with clients and employers. Because these guidelines fail to recognize or emphasize the broader social context within which technical writing is immersed (although the public good, as an abstraction, is present in the guidelines), the guidelines effectively reinforce the separation between professional good practice and broader social responsibilities. Given this emphasis, the single perspective of management threatens to drown out a multiplicity of other potential voices. Dale Sullivan (1990) notes much composition instruction casts the writing process, "in terms of problem solving, stresses objectivity and thereby denies a writer's social responsibilities, distances the interaction between writer and reader, deals with abstract issues, and denies politics" (p. 375). If rhetoric is to be not merely vocational but is instead to be practical in the sense that it is a form of conduct and an ethics, than a wider context of evaluation must be identified.

Given the need for a deep context of evaluation, the field of Science and Technology Studies (STS) can make an important contribution to technical writing. The central intellectual project of STS is a thoroughgoing critique of rationality, pressing this critique to bear upon the social institutions, representations, and practices associated with science and technology. If the practice of technical writing is to be responsive to society, the ways in which STS unravels the tangled relations among science, technology, writing, and society can serve as a locus for developing critical awareness of the rationality implicitly or explicitly built into the technical writing process. STS is less an established discipline than it is an interdisciplinary field drawing on the work of sociologists, philosophers, historians, anthropologists, and others in related disciplines to examine the interrelationships among science, technology, and society. This field is not united by method; indeed, STS utilizes methods from all of its contributing disciplines, including quantitative approaches such as surveys, citation analysis, and scientometrics, as well as qualitative methods such as discourse analysis, ethnography, interpretive methods, grounded social inquiry, and political critique. The STS project parallels and overlaps the project of feminist scholars (Lay, this volume) who open up the process of fact construction to lines of inquiry that can identify the plurality of voices and values that reside behind every "objective" fact.

It is often difficult to connect a particular piece of technical writing to its broader social import. This is especially true for technical writing practitioners. In their fieldwork in corporate offices, Geoffrey Bowker and Susan Leigh Star (1999) notice that although "[I]nformation scientists work every day on the design, delegation, and choice of classification systems and standards, few see them as artifacts embodying moral and aesthetic choices that in turn craft people's identities, aspirations, and dignity" (p. 4). It is often difficult as well for technical writing academicians to trace these connections. Carl Herndl diagnosed a number of problems with the limited, descriptive focus of research in technical writing, among them the lack of analysis of the social, political, and economic sources of power that authorize this production or the cultural work such discourse performs (1993, p. 351). This imbalance is beginning to be redressed in the calls that Bernadette Longo (1998), for example, makes for the kind of research needed to situate technical writing as a cultural form in a larger system of social relations.

Technical writing crafts representations. These representations shape social understandings and practices in a global, information age where such representations coordinate action across distance, cultures, and a wide variety of knowledge specialties. Such representations risk failure, albeit at times in indirect or obscure ways, when the differences inherent in bridging diverse perspectives are rendered invisible because a unitary managerial perspective is unreflectively and automatically adopted. These representations hold a profound influence on how we collectively think about individual agency, expertise, and political power. STS begins from the premise that science and rationality are varieties of tools, representations for getting along in the world. This world is not a mystical, transcendent or Platonic sphere but the messy, complex world of human activities. The strength of STS is that it explores otherwise taken-for-granted understandings of rationality, an exploration that opens rationality to significant social and political questioning. The distance between traditional understandings of technical writing and STS may be difficult to cross because the fundamental presuppositions of these traditions are in so many ways opposites, but this distance itself might be a measure of the payoff that can be earned when the boundaries between technical writing and STS are successfully crossed.

In this chapter I analyze and critique the narrow conception of rationality that stands behind and frames so much of our commonsense understanding of the world, including technical writing. This conception of rationality emphasizes clarity, proper organization, closure, language as a transparent medium, and, most important, efficiency. Drawing on philosophers, feminist theorists, and technology critics who work within the STS rubric, I identify an alternative model of rationality more adequate to the development of a meaningful, sustainable, and egalitarian society. To generate a more vigorous public dialogue, a more robust objectivity, we must be sensitive to submerged social mechanisms and identify those mechanisms through which power relations are made to seem natural and necessary. I then address three case studies that show how the alternative model of objectivity shifts the focus of technical writing activities, highlighting important social and political concerns. Emily Martin's (1994) work on immunology reveals how assumptions made in scientific writing reinforce cultural categories that lead to political disempowerment and injustice, Constance Perin (1998) examines how the narrow conception of rationality and safety built into the design documents and operating procedures that guides organizational practice diminishes nuclear power plant safety, and Susan Leigh Star (1995) calls for a new politics of accountability for the formal representations used to engineer advanced computer chip designs. These case studies can be used as models to develop a rhetoric that is practical in the sense that it is a form of conduct, an ethics, making visible connections that are otherwise made invisible when a thin form of rationality is adopted. They point toward the kind of technical writing research that can extend and deepen lines of STS inquiry to transform long-held views of the writing process.

SCIENCE AND TECHNOLOGY STUDIES AS A CRITIQUE OF "SCIENTIFIC" RATIONALITY

The development of and belief in scientific realism arose in Europe between the seventeenth and nineteenth centuries. This epistemology places emphasis on universal abstract truth and methodological individualism. Scientific realism is aligned with a correspondence theory of truth that seeks to match the representations within the heads of individuals to a pre-existent "natural" reality. Language is, or should be, a neutral medium to convey an accurate picture of the objective world into each individual's mind. This perspective frames much of our commonsense understanding of the world, and it is prevalent in the mind-set of technical writing professionals. This set of assumptions, as Carl Herndl (1996) noted, narrows the ethical horizon, "The objectivity of a technical discourse grounded in an unproblematic relation between experience and writing ... leads to a monologic view of writing that excludes questions of power, values, or interest and considers technical and professional writing as an instrumental discourse designed for stating the facts clearly and efficiently" (p. 23). This set of assumptions is codified in the STC Ethical Guidelines for Technical Communicators. Technical writers must be truthful, accurate, honest, and fulfill negotiated roles in a timely, responsible manner. Such requirements are laudable; however, they do not require technical writers to reflect upon or incorporate the multiple perspectives into the technical documents they produce. Indeed, because of the heavy emphasis this code places on meeting contractual expectations, it serves to reinforce, instead of erode, a distinction between professional practice and social accountability.

This conception of rationality requires a universal standpoint, outside of language, that underwrites the true picture of the world. Much to the dismay of realists, efforts to find a convincing transhistoric definition of rationality that holds for the very wide variety of historical case studies available have proved as yet unsuccessful. W.V.O. Quine (1980) demonstrated that all distinctions rest on a set of more fundamental assumptions, so there exists no noncircular possibility of getting outside a system of meaning. Critiques that press this argument recognize that theory is always underdetermined by evidence and observations are inherently theory-laden, blurring the demarcation between the social factors and the realist "nature" that determine theory acceptance. Because ideas must be represented to be communicated, ideas are always products of and sustained by social practices. Ideas are linked to interests; they are claims on cultural and material resources.

An extensive literature demonstrates the impossibility of finding an "objective" standpoint outside language and the social positions we inhabit. Hess (1997) and Martin (1998) trace the philosophical and methodological developments within the field of STS that reveal how even the most "objective" scientific findings and technological artifacts—quarks, bacteria, missile guidance systems—arise through a process of social negotiation, argument, and construction. Longo (1998) and Herndl (1993) trace a parallel philosophical critique of Western epistemology in terms of technical writing. Scientific entities (and for that matter, all entities) are projections and are tied to the theory, ideology, and culture that project them. Given this more robust definition of social reality, social constructionism is compatible with the forms of realism that hold that a reality exists independently of human perception. Indeed, constructivist approaches direct analytical attention toward the central activities of technical writing: methods of inscription, problem formulation, negotiations of reproducibility and confirmation, and funding decisions; that is, the processes that produce, extend, maintain, and call into question the collective representations through which we understand our world. In contrast, the more epistemologically pure approaches that appeal to the pre-existence of mind-independent real entities direct attention away from the world encountered in social reality to some kind of quasi-Platonic immaterial sphere of pure concepts.

Wanting to "read from the book of nature," epistemological realists fear that letting go of a foundational epistemology leads to chaos, that anything goes. They mistake sensitivity toward social factors as relativistic license for chaos. These fears are misguided. As social beings we are far from unconstrained. What counts as a problem, what counts as an important problem, what counts as a solution, what counts as replication: All these are constituted through social processes. Individuals are not free to accept or reject these processes at a whim, and it is to these processes that STS might lend technical writers guidance. Technical writing is not a writing of the "book of nature." Technical writing is not a simple, neutral lens to a pre-existing physical world; technical writing is a (perhaps *the*) social practice that mediates knowledge and experience. From a close examination of the actual work practices of scientists, Karen Knorr Cetina (1993) identifies the centrality of rhetorical practices in even the purest and hardest of sciences,

> ... "the work" of translating scientific accounts into practice, of solidifying objects which exist only on a laboratory scale or only as representations, of making these objects recur outside the laboratory, of construing contexts in which occurrence and encounterability are possible, of construing a new world together with new scientific entities. (p. 559)

That individuals always do this work does not remove the phenomenon from the social realm. Verification practices are both "internalized" as individuals make judgments about their environments without standards being present, and "externalized," as earlier encounters structure experience, conferring an "independent reality" on what has already been pre-interpreted. As verification practices are social practices, objectivity is a property of social collectives. Demands that scientists, technologists, and other "realists" make for the recognition of the purity and special rationality of science are political moves. They are attempts to erect boundaries and claim special treatment for privileged activities so that they are immune from critical analytical inquiry. Steven Katz has forcefully revealed the consequences of these special claims in a complex society. Demands for a "pure" form of objectivity lead to an impoverished decision-making process. Katz (1992) stresses that "[t]he ethic of expediency is an exclusively logical, systemic, even quantifiable one, can lead to a rationality grounded in no other ethic but its own, and is symptomatic of a highly scientific, technological age" (p. 266). When all values but efficiency are removed, Katz concludes, even the death-dealing machines of the Holocaust can be understood by a society as rational. Our complex society requires a less pure, more balanced rationality.

CRAFTING A RATIONALITY THAT WORKS

Rationality must not be reduced to efficiency. If our sense of rationality is to incorporate the full range of values we care about, it cannot be abstract, timeless, and universal. Rational methods might be defined as the best contemporary and socially available tools for achieving socially given goals. Rationality would then describe a set of socially embedded practices for conducting arguments, a set of culturally specific norms for creating and contesting the credibility of knowledge claims. In an earlier era, John Dewey (1927) recognized that objects are the outcomes of community experience, constituted by interventions—that tests are never independent from the underlying intentions that prompted attention to the particularity of experience. In our age, an era of technoscience with a rapid and easy mutual transformation between scientific knowledge and power, attention must be directed to the work that goes into "making the world," as well as the technologies and tools that enframe our world, giving rise to the novel wired cultural representations of our media-saturated social sensorium. In his critique of the rationality of techno-society, German philosopher and social theorist Jürgen Habermas (1984) distinguishes between administrative and corporate "system imperatives" that are strictly oriented toward accomplishing a single end via the most efficient means possible and the "lifeworld" which provides individuals in a society with their sense of meaning, understanding and purpose. Habermas keeps the relationship between "system imperatives" and "lifeworld" at the core of his theoretical framework, preventing an easy slippage into the kind of functionalism that prevents the scrutiny of ends, when the efficient organization of means is transformed into an end in itself. Habermas argues that the Gulags, gas chambers and mind-numbing assembly lines associated with modernity, are not indictments of rationality per se, but indict reason as developed under and directed toward meeting the demands of a capitalist social order.

The ability to test positions, the capacity for criticism, and reflexivity can be built into the social structures that institutionalize inquiry. To further rationality and objectivity, we need not more rigorous formal epistemological methods, but an open, decentralized, participative social order where the cultural and material resources to support inquiry are broadly distributed (Restivo, 1989). Habermas (1984) stresses that the notion of ideal universal agreement must be understood in relation to an actual community of scientists—not as an abstraction. The discovery of causal laws occurs only in the course of instrumental interventions in nature. The scientific method transforms feedback-monitored behavior into a cumulative learning process by isolating causal chains under controlled conditions. Nature is thus a product of human measuring activity directed by preinterpreted scientific categories. Pragmatic interests shape our self-understanding, not the correspondence of interpretation to a brute, independently existing reality. Pragmatic interests are always embedded within the context of intersubjective agreement; communicative action underscores the contextuality of knowledge and the role of human choice. In this way, Habermas develops exactly the kinds of independent evaluative criteria that Carolyn

Miller (1989) calls for, so that technical writing as a discipline could determine whether a practice is good or bad instead of merely asking whether a practice is common or rare.

A fuller conception of objectivity presumes a real dialogue, a dialogue of challenge and justification in which facts and values are no longer conceptually severed. Following John Dewey (1927) and George Herbert Mead (1934), Habermas (1984) finds that the linkage between dialogic, communicative rationality and the institutionalization of democratic forms of political life requires an understanding of the dynamics of practical sociality. The move toward an open, egalitarian dialogue requires, among other things, the creation of subculturally protected communication groups that further the search for individual and collective identity. Nancy Fraser (1989) extends this line of reasoning, arguing for the need to recognize the range of vocabularies, idioms, gestures, and rhetorical devices—the sociocultural means of interpretation and communication—available to diverse groups for pressing claims. A more radical critique is developed in the standpoint feminist epistemology associated with Dorothy Smith, Nancy Hartsock, and Hilary Rose. Sandra Harding (1991) brings this project to bear on epistemological questions within the science studies field. Although Harding's "strong objectivity" holds that truth is historically relativized, she does not reject the ideals of objectivity, but does remain suspicious of calls for "neutrality" that serve to "depoliticize" science in ways that silence critical voices and legitimate expressions of male supremacy, class exploitation, racism, and imperialism. Critical analytic categories in this frame of reference include commodification, appropriation, exploitation, and oppression. The ideals of fairness, honesty, and detachment are not separated from the analyst as an asocial knower, but mark the ability of the theorist to maintain a critical distance from the assumptions that shape his or her own spontaneous perceptions and convictions.

Harding (1991) holds that knowledge is socially situated and convictions belong to communities. This recognition requires the institutionalization of reflexivity. Social roles must be crafted to recognize the contribution that those in determinate, objective locations of marginalization "outside" the dominant power structure can contribute to an enlarged perspective. The first step is listening to, and taking seriously, these perspectives, not a chimerical search for the irrefutable grounds of knowledge. Difference, incommensurability, and communication failure must not be perceived as silence; invisibility must not be taken to mean acceptance and agreement. Differences need to be highlighted, not submerged.

Standpoint perspectives are subject to difficulties in identifying marginalized positions, as tensions are felt between identities shaped by class, gender, and ethnicity. Donna Haraway (1990) recognizes no boundary between the inside and outside of science; sciences are woven of social relations throughout their tissues. To speak of science is always at the same time to speak of representation, intervention, power, and politics. Haraway opposes a standpoint epistemology that privileges the worldviews and experience of individuals able to maintain coherent identities, but like the standpoint perspective, her position depends on development of oppositional consciousness and is intensely political. Haraway stresses that we cannot remain nostalgic for a "pure nature," as the essentialist dualisms of male/female, nature/culture, human/machine, physical/nonphysical, public sphere/private sphere, and difference/unity unravel. These dualisms erode in the face of the postmodern impulses of technoscience that reconstruct the world into a control problem for cybernetic information technologies and deterministic genetic engineering practices and techniques. Sociobiological narratives represent the body as a private satisfaction and utility-maximizing machine, opening paths for the instrumental moves of "visualization" and "intervention," again raising the specter of determinism.

The fields/disciplines/movements of science and technology studies and feminism share important orientations. Both have roots in the critical social movements of the 1960s, both make visible asymmetries in power relationships that have been taken as natural and unproblematic, and both bridge political activism in the academy, the corridors of power, and the mainstreams of society. These efforts demand humility in theory production, including our own, so that positions are not reified, ahistorical, and permanent but understood to be situated, nuanced, and contingent.

APPLYING ALTERNATIVE MODELS OF RATIONALITY IN TECHNICAL WRITING RESEARCH

Technical writing is often produced in organizational contexts that primarily value efficiency, closure, and a detached, third-person form of objectivity. These priorities almost necessitate adopting the narrow kind of rationality STS critiques, a rationality that tends to highlight the interests of powerful groups and tends to make invisible the interests of less powerful groups. What would it mean, however, for technical writers to adopt a more reflexive, democratic model of rationality? How can the insights developed in Sandra Harding's (1991) model of strong objectivity inform technical writing research? Three case studies answer these questions in slightly different ways, shedding light on the relationship among technical writing, technical knowledge, and social and political contexts. The technical writing process mediates the movement of ideas through social contexts in a diverse array of documents, including medical textbooks, scientific journals, clinical handbooks, public service announcements, chemical and radiological analysis forms, standard operating procedures, and formal systems of classification.

A broader conception of objectivity can open this mediation. The technical writing process can be crafted to include values beyond efficiency and incorporate the diversity of voices needed to test key assumptions. Each of the case studies explores the values incorporated in the technical writing and documents a distinctive domain of technical expertise. Emily Martin (1994) identifies connections between the science of immunology and widespread social values, Constance Perin (1998) examines the effect that organizational culture has on nuclear power plant safety, and Susan Leigh Star (1995) explores the politics of the process of formalization, the creation of technical representations used for the construction of advanced computer chips.

Emily Martin (1994) examines a wide range of technical writing to trace connections across representations of the body, science's understanding of the immune system, and larger cultural and social formations. In a present termed "postmodern" or "late capitalist," flexible accumulation has become the key attribute of success, whether one is considering a corporation, worker, or city. In this era, the body is conceived of as a self-regulating system where constant change transforms the experience of space and time, self and other. With the social emphasis on a narrow conception of efficiency, bodies that fail to adapt rapidly enough are labeled as marginal, redundant, inefficient, or even threatening. The worst forms of social injustice can be cloaked in neutral categories developed by an objective medical science.

How can the connections between social values and scientific writing be identified? As the interpenetration of science and society intensifies, the sites at which knowledge production takes place multiply. As a cultural anthropologist, Emily Martin is well situated to trace the paths and implications of the metaphors that travel across social experience. Martin and her team of researchers conducted extended informal interviews with more than two hundred people from diverse socioeconomic backgrounds to understand how the concept of health had changed. Martin participated in training courses for workers and managers in corporations, training courses that teach new ways of organizing the workforce and new ways of interacting. She also spent a year of fieldwork in an immunology research laboratory, attending graduate classes, departmental seminars and planning sessions, carrying out experimental procedures, reviewing textbooks, scientific journals, and clinical handbooks. Martin volunteered in an AIDS service organization and was active in the political protests of a local chapter of ACT UP. This diverse set of research activities allows Martin to deliberately cross back and forth across the borders between the institutions in which scientists produce knowledge, for instance, an immunology research laboratory, and the wider society (neighborhoods, places of work) where the direct and indirect consequences of immunological knowledge are expressed.

In context after context, Martin has identified a shift in the way we, broadly speaking, understand ourselves, broadly speaking. In the social worlds of science, health care, neighborhoods, and corporations, a new emphasis on flexibility and competition is apparent. The key metaphors used in popular accounts of immunology depict the body as "a regulatory communications network." Where boundaries within the body are fluid and control is dispersed, the boundary between the body (self) and the external world (nonself) is rigid and absolute. Added to the conception of a clear boundary between self and nonself is a conception of the nonself as foreign and hostile. As a measure of the extent of this threat, the body is depicted in contemporary popular publications as the scene of total war between ruthless invaders and determined defenders. Uncritically adopting metaphors that describe the body as flexible and violently competitive also risks adopting a related set of political values. These metaphors make violent destruction seem ordinary and part of the necessity of daily life. They also project a bodily hierarchy onto society as a whole, so that social hierarchies are seen as natural, legitimate, even functional. If we live in an age that requires competitive flexibility, individuals whose immune systems lack competitiveness can be discarded by society; they are expected to, even deserve to, fail. Because medical science frames these failings "objectively," a hidden, particularly dangerous form of inequality becomes entrenched in society.

The dominant metaphors used by immunologists to make sense of the body are not the only or even the best way to make sense of how the immune system functions. When a narrow, "pure" form of scientific rationality is used to understand the world, other possibilities are lost. The social and political values implicit in the metaphors scientists use to describe the world come to be understood as natural and inevitable, instead of malleable and open to challenge. Far from maximizing the diversity of voices that participate in the social dialogue, new conceptions of immunology threaten to reinforce and intensify, as fixed and natural, already existing social inequalities. Anthropology's technique of comparative research helps highlight alternative conceptualizations, providing the intellectual resources necessary to imagine a more egalitarian, democratic social order.

From Emily Martin's (1994) study of immunology, it is clear that narrow forms of rationality have social and political ramifications. A too narrow form of rationality risks dreadful safety and environmental consequences as well. Rhetoric can slide into a stance of adopting the ethic of efficiency for ethics as a whole; this is particularly troubling in regard to dangerous technologies. Steven Katz warns, "Rhetoric is increasingly called upon and used to make or justify decisions based on technological expediency—to create the necessary technological *ethos* for accepting actions or events, in the management of risky technologies such as hazardous waste disposal facilities or nuclear power plants" (1992, p. 271). A technical writing context that stresses efficiency, closure, and clarity misses the chance to learn from experience. Constance Perin (1998) explored the negative and possibly disastrous consequences of adopting a narrow form of rationality in the nuclear energy industry. A cultural anthropologist specializing in work and organizations, Perin spent time at thirteen nuclear power plants in the United States, Europe, and Latin America. This experience lead Perin to understand nuclear power plants not as fixed systems, but as open, ongoing, evolving enterprises. She found social, cultural, and technical issues intertwined at every level of the nuclear power generation enterprise. The technical documents that defined and codified nuclear power plants were created in a way that constructed a boundary protecting pure, uncontaminated technical knowledge. Because of the ways in which technical documents and procedures explicitly and implicitly separated social, cultural, and technical issues, these connections remained invisible, seemingly nonexistent, and impossible to be incorporated into understandings that could lead to more robust levels of safety.

The risk assessment process, constituted by an array of design documents, operating procedures, maintenance records, and accident reports, highlights the complexity of the technical writing context in a large, sophisticated, highly regulated, capital intensive context. Conventional understandings of nuclear power plants are premised on assumptions of predictability and control; nuclear power plants are closed systems that function according to the design documents. However, the need to refuel, test safety equipment, and continuously upgrade plant design in the social and cultural context of markets, regulations, and work systems means that nuclear reactor systems are in a state of near constant change. Power plants are not closed systems flawlessly performing according to design specifications. But the assumption that these plants are closed systems is meticulously crafted into the 4,303 separate written procedures covering the administration, operations, and maintenance, radiation protection, and chemical and radiological analyses, as well as surveillance and other testing activities of the organization (Perin, p.105).

Because of the assumption that these technologies will function according to plan, much potentially meaningful information is invisible, unnoticed, ignored, or misinterpreted. Artifacts are expected to perform as precisely as the axioms and algorithms used to design them; technologists in the nuclear power industry are more oriented toward fixing than understanding. This attitude is institutionalized and deeply embedded in organizational culture. There is a notable lack of documentation and analysis of the context and conditions of errors.

Perin discovered that nuclear power plant corporations maintained a clear distinction between issues of technical design and organizational dynamics. STS rationality theorists, extending an intellectual line connecting Dewey, Habermas, Fraser, Harding, and Haraway, explain how rationality is enhanced with a diversity of voices, and that these voices require institutional support. Unfortunately, nuclear power plant managers sharply separate technical issues from organizational issues. There are, therefore, no forums in which and no language through which organizational dynamics can be discussed together with technical matters. Indeed, these organizations diminish the diversity needed for a robust rationality by institutionally marginalizing those most in position to understanding the operating characteristics of the plant. Social and cultural practices imported into high-hazard environments from daily lifeworlds are often implicated in accidents and incidents, but the day-to-day knowledge of operations personnel and safety specialists is dismissed by "an epistemological caste system that does not value knowledge that is specific, homegrown, and based on experience" (1998, p. 115).

What could lead to a richer form of rationality? Perin argues that nuclear power plant organizations ought to think like scientists. To scientists, surprises and disappointments produce valuable new knowledge about the merits of a hypothesis. Surprises and disappointments should not be silenced. For nuclear power plants to become more rational, organizational norms should reward clear statements of problems that do not already have solutions attached to them. Curiosity, doubt, and interpretation would have to become as highly valued as certainty; discovering undesirable consequences of technical logics and of the gray area of organizational policies and social arrangements would have to become good news. Reading plant dynamics as "experiments" suggests an alternative epistemology combining science's values of doubt, uncertainty, discovery, and documentation with engineering's values of efficiency, optimization, and problem solving. New epistemological standpoints could be institutionalized, "redefining plant-based risk handlers as ethologists, geologists, and anthropologists of an ecology of visible and invisible hazards" (1998, p. 98).

The connections between a nuclear power plant and society are as clear as the cement cooling towers that rise above and dominate a city's landscape. But just how far and how deep do the connections between technical writing and society go? Susan Leigh Star (1995) elaborates a version of this question when she asks, "How are formal (mathematical, computational, abstract) representations defining the space of our world? What are the moral consequences of using formal representations?" (p. 89). Star is a qualitative sociologist working in the tradition of grounded theory developed by Barney Glaser and Anselm Strauss. Grounded theorists generate their social theory concepts out of the specific social contexts they study. The particular context Star explores is the community of VLSI CAD engineers who design computer chips; her understanding of this context developed from her teaching in a computer science department and her work with computer scientists.

Like Perin, Star also found the individuals in the community she studied held a sharp distinction between technical factors and social factors. In the VLSI CAD community, technical factors are understood to be separate from, and more important than, social factors. "The values of quantification are deeply embedded in that community. Numbers, algorithms, abstractions are valued over qualities, emotions, and deep descriptions. These values are linked with precision, portability and speed" (1995, p. 89). As in the contexts of immunology and nuclear power, this separation and denigration of the "social" in the context of computer chip design creates deep-seated problems. Social and technical contexts are inseparable in all human activities, and when they are analyzed separately, crucial aspects of these activities become invisible. This remains true even in the abstract technical field of computer chip design. A deep form of rationality requires a dialogue among a diverse range of actors. When organizations institutionalize the separation of social and technical domains, acquiring systematic knowledge of organizational behavior becomes nearly impossible. Furthermore, the very people who have expertise in studying organizations are often alienated from working within engineering culture, and find it impossible to obtain the necessary resources to do research.

The creation of abstract, formal knowledge is always political. Technical writing always includes abstraction from a particular situation and simplification, reducing complexity of real-life situations to make them tractable. Creating formal representations requires the following kinds of work: abstracting, quantifying, making hierarchies, classifying and standardizing, and simplifying. Such choices revolve around what to keep in as important and what to keep out as unimportant. These choices pose special challenges for technical writing. These political choices have an increasingly weighty significance, as the formalisms associated with information technologies extend ever deeper into the fabric of everyday life; at the same time, the neutrality and objectivity associated with these formalisms make the political choices themselves invisible.

Political choices are not made by specific individuals; choices are produced by a complex network of people and things. If moral and ethical decisions are embedded in computer systems, a new process of accountability is needed. Star calls for a reformulation of the legal concept of due process. Instead of valuing clarity and simplicity, it is important for technical writers to document the history of the trade-offs that lay behind decisions and interpretations, for these decisions may migrate across great organizational and social distances over time.

> The simultaneous existence of multiple viewpoints and the need for solutions that are coherent across divergent viewpoints are driving considerations here. The term (due process) is borrowed from a legal phrase that refers to collecting evidence and following fair trial procedures. The due process problem in either a computer or human organization is this: in combining evidence from different viewpoints, how do you decide that sufficient, reliable, and fair amounts of evidence have been collected? Who, or what, does the reconciling, and according to what set of rules? (1995, p. 117)

In the present era, technical infrastructures penetrate more and more deeply into the background of everyday life. Work is done so that the categories these infrastructures rely upon are naturalized and invisible. It is politically and ethically crucial to recognize the vital roles infrastructures play in the built moral environment. Seemingly purely technical issues like how to name things and how to store data in fact constitute much human interaction and much of what we come to know as natural.

RESEARCH FOR A PRACTICAL TECHNICAL WRITING

Industry turns to technical writing for guidance in grammar, logic, organization, and clarity. But if technical writing is to be not merely an instrumental tool designed to implement predetermined ends, technical writing requires a practical rhetoric; a code of conduct, a locus for questioning, and accountability to the human community as a whole affected by its practice. Each of the three case studies illustrates the trade-offs inherent in the technical writing process. Technical writing always involves a balance between the universal and the local, a series of trade-offs among, on the one hand, the universal factors of generality, reliability, portability, and integration, and on the other hand, the particularistic factors of customization, uniqueness, and goodness of fit with local work arrangements. The case studies demonstrate how problems arise when the universal side of the equation is taken for the whole and local conditions are ignored.

The attitudes and methods associated with STS help to redress this balance and make otherwise invisible implications, visible. The case studies show both the inherent interconnection between technical and social factors, as well as the risks of ignoring these interconnections. Because technical writing mediates relationships at the heart of the complex, global social order, technical writing scholars and researchers are positioned to make significant social and intellectual contributions. This position is especially important because the technical writing process articulates expert knowledge across the full range of laboratory, corporate, institutional, and media contexts; providing the interconnections between technical and social factors is a hallmark of technical writing. An explicit reconceptualization of rationality, with an emphasis on dialogue and open-ended inquiry, can counteract this trend, primarily by ensuring that a diverse set of standpoints can contribute to the technical writing process. Striking the right balance will lead to a safer, more intelligent, more democratic social order.

Steve Katz asks whether "deliberation, phronesis, or even democracy itself, is possible in a technological society, especially in regard to risk technologies?" (1993, p. 61). Geoffrey Bowker and Susan Leigh Star argue that ethnographic and historical research is needed to develop an analytic vocabulary so that we can recognize, learn, and plan how invisible organizational structures influence the design of information technology and classificatory systems (1999, p. 323). STS research methods promise to open new lines of inquiry. Close, detailed, and specific analyses of the technical writing process are required if these lines of inquiry are to be more than a promising potential. In order to explore the relations between specific discourses and structural properties, sources of power and authority in discourse, an expanded body of research in professional and technical discourse will be essential.

REFERENCES

Bowker, G, & Star, S.L. (1999). *Sorting things out: Classification and its consequences*. Cambridge, MA: MIT Press.

Dewey, J. (1927). *The public and its problems*. New York: Henry Holt and Co.

Fraser, N. (1989). *Unruly practices: Power, discourse, and gender in contemporary social theory*. Minneapolis: University of Minnesota Press.

Habermas, J. (1984). *The theory of communicative action* (Vol. 1), *Reason and the rationalization of society* (T. McCarthy, Trans.). Boston, MA: Beacon.

Haraway, D. (1990). A Manifesto for cyborgs: Science technology and socialist feminism in the 1980s. In L.J. Nicholson (Ed.), *Feminism/postmodernism*. New York: Routledge.

Harding, S. (1991). *Whose science? Whose knowledge? Thinking from women's lives*. Ithaca: Cornell University Press.

Herndl, C. (1993). Teaching discourse and reproducing culture: A critique of research and pedagogy in professional and non-academic writing. *College Composition and Communication, 44, 3*, 349–363.

Herndl, C. (1996). The transformation of critical ethnography into pedagogy, or the vicissitudes of traveling theory. In A.H. Duin and C.J. Hansen (Eds.), *Nonacademic writing: Social theory and technology*. Mahwah, NJ: Lawrence Erlbaum Associates.

Hess, D. (1997). *Science studies: An advanced introduction*. New York: New York University Press.

Katz, S. (1992). The ethic of expediency: Classical rhetoric, technology, and the Holocaust. *College English, 54, 3*, 255–275.

Katz, S. (1993). Aristotle's rhetoric, Hitler's program, and the ideological program of praxis, power, and professional discourse. *Journal of Business and Technical Communication, 7, 1*, 37–62.

Knorr Cetina, K. (1993). Strong constructivism from a sociologist's point of view: A personal addendum to Sismondo's paper. *Social Studies of Science, 23*, 556–562.

Longo, B. (1998). An approach for applying cultural study theory to technical writing research. *Technical Communication Quarterly, 7*, 53–73.

Martin, E. (1994). *Flexible bodies: Tracking immunity in American culture from the days of polio to the age of AIDS*. Boston, MA: Beacon Press.

Martin, E. (1998). Anthropology and the cultural study of science. *Science, Technology and Human Values, 23, 1*, 24–44.

Mead, G.H. (1934). *Mind, self, and society*. Chicago: University of Chicago Press.

Miller, C.R. (1989). What's practical about technical writing? In B.E. Fearing and W. Keats Sparrow (Eds.), *Technical writing*. New York: Modern Language Association of America.

Perin, C. (1998, Winter). Operating as experimenting: Synthesizing engineering and scientific values in nuclear power production. *Science, Technology and Human Values, 23, 1*, 98–128.

Quine, W.V.O. (1980). Two dogmas of empiricism. In H. Morick (Ed.), *Challenges to empiricism*. Indianapolis, IN: Hackett Publishing.

Restivo, S. (1989). In the clutches of Daedalus: Science, society, and progress. In S.L. Goldman (Ed.), *Science, technology and social progress*. Bethlehem, PA: Lehigh University Press.

Star, S.L. (1995). The politics of formal representations: Wizards, gurus, and organizational complexity. In S.L. Star (Ed.), *Ecologies of knowledge: Work and politics in science and technology*. Albany, NY: State University of New York Press.

Sullivan, D. (1990). Political-ethical implications of defining technical communication as a practice. *Journal of Advanced Composition, 10, 2*, 375–386.

CHAPTER 12

Technical Communication Research in Cyberspace

Laura J. Gurak and Christine M. Silker

Over the past few years, researchers in technical communication have begun to realize that the interactions taking place via computer-mediated communication present a rich spectrum of data for research. Electronic discussion lists and Usenet newsgroups, for example, are often focused around specific technical topics and thus provide interesting evidence about transmitting technical material to a wide range of audiences. Electronic mail is also a source of relevant data because the use of electronic mail, it has been argued, helps "flatten" corporate and other communication hierarchies (Sproull & Kiesler, 1991) and therefore offers the possibility of more input from employees at all levels. Similarly, real-time (synchronous) discussions offer an opportunity to study collaboration, gender issues, and the notions of speaker/audience within a context that often spans corporate, professional, and international boundaries. In one recent study, technical communicators expressed a strong interest in using the wealth of information available via the Internet to learn more about users, tasks, technologies, and accessible information structures (Silker & Gurak, 1996).

Yet at present, technical communication researchers have few guidelines to follow when their primary data consist of electronic exchanges on computer-mediated communication systems (such as the Internet). Traditional research questions such as the selection of an appropriate method, the need to obtain permission from subjects, and issues of private versus public information become blurred in the cyberspace research site. What at first appear to be "texts," for example, may in fact be closer to conversations, and what at first seem like public postings may turn out to be posted to quasi-private sites. In addition, the names of authors on Internet postings are often pseudonyms or "handles," not real names, so obtaining accurate permissions or demographic data is often impossible.

Researchers in other related fields have also begun to notice that discourse from the Internet raises new and novel questions about traditional research methods. In her latest book, a case study of communication over MUDs and MOOs (real-time virtual communication spaces), psychologist Sherry Turkle (1995) adds what she calls "a note on method"; this appendix describes her experiences of conducting ethnography in cyberspace and her reasoning for disguising the identities of the people whose Internet chats she observed. Similarly, Laura Gurak (1997a) describes her methodological decisions in choosing to use entire e-mail messages but make names anonymous and remove actual e-mail addresses. Christina Allen, in a special issue of the journal *The Information Society* devoted solely to "the ethics of fair practices for collecting social science data in cyberspace," also discusses the challenges of participant observation and ethnography conducted via the Internet, noting that "[i]n cyberspace, the sites of inquiry, reporting, and critical response have collapsed into one medium" (1996, p. 182). Other articles in this special issue debate the ethical and methodological issues of researching in cyberspace, asking if and how traditional human subjects boards should be involved in the monitoring and regulation of cyberspace research (King, 1996) and whether distinctions based on public or private newsgroups are of use in determining when permissions must be obtained (Herring, 1996b; Waskul & Douglass, 1996).

In this chapter, we attempt to sort out some of these methodological issues as appropriate for technical communication research and raise some initial exploratory questions about how to conduct research in cyberspace. As Internet technologies change, these issues will change; some practices will begin to become formalized, and other practices will not be relevant when technologies evolve or disappear. Given these inherently dynamic conditions, researchers will need to continue evaluating their decisions against currently accepted research standards and ongoing technological changes.

The scope in this chapter is to discuss three now-standard technical communication research methods (ethnographic research, rhetorical analysis, and surveys), noting first how these approaches have traditionally been used in technical communication research and then exploring certain nuances and complexities raised when these approaches are used in cyberspace. In addition, we comment on research of Web sites. We then provide an example of a research project that used one of these approaches. Although our categories are by no means comprehensive, we nonetheless hope this comparative approach will have at least two benefits: it will introduce new researchers to some of the tools of the discipline, and it will challenge all of us to rethink our approaches to cyberspace research. In addition, our choice of these methods allows us to address two points of view: studying discourse that takes place on the Internet (via ethnographies and rhetorical analyses) and using cyberspace as a site for conducting research (via surveys). We strongly believe that research on and via the Internet offers new and exciting possibilities for the profession, and we should begin to explore how traditional approaches can be adapted and modified to function in cyberspace.

ETHNOGRAPHIES AND FIELD STUDIES

The use of ethnographic and field study research in technical communication has its roots in the discipline of anthropology. These methods have been adapted by many other disciplines, including composition studies (Doheny-Farina & Odell, 1984) and software design (Simonsen & Kensing, 1997); ethnography is currently an accepted method in the technical communication researcher's tool kit (see, e.g., Spilka, 1989, and Katz, in this volume). Ethnography and field study involve the use of participant observation. In regard to the other two methods we have chosen to discuss, ethnography and field study are more closely aligned with rhetorical analysis than with survey research, in that for the most part, ethnographers and field researchers work in the qualitative realm and recognize that their findings, although useful in a somewhat broad manner, are based on their particular subjective interpretation; or, put another way, "[q]ualitative research is unabashedly interpretive, but it is not idiosyncratic" (Anderson, 1987, p. 253). These researchers are aware that their personal backgrounds, training, and viewpoints act as what Burke (1966) called a "terministic screen" through which their observations are colored and shaped. But this perspective is not seen as problematic; rather, it is considered a part of the process. Each ethnography or field study is thus unique, yet as new researchers study similar cases and sites, it is hoped that some broadly applicable understandings of a given culture or phenomenon may be reached. As with rhetorical analysis, these conclusions are subject to change, yet they work somewhat empirically to capture an idea of how a culture, be it corporate or ethnic, functioned at a particular point in time.

Ethnography and Field Research IRL

Internet users often invoke the acronym "IRL" (in real life) to describe life outside the virtual forum of cyberspace. When ethnographers and field researchers perform their studies IRL, they do so in defined physical locations. Researchers interested in corporate communication, for example, may spend time at a software company's corporate headquarters or research and development labs, listening, observing, and participating in the culture of that organization. Researchers often must physically move to a new city or country in order to be part of this organizational culture. They must get dressed each day and essentially go to work at this site. Employees at the site are obviously aware of a researcher's presence, as they would see the researcher observing at meetings, taking notes, and making tape recordings.

Ethnography and Field Research in the Cyberfield

These forms of research take on some new shapes when performed in virtual space. The most obvious difference between ethnography/field research IRL and the same research conducted virtually is the fundamentally different sense of place. Take, for example, a real time (synchronous) chat situation. Ethnographers might be interested in studying the culture of an online community of software engineers who "meet" twice a week in an online chat session. Researchers still must "go" to this location, but they can do so from the comfort of home, connected via modems, and dressed however they wish. They can also choose to make themselves invisible by "lurking" or observing the chat without announcing their presence. This choice is made possible solely by the technology; ethnographers IRL cannot suddenly become invisible.

For many ethnographers and field researchers, the choice to lurk is inviting, because it offers the opportunity to be the proverbial "fly on the wall." (Ethnographers talk about "the observer affect" and argue as to how much the researcher's presence impacts the actions and behaviors of those being observed.) But is it ethical not to announce one's presence, or, to use another feature of online technology, to take the notion of participant observation one step further by pretending to be a member of the group? "The Strange Case of the Electronic Lover" (Van Gelder, 1990) is a perfect example of the new and troubling possibilities for ethnography and field research in cyberspace. In this case, now famous among Internet researchers, a male psychologist joined an online chat with the intent of observing, pretending to be a disabled woman named Joan. Months later, he revealed himself to be both a man and a researcher, much to the alarm and dismay of the other listed participants.

Ethnographers and field researchers usually announce and explain their presence, often requesting signatures on a consent form before proceeding with their observation (House, 1990). In fact, in the field of psychology, informed consent is written into the guidelines of the governing professional organization (the American Psychological Association) "unless the research involves simply naturalistic observations in public places" (King, 1996, p. 125). But is online discourse public or private? As Reid (1996) and others have noted, there is still little agreement as to whether consent is required for such discourse. In addition, as mentioned previously, the "lurking" factor presents a new conundrum: In real life, observers are evident by their physical presence in the room. Participants in the meeting or activity may notice a person who is not a member of the group and question his or her presence. If they discover that this newcomer is a researcher, they may decide that they do not wish to be studied. But in cyberspace, participants may never even know that they are being watched and logged. This panoptic effect puts the researcher into a unique position and forces the researcher to ask some serious ethical questions.

In this regard, Human Subjects Review Boards (also called Institutional Review Boards or "IRBs") may not be of any assistance. Although these boards exist ostensibly to protect the interest of research subjects, "[i]t would be rare ... to find an IRB board currently aware enough of the nuances of cyberspace interpersonal dynamics to foresee the need to protect the perception of privacy with which some participants post to public forums" (King, 1996, p. 121). Also, it would no doubt be difficult to find an IRB board that understands the dynamic and anonymous nature of online discourse. Many researchers, for example, have concluded that it is impossible to obtain consent forms in synchronous chat-type sessions: because users often don't use their real names and because they can log in and out of a chat session with incredible speed, researchers will have a difficult time tracking down any given user and then proving that the form was actually signed by the person who originated a particular piece of electronic discourse. (See Kastman Breuch, et al. in this volume for more on Human Subjects Review Boards.)

The amount of ethnographic and field research that can be performed in cyberspace is truly endless. Turkle (1995), a psychologist, has used ethnographic research to study the concept of identity as it is exhibited

and modified via a MOO (a synchronous "chat" technology that is structured around virtual rooms, buildings, and character names). Indeed, her
study richly describes how communication takes place via this technology, but she is careful in the appendix of her book to describe the novel
methodological choices that she faced. She chose, for example, to use
pseudonyms in place of the actual character names she observed on the
MOO. This choice reflects the traditional nature of ethnographic and field
research, where individual names are usually changed before publishing
research results. Yet others who perform similar cyber-ethnographies feel
an obligation to announce their presence, check with the moderator, and
even attempt to seek permission from many of the participants (Reid, 1996).
As more and more researchers become aware of the overall lack of privacy
on the Internet, one might argue that at some point using pseudonyms is
not necessary because individuals should not expect any sort of privacy in
a space where their names and comments can easily be rebroadcast across
the entire Internet. On the other hand, the very lack of privacy that is
inherent in most Internet communication may be reason enough to seek
permission to use Internet logs and texts. As with the next two items we
discuss (rhetorical analysis and survey research), ethnography and field
study methods in cyberspace "pose complex ethical issues that may lack
exact analogs in other types of inquiry" (Thomas, 1996, p. 108). These
methods will need to be thought through and modified to adapt to the
features of online communication technologies.

RHETORICAL ANALYSIS

Rhetorical analysis, also called rhetorical criticism, normally involves
the critique of speeches or texts using elements from rhetorical theory. A
very simple example from an Aristotelian perspective might be applying
the rhetorical appeal of *ethos*, or credibility, to the transcript of a presidential address to determine how the president made his arguments by
drawing on his credibility as the holder of the highest office in the land.
This sort of analysis has been a central part of research in technical communication, in part because the discipline of technical communication
arose to a certain extent out of English departments (mostly in engineering and land grant institutions) and therefore out of people trained in language analysis (Connors, 1982). These scholars began applying the same
rhetorical concepts once reserved for public discourse to genres such as
software manuals, training materials, computer interfaces, professional discourse (memos, proposals, feasibility reports), and so on.

Although occasionally practiced with a leaning toward social science, rhetorical analysis is purposefully and inherently a subjective mode of research, more closely aligned with literary criticism than with social science in this regard. This approach does not mean that rhetorical analysis is not empirical, for it is. As S. Michael Halloran (1984) argues, rhetorical analysis has always been highly empirical in that it functions by researching individual cases and instances to build theory. But that theory is not considered fixed and eternal; it is what Trevor Melia (1984) called "a relative fix" like the pole star, he says, fixed in a position for a time but eventually shifting as time moves on. The purpose of rhetorical analysis, then, is to "document social trends" and "provide general understandings via the case method" (Hart, 1990, pp. 33–34).

The Traditional Approach

One need only casually peruse the technical communication journals to find numerous examples of the use of rhetorical analysis as a research method in the discipline. Rhetoric has played a major role in the development of technical and professional communication theory and practice, from theoretical discussions of rhetoric and technical writing (Miller, 1989) to heuristics for a "rhetoric of technical copywriting" (Henson, 1994). Traditionally, elements of rhetorical theory are used as tools to analyze scientific, technical, and professional documents. For example, a rhetorical approach to technical documentation might involve applying the Aristotelian common and special topics to technical reports (Miller & Selzer, 1985).

Paper documents are often clear as to type and accessibility. For example, paper documents usually fall into recognizable genres: feasibility study, proposal, report, and so on. With regard to accessibility, if documents are from a public source, such as the U.S. Government Printing Office, it is usually not necessary to obtain permission to use the material (this may not be the case with documents from other countries, however). Even when material is from a private source, such as a corporation, there is an identifiable agent who can be asked for permission (if permission is required—we consider fair use later in this discussion). Traditional documents also tend to have a traceable path of development and authorship. Finally, researchers usually do not need any special technical skills (such as Internet search skills) in order to read or obtain these documents, though researchers often need diplomatic skills to convince an organization to give up its texts.

Rhetorical Analysis in Cyberspace

In the virtual research site, many aspects of rhetorical analysis are the same, whereas many are unique and difficult to determine. Probably the most fundamental similarity is the desire on the part of the researcher to use rhetorical theory to understand and explain the policies, motives, arguments, and structures in certain documents. Beyond this point, however, the similarities often cease. Documents obtained from the Internet present many challenges to the rhetorical critic. At the highest level is the definitional question of whether the material is a published document, an unpublished document, or a transcript of oral conversation. These most basic distinguishing features are easily identified with traditional materials but can be confusing to identify on the Internet, yet it is these distinguishing features, along with the legal doctrine of fair use, that significantly impact whether a document can be studied with or without having to obtain permission.

The following example, based on the experience of one of us, illustrates this point. During Gurak's work on the Lotus MarketPlace case (Gurak, 1997a), she discovered many Usenet newsgroups that discussed MarketPlace, computer privacy, and related topics. Seeing these sites as rich sources of material for her research, she decided to use rhetorical analysis to study the texts of this newsgroup. But, she asked, are these Usenet postings *texts* or, instead, written forms of oral conversations? They look like texts, but after reading through a few, Gurak noted that these "texts" sounded more like conversation, because people post messages in short bursts, often without regard for spelling. Each of these possibilities presents the researcher with a different series of required steps. If these are texts, can they be used without seeking permission, especially as this newsgroup is public? Researchers today would note that others have made this claim (Gurak 1997a, Herring, 1996a), but would also note that still others (Waskul & Douglass, 1996) have criticized the public/private distinction as an ethical basis for using electronic texts without permission. If these "texts" are more akin to conversations, researchers might wish to seek permission, make names anonymous, and follow other conventions used by those who study "live people" instead of texts. But again, others would argue that even though real-time chats may *seem* like conversations, they are being posted to a public space where anyone with an Internet connection might view the conversations; thus, these chats more closely resemble public meetings than private conversations.

Some legal considerations might help researchers at this stage. Specifically, if researchers decide to view the material as text (even the "live conversation" of real-time chats are typed in via a keyboard), the legal doctrine of copyright and fair use would provide some guidelines as to whether material can be used and how much may be used. Copyright law states that whenever the expression of an idea becomes fixed in a tangible medium, that expression is protected. No one besides the author or creator can reproduce this expression (including downloading the file, which is in fact making a copy) without permission of the author. As Cavazos and Morin indicate, "the existing copyright system seems to hold up rather well" in cyberspace (1994, p. 48), thus copying Internet text would constitute a violation. Except, as our Gurak learned, the doctrine of fair use allows certain conditions under which copies can be made without permission. One criterion for determining if the use is fair is whether such use is educational. Another is if the original material is published or unpublished. Clearly, the use is educational (although if the researcher later decides to publish a book, the use may become more commercial). But is electronic discourse published? Gurak decided "yes" based on consensus among other computer-mediated communication (CMC) scholars, though noting that this decision is questionable. The final two criteria (amount of material used, impact on the original) are also taken into consideration. Fair use does not often apply when an entire text is used. But what constitutes an entire text? Does removing the header or signature file count? As for impact on the original, this seems easy enough, because Gurak did not see any possible damage she would have caused to the original posting or e-mail message by using the material in her study. In sum, researchers can look over several articles about the subject (Gurak, 1997b; Lefevre, 1992; Lunsford & West, 1996; Woodmansee & Jaszi, 1995) to determine if their use (of the material that resembles text, that is) is fair. However, if their experience is like Gurak's, they will also recognize that fair use is not a black-and-white issue: "Despite its longevity," write Patterson and Lindberg, "the fair use principle is perhaps the most debated and least understood principle of copyright law" (1991, p. 66).

Yet even with a general understanding of these legal concepts, complications continue. It is difficult if not impossible to accurately trace the origins of many Usenet and e-mail messages and thus confirm their actual authorship, because people on the Internet often use pseudonyms. In fact, some of the postings might have been made by a "bot," or Internet robot. And if the work is funded, a researcher might be concerned about his or her school's IRB, fearing that they may not understand these postings to be text, not conversation, and thus may demand permission forms if the researcher is to receive funding. Despite these difficulties, researchers should forge ahead, recognizing the vast amount of rich and informative

material available on the Internet. Web pages, which appear more like traditional printed pages, may help answer some of this questions; so too does
the appearance of more and more commentary on performing Internet research (Gurak, 1997a; Herring, 1996a; King, 1996; Turkle, 1995). In the
end, as with cyber-ethnography, Gurak drew on her own ethical instincts,
understanding of copyright law and the doctrine of fair use, and the
methodological choices made by others doing similar research.

SURVEYS

Ethnography and rhetorical analysis are used primarily to study discourse
that is taking place on the Internet. Survey research, on the other hand,
is used to collect information. Survey research is a widely used method in
a variety of disciplines and situations; Babbie notes that it "is perhaps the
most frequently used mode of observation in the social sciences" (1990,
p. 261). As with rhetorical analysis, survey research is quite common and
well utilized among technical communication researchers, serving as "a
powerful tool for studying technical communication" (Plumb & Spyridakis,
1992, p. 625). (There are numerous surveys in technical communication;
for example, see MacNealy, 1992; Mirel, 1992; Norman & Stohrer, 1990.)
Although survey research encompasses not only self-administered mail
questionnaires but also telephone surveys and face-to-face interviews, our
discussion of survey research here concentrates on self-administered mail
surveys, which are most similar to surveys that are conducted online.

The Traditional Approach

Mail surveys have a number of advantages that contribute to their popularity and widespread use. One advantage is their relatively low cost when
compared with methods such as telephone surveys and face-to-face interviews because mail surveys can be conducted with minimal staff and facilities (Dillman, 1978; Fowler, 1993). Mail surveys also allow researchers
to have a wider geographic reach than is generally possible with personal
interviews (McDowell, 1993; Plumb & Spyridakis, 1992). Another advantage of mail surveys is that respondents are not "on the spot"; they have
time to consider their answers and consult other materials if necessary (Rea
& Parker, 1992). Additionally, respondents feel that their responses are
more anonymous because they do not have to share their responses with
an interviewer, either in person or over the phone (Dillman, 1978; Fowler,
1993). And because survey forms are standardized, all participants receive
the same instructions and definitions.

However, mail surveys have disadvantages as well. Because mail surveys must be standardized across respondents, they "often appear superficial in their coverage of complex topics" (Babbie, 1990, p. 279). In addition, mail surveys lack an interviewer, which can be disadvantageous in several ways: it may not be possible to ensure the questions will be completed (Dillman, 1978); confusing questions cannot be explained or clarified (Rea & Parker, 1992); and self-selection or respondent substitution cannot be determined (Plumb & Spyridakis, 1992). Mail surveys are also not always effective in "enlisting cooperation" to the extent that a personal contact would be (Fowler, 1993). Additionally, mail surveys often take longer to implement than other types of research because of the traditional cycle of mailing the survey, waiting for responses, sending a reminder, waiting for responses, sending a new survey, and waiting for responses (Dillman, 1978; Rea & Parker, 1992).

Surveys in Cyberspace

Conducting surveys over the Internet, either via electronic mail or a Web page, is a relatively new phenomenon that, like traditional mail surveys, offers both plusses and minuses. Few guidelines exist about the ways in which online survey research differs from traditional methods (Penkoff, Colman, & Katzman, 1996). Again, as in the other two methods mentioned here, because the issues surrounding electronic surveys are still so new, many researchers do not reflect on or describe their methods beyond "I made up a survey which I sent to [a list or newsgroup]" (Herring, 1996a; We, 1994). This approach is potentially problematic, as Penkoff and her colleagues note that

> computer-mediated research needs specific and carefully designed instruments that not only accommodate but exploit the features of the electronic environment to attract respondents who, otherwise, may have their fingers on a "delete" key. Researchers cannot merely import paper-and-pencil methodologies to on-line studies, but must adapt them to the electronic environment and create new methods to expand our knowledge in and of computer-mediated communication. (1996)

Although Internet surveys are still a somewhat new method for gathering research data, some of their advantages and disadvantages are already clear. One previously mentioned advantage that traditional mail surveys have over other methods is that mail surveys are relatively inexpensive to conduct (Sheehan & Hoy, 1999). Unfortunately, mail surveys generally cannot be implemented quickly—it can take several months to conduct such a survey. However, Internet electronic surveys, although remaining inexpensive, increase the speed with which surveys can be conducted (Mitchell, Paprzycki, & Duckett, 1994). Additionally, electronic surveys may overcome one of the disadvantages of open-ended questions noted earlier—that surveys requiring "original written responses" generally received fewer responses (MacNealy, 1992). In a recent survey by Silker and Gurak (1996), the researchers noted that e-mail responses were longer and friendlier than responses to a traditional mail survey.

A significant disadvantage of e-mail surveys is that they are not anonymous unless the respondent goes to a great deal of trouble to use an anonymous re-mailer (Penkoff, Colman, & Katzman, 1996). Additionally, some members of the Internet community are especially belligerent about receiving unsolicited e-mail (sometimes known as "spam"). To avoid irritating their sample with a long, unsolicited e-mail survey, Penkoff and her colleagues sent an initial short e-mail message to their sample. This e-mail explained what the study entailed and provided a way for sample members not to receive the survey if they did not wish to, allowing members of the sample some measure of control over the situation. An additional disadvantage of electronic surveys is that computer problems can result in surveys being lost because e-mail is still not as reliable as traditional mail (Mitchell, Paprzycki, & Duckett, 1994). Finally, electronic surveys are still, by the very nature of the Internet, somewhat self-selecting, because only a small percentage of citizens use the Internet (focused in a rather specific demographic grouping, though this is changing).

At this time, two main types of Internet electronic surveys exist: e-mail surveys and Web-based surveys. Although some researchers have also tried newsgroups and bulletin boards for surveys, the most popular approach has been e-mail and, increasingly, the Web. The advantage of an e-mail survey versus a Web-based survey is that the e-mail survey arrives in respondents' electronic mailboxes; respondents do not have to cut and paste a URL into a Web browser to go to the survey or launch a Web browser (if they receive the announcement for the survey via e-mail) or follow a link (if they read the announcement for the survey on the Web). Additionally, by e-mailing surveys to a sample, the researcher has more control over who the respondents actually will be than generally is possible with a Web-based survey.

Web-based surveys have become increasingly popular for a number of reasons, as noted in an e-mail message from a communication researcher who indicated that sending a survey as a simple e-mail message requires much time on the part of the researcher to compile and organize, whereas Web-based surveys can automate many of the data collection tasks (Harding, 1995). Harding's arguments are compelling and support the findings of Penkoff and her colleagues (1996), indicating that technical communication researchers need to decide carefully whether to administer an electronic survey by e-mail or via the Web. This decision will depend on whether the target population will have access to Web browsers and fast Internet connections. In addition, surveys conducted for educational research require additional considerations, such as obtaining student permission forms (Kastman & Gurak, 1999).

CASE EXAMPLE: THE CASE OF LOTUS MARKETPLACE

In April 1990, Lotus Development Corporation announced a product called MarketPlace: Households, a direct mail marketing database that would contain name, address, and spending information on 120 million American consumers. After MarketPlace was announced, the Internet was full of debates, discussions, and online petitions over the product. In what was the first such action in cyberspace, MarketPlace was quickly defeated: over 30,000 people contacted Lotus and asked that their names be removed from the database. The product was never released. One of us (Gurak) analyzed the Lotus and Clipper protests from a rhetorical perspective. Gurak's (1997a) analysis (subsequently published as *Persuasion and Privacy in Cyberspace*) argues that the Lotus protest community was a new kind of rhetorical entity: a community whose use of language was focused around social action but whose use of this language took place in a new social space, a virtual place of incredible speed and reach. Gurak argued that two rhetorical features, community *ethos* and the novel mode of delivery on computer networks, are critical to rhetorical online communities because these features sustain the community and its motive for action in the absence of physical commonality or traditional face-to-face methods of establishing presence and delivering a message.

In order to perform this study, it was necessary to use rhetorical analysis techniques in a virtual setting, Unlike the study of traditional printed documents, analyzing texts from the Internet presented privacy considerations. Therefore, it was necessary to develop an approach that reflected a balance between the use of such material and the privacy of those who posted it. Postings on the Internet, especially those in publicly accessible forums, can certainly be viewed as published material and are increasingly being seen as such by publishers. Yet the intent of the Internet author usually is for his or her material to be seen within the context of the

Internet and not more broadly in a published research paper or book. As the Internet continues to grow and expand, this expectation will probably decrease, but at this time, it was necessary to balance the expectations of authors of Internet postings with the need to use this material for academic purposes. After all, it would be impossible to document these cases without using the actual postings, and the authors of these postings, being computer experts, were certainly aware that their material would be posted and reposted across cyberspace. What is the difference, then, if this material, properly credited and in conformance with fair use, is reprinted in a paper document?

These factors being the case, Gurak began by removing the actual e-mail addresses, physical addresses, and references to other persons or corporate affiliations from all of the postings. She then changed the name of the author, adding quotes ("Jane Doe") around the changed name in the footnote. (Other researchers have chosen to make completely anonymous all material taken from the Internet, and this model is based on the notion that Internet texts are not texts at all, but rather are written versions of spoken conversations. In some cases, this model is valid: a real-time chat or a MOO or MUD may be closer to conversation, and thus, scholars may see themselves as observers of "research subject," and are thus required to follow standard human subject procedure.) In this book, however, none of the material is from synchronous communication. The postings used here are much closer to published articles in magazines or newspapers. Therefore, Gurak could have easily made the case that the use of real names in Internet postings was justifiable and legal. Yet, given that the authors of these postings are privacy advocates who did not expect their postings to go anywhere outside the Internet, Gurak took the additional step of using pseudonyms.

FINAL NOTE: RESEARCH ON THE WEB

The latest twist on research in cyberspace involves research that takes Web sites as its primary data source. This topic is certainly one which could become its own chapter or book, and it is beyond the scope of what we intended in this chapter. Yet much current technical communication research involves the Web as artifact. It is important for the researcher to note that Web pages are sums of parts; that is, a Web page can involve all of the items suggested in this chapter (participant conversations, text, survey material). In addition, Web pages involve color, sound, graphics, issues of navigation, interactivity, and so on. The study of these features is often grounded in cognitive psychology and human-computer interaction

(HCI) studies, including usability (see Grice in this volume for more on usability), and technical communication researchers would be wise to turn to these bodies of study, in combination with rhetorical and ethnographic analysis, when studying the Web as artifact. In addition, a body of research since the 1980s, often called "computer-mediated communication" and increasingly referred to as "Internet studies," although based primarily in text-based analysis, provides a basis for such considerations. Because "the Web" is not one entity but many, many different pages consisting of many content areas and delivery mechanisms, many new researchers are finding that they must bring together several different disciplinary bodies of work in order to perform a Web analysis.

One example of a study using the Web as artifact is the thesis of Gretchen Haas, who looked at the use of the Web in the election campaign of three Minnesota state Senate candidates. She needed to be versed in political communication, Internet studies, and the complexities of doing Internet research:

> Because of the relative youth of the Web, little research has taken politics and the Web together as its object of study. In this literature review, I will describe the sparse landscape of studies involving politics and the Web and augment that literature with work in computer-mediated communication (CMC) and political communication.
>
> A review of current scholarship on politics and the Web reveals that the jury is still out when it comes to gaining a cohesive sense of what the Web means for politics. Little work involving politics and the Web has actually focused on political campaign sites. Some researchers have examined how various levels of government implement their Web sites (Stowers; Steyaert). Research on political portals puts the same emphasis on service as do the studies of government Web sites; that is, what services do political portals offer to site visitors? (Dutton, Elberse and Hale). The little work that does exist in the area of political campaigns and the Web tends toward description of campaign sites.
>
> This work has done much to establish a baseline of what political campaign Web sites consist of, for example, that they utilize their sites to publish more information pertaining to issues than traditional media channels (McKeown and Plowman) and that campaign Web sites essentially function as "electronic pamphlets" (Schneider and Larsen). The drawback of studies like these is that they lack grounding in a theoretical framework and rarely move beyond pure description. (Haas, p. x)

Many emerging scholars in technical communication and Internet studies are also exploring the ethical and methodological implications of studying the Web. In 2000, a group of researchers met at the Annenberg

School at the University of Pennsylvania to explore the methods people were using to research the Web. This group continues to meet at the annual Association of Internet Researchers conference (www.aoir.org). In addition, one of us (Gurak) is currently a co-PI on two grants at the University of Minnesota Medical School involving the use of the Internet in HIV/AIDS prevention in two discrete populations of high-risk people. As these and other studies become more common, we will see an increasing number of publications in this area. In fact, several edited collections and essays on this topic are currently in press. Technical communication scholars are advised to stay in touch with appropriate organizations and published research in order to keep on top of this changing area.

SUMMARY: RESEARCH FROM TRADITIONAL TO VIRTUAL

Research in technical communication, it can be argued, has changed the field from an occupation to a discipline and profession (Smith, 1992, p. 521). This research has become increasingly interdisciplinary, drawing from rhetorical theory, cognitive science, psychology, education, and anthropology. Technical and professional discourse-producing sites have always been rich with potential areas for study, and now Internet technologies are providing even more texts, research subjects, and field sites. We owe it to ourselves and to the future of the discipline to use the opportunities available in cyberspace to perform our research.

Yet traditional, established research practices may require some adjustments and rethinking if they are to be used in these new virtual research forums. This fact should not deter our efforts; instead, it should invite us to examine technical communication research in light of the possibilities of such online research and then seriously consider how to conduct informative, useful, and ethical research in these new forums. As Herring notes, research involving computer-mediated discourse up until now has left most of us with "no choice but to make up rules and procedures as we went along" (1996b, p. 153). Her suggestion for solving this idiosyncratic approach is to examine and design appropriate methods and guidelines for cyberspace research on a discipline-by-discipline basis. This approach makes sense, because each discipline has unique methodological conventions and situations; psychologists, for example, are accustomed to thinking in terms of obtaining permissions and seeking IRB approval, whereas rhetoricians, who generally deal with texts, are not. In technical communication, where we draw upon the methods of many disciplines, our task might be a bit more complicated. But it would be worthwhile to begin a discussion about the topic.

In this chapter, we have only scraped the surface by raising some of the major issues and questions in this area. These issues focus around several key themes:

- Obtaining (or not) permissions
- Deciding if material is textual or more like a recorded conversation
- Deciding if material is public or private
- Determining if the doctrine of fair use applies
- Using the technology to "lurk" or disguise one's true self or announce one's presence
- Choosing (or not) to seek IRB approval
- Choosing the speed of an e-mail survey response over the use of a Web page

Many other topics that we did not explore would include other issues of copyright beyond fair use (who actually owns the texts created via a collaboratively created e-mail message or Web page, for example?) and citation methods (how does one cite an e-mail message that has been forwarded several times?).

We believe that the future of the most fruitful and exciting research in technical communication is based in the digital realm. The ability to communicate across distance, time, and national boundaries offers great possibilities for studying the ways in which technology and technological discourse are shaped, used, and disseminated; the many recent doctoral dissertations that treat some aspect of technical communication and cyberspace testify to the increased focus on the Internet for research in our discipline. Thus, technical communication scholars should begin a serious conversation about the methodological issues of conducting research in cyberspace. We should consider creating research guidelines, much like the APA, but with a focus on the nuances of electronic discourse. (Sharon Boehlefeld [1996], writing about ethics and cyberspace research, notes that the ethics statement of the Association of Computing Machinery might be useful in this regard.) Such guidelines would be informative to both seasoned researchers and emerging scholars, and they would also give us a proactive position for use with our institutional review boards, grant proposals, and the like. Of all the disciplines, technical communication, with its traditional emphasis on the relationship between technology and human communication, should take the lead in examining research in the virtual forum.

REFERENCES

Allen, C. (1996). What's wrong with the "Golden Rule"? Conundrums of conducting ethical research in cyberspace. *The Information Society, 12 (2)*, 175–188.

Anderson, J.A. (1987). *Communication research: Issues and methods*. New York: McGraw-Hill.

Babbie, E. (1990). *Survey research methods* (2d ed.). Belmont, CA: Wadsworth Publishing Company.

Boehlefeld, S.P. (1996). Doing the right thing: Ethical cyberspace research. *Information Society, 12 (2)*, 153–168.

Burke, K.L. (1966). *Language as symbolic action*. Berkeley: University of California Press.

Cavazos, E.A., & Morin, G. (1994). *Cyberspace and the law: Your rights and duties in the online world*. Cambridge, MA: MIT Press.

Connors, R.J. (1982). The rise of technical writing instruction in America. *Journal of Technical Writing and Communication, 12 (4)*, 329–351.

Dillman, D.A. (1978). *Mail and telephone surveys: The total design method*. New York: John Wiley & Sons.

Doheny-Farina, S., & Odell, L. (1984). Ethnographic research on writing: Assumptions. In L. Odell & D. Goswami (Eds.), *Writing in nonacademic settings* (pp. 503–535). New York: Guilford Press.

Dutton, W.H., A. Elberse, & M. Hale. (1999). A case study of a Netizen's guide to elections. *Communications of the ACM, 42,12*, 48.

Fowler, F.J., Jr. (1993). *Survey research methods* (2d ed.). Newbury Park, CA: Sage Publications.

Geertz, C. (1973). *The interpretation of cultures*. New York: Basic Books.

Geertz, C. (1983). *Local knowledge*. New York: Basic Books.

Gurak, L.J. (1997a). *Persuasion in cyberspace: Privacy, community, and the online protests over MarketPlace and Clipper*. New Haven, CT: Yale University Press.

Gurak, L.J. (1997b). Technical communication, copyright, and the shrinking public domain. *Computers and Composition, 14*, 329–342.

Gurak, L.J., & C. Silker. (1997). Technical communication research: From traditional to virtual. *Technical Communication Quarterly, 6.4*, 403–418.

Haas, G.M.A. (2001). *New tools, new politics? A rhetorical analysis of the Minnesota Fourth Congressional District Campaign Web sites*. Unpublished thesis, University of Minnesota.

Halloran, S.M. (1984). The birth of molecular biology: An essay in the rhetorical criticism of scientific discourse. *Rhetoric Review, 3*, 70–83.

Harding, D.C. (1995, October 24). RE: Special Issue of Technical Communication CFP. [Personal e-mail].

Hart, R.P. (1990). *Modern rhetorical criticism*. Glenview, IL: Scott, Foresman and Company.

Henson, L. (1994). A preliminary rhetoric of technical copywriting. *Technical Communication, 41 (3)*, 447–455.

Herring, S. (1996a). Bringing familiar baggage to the new frontier: Gender differences in computer mediated communication. In V.V. Vitanza (Ed.), *CyberReader* (pp. 144–154). Needham Heights, MA: Allyn & Bacon.

Herring, S. (1996b). Linguistic and critical analysis of computer-mediated communication: Some ethical and scholarly considerations. *Information Society, 12 (2)*, 153–168.

House, E.R. (1990). An ethics of qualitative field studies. In E.E. Guba (Ed.), *The Paradigm Dialog* (pp. 158–164). Newbury Park, CA: Sage Publications.

Kastman, L.A., & Gurak, L.J. (1999). Conducting technical communication research via the Internet: Guidelines for privacy, permissions, and ownership in educational research. *Technical Communication, 46 (4),* 460–469.

King, S.A. (1996). Researching Internet communities: Proposed ethical guidelines for the reporting of results. *Information Society, 12 (2),* 119–128.

LeFevre, K.B. (1992). The tell-tale "heart": Determining "fair" use of unpublished texts. *Law and Contemporary Problems, 55,* 153–183.

Lunsford, A.A., & West, S. (1996). Intellectual property and composition studies. *College Composition and Communication, 47 (3),* 383–411.

MacNealy, M.S. (1992). Research in technical communication: A view of the past and a challenge for the future. *Technical Communication, 39 (4),* 533–551.

McDowell, E.E. (1993). *Research methods in scientific and technical communication.* Edina, MN: Burgess Publishing.

McKeown, C.A., & Plowman, K.D. (1999). Reaching publics on the Web during the 1996 presidential campaign. *Journal of Public Relations Research, 11,(4)* 321–347.

Melia, T. (1984). And lo the footprint ... Selected literature in rhetoric and science. *Quarterly Journal of Speech, 70,* 303–334.

Miller, C. (1989). What's practical about technical writing? In B.E. Fearing & W.K. Sparrow (Eds.), *Technical writing: Theory and practice* (pp. 14–24). New York: Modern Language Association.

Miller, C., & Selzer, J. (1985). Special topics of argument in engineering reports. In L. Odell & D. Goswami (Eds.), *Writing in nonacademic settings* (pp. 309–341). New York: Guilford Press.

Mirel, B. (1992). Analyzing audiences for software manuals: A survey of instructional needs for "real world" tasks. *Technical Communication Quarterly, 1 (1),* 13–40.

Mitchell, T., Paprzycki, M., & Duckett, G. (1994, September). Research methods using computer networks. *Arachnet Electronic Journal on Virtual Culture, 2*(4). Available: http://www.lib.ncsu.edu/stacks/e/ejvc/aejvc-v2n04-mitchell-research.txt.

Norman, R.L., & Stohrer, F.F. (1990). Survey of graduate and undergraduate internships in technical communication. *Technical Communication, 37*(3), 252–261.

Patterson, L.R., & Lindberg, S.W. (1991). *The nature of copyright: A law of users' rights.* Athens: University of Georgia Press.

Penkoff, D.W., Colman, R.W., & Katzman, S.L. (1996, May). From paper-and-pencil to screen-and-keyboard: Toward a methodology for survey research on the Internet. Poster session presented at the 46th Annual Conference of the International Communication Association, Chicago.

Plumb, C., & Spyridakis, J.H. (1992). Survey research in technical communication: Designing and administering questionnaires. *Technical Communication, 39 (4),* 625–638.

Rea, L.M., & Parker, R.A. (1992). *Designing and conducting survey research: A comprehensive guide.* San Francisco, CA: Jossey-Bass Publishers.

Reid, E. (1996). Informed consent in the study of on-line communities: A reflection on the effects of computer-mediated social research. *Information Society, 12 (2),* 169–174.

Schneider, S., & Larsen, E. (2000). The 2000 presidential primary candidates: The view from the Web. Paper delivered at the Annual Meeting of the International Communications Association, Acapulco, Mexico.

Sheehan, K.B., & Hoy, M.G. (1999). Using e-mail to survey Internet users in the United States: Methodology and assessment. *Journal of Computer-Mediated Communication, 4 (3).* Available:http://www.ascusc.org/jcmc/vol4/issue3/sheehan.html.

Silker, C.M., & Gurak, L.J. (1996). Technical communication in cyberspace: Report of a qualitative study. *Technical Communication, 43 (4)*, 357–368.

Simonsen, J., & Kensing, F. (1997, July). Using ethnography in contextual design. *Communications of the ACM, 40 (7)*, 82–88.

Smith, F.R. (1992). The continuing importance of research in technical communication. *Technical Communication, 39 (4)*, 521–523.

Smith, L.H. (1990). Ethics, field studies, and the paradigm crisis. In E.G. Guba (Ed.), *The paradigm dialog* (pp. 139–157). Newbury Park, CA: Sage Publications.

Spilka, R. (1989). Interacting with multiple readers: A significant component of document design in corporate environments. *Technical Communication, 36 (4)*, 368–372.

Sproull, L., & Kiesler, S. (1991). *Connections: New ways of working in the networked organization*. Cambridge, MA: MIT Press.

Steyaert, J. (2000). Local governments online and the role of a resident: Government shop versus electronic community. *Social Science Computer Review 18 (1)* 3–16.

Stowers, G. (1999). Becoming cyberactive: State and local governments on the World Wide Web. *Government Information Quarterly 16 (2)* 111–127.

Sullivan, P., & Spilka, R. (1992). Qualitative research in technical communication: Issues of value, identity, and use. *Technical Communication, 39 (4)*, 592–606.

Thomas, J. (1996). Introduction: A debate about the ethics of fair practices for collecting social science data in cyberspace. *Information Society, 12 (2)*, 107–118.

Turkle, S. (1995). *Life on the screen: Identity in the age of the Internet*. New York: Simon & Schuster.

Van Gelder, L. (1990). The strange case of the electronic lover. In G. Gumpert and S.L. Fish (Eds.), *Talking to strangers: Mediated therapeutic communication* (pp. 128–142). Norwood, NJ: Ablex.

Waskul, D., & Douglass, M. (1996). Considering the electronic participant: Some polemical observations on the ethics of on-line research. *Information Society, 12 (2)*, 129–140.

We, G. (1994, July). Cross-gender communication in cyberspace. *Arachnet Electronic Journal on Virtual Culture, 2 (3)*. Available: http://www.inform.umd.edu/EdRes/Topic/WomensStudies/Computing/Articles+ResearchPapers/ArachnetJournal/we.

Woodmansee, M., & Jaszi, P. (1995). The law of texts: Copyright in the academy. *College English*, 769–787.

Portions of this chapter originally appeared in Laura J. Gurak and Christine Silker, "Technical Communication Research: From Traditional to Virtual," *Technical Communication Quarterly*, 6.4 (1997): 403–418. Courtesy of the Association of Teachers of Technical Writing. Portions of the "MarketPlace" database discussion (pp. 241–242) are adapted from Gurak (1997a).

Index

Allen, Christina: on ethics in research in cyberspace, 230

Allen, Jo, 173; and responsibility of researchers to audience, ix, 1–2, 131

American Psychological Association (APA), 233; Code of Ethical Standards, 9; research guidelines of, 245

American Society of Engineering Education: proceedings of, 83-84

Anderson, Kathryn: on interviewing, 171

Anderson, Paul V., 6; and ethics, 2, 3

Annenberg School: and research methodology for work on world wide web, 244

Annual Review of Psychology, 102

lNanthropologists, anthropology, 8, 10; develop ethnography, 24; techniques used in technical communications research, 6

"APA Ethical Principle 9: Research with Human Participants" (APA), 9

Applied Psychological Measurement, 102

archaeologists: and analysis of artifacts, 76

archives: corporate, 86; as depositories of primary sources, 74, 82–83

artifacts, 48, 76; importance of, 223

Asher, J.W., 133

Association of Teachers of Technical Writing (ATTW), xii: Code of Ethics of, 1, 2, 5,

19; issues of security, confidentiality and privacy, 2

Association of Internet Researchers, 244

Atkinson, Dwight, 47, 51, 61, 62: and careful choice of data set, 55; and intertextuality, 52; procedures used by, 56; use of rhetorical and multidimensional analysis, 55, 56

audience, vii, ix, 2; academic, 201–202; and anonymity, 138; bosses, 137, 138, 143–44; characteristics based, 145–46; colleagues, 137, 138, 140; directs choices when writing study, 38; and ethics, 135, 137; failures to address needs of, 135, 136; "gate-keepers," 137, 138, 140–42; identification, 2; identifying for technical communication research, 131–47; methods to accommodate, 144–45; "nonnative practitioners," 137, 138, 142–43; participants, 38, 39, 137, 138, 139–40; poorly defined, 136; researcher's relationship with, 4; role of, 38–39; role based classification of, 132, 142; scholarly, 38; textbooks do not address needs of, 133; and women, 174

audiotapes: contribute to thick description, 52; of meetings, 31, 34

12; demonstrates respect for participants, 11; in surveys, 105, 107
consent: *see* informed consent
control group: *see* experimental research
control variables: *see* experimental research
Constantinidies, Lenna, xi
Cook, Judith: on feminist research, 167
Cook, Thomas, 116, 124, 125, 127
Crick, Francis: work on double helix, 50
Cross, Geoffrey, 25, 26
cultural studies, vii, 47, 185–207; and academic audiences, 201–202; agency and social action, 186; and Centre for Contemporary Cultural Studies, 186; and contextualizing, 196, 197; critiques objectivism, 205; empowerment, 193–95; and ethics of research, 205; focus on articulations, 194–95; focus of research, 188–89; instability of linkages, 191–92, 206; and interdisciplinary approach, 185, 186; and linkages, 189–92, 198; opposes reductionism, 196; origins of, 186–88; poststructuralist orientation of, 187; purpose of, 192; quantitative and qualitative approaches to, 187; research orientation, 185; and self-reflexivity, 198, 205–206; in technical communications research, 195; view of power, 192–93
Currie, Dawn: on feminist research, 167
cyberspace, vii; issues of copyright and fair use, 237; research and privacy issues, 241–42; rhetorical analysis in, 236–38; and surveys, 107; technical communications in, 229–45

Darwin, Charles, 50
data: gathering, viii, 29–34; analysis, viii, 34–35, 108–109; changing, 13; choice of, 55–56; citing field notes, 31; dropping, 13; establishing relevance of, 87–88; falsifying, 13; manipulation of, 2, 4, 5, 10, 13; observation, 29–31; and outliers, 13; note taking, 30; selective use, 13; storage, use and confidentiality

of, 28; synthesis of qualitative, 13; and thick description, 30
Dautermann, J., 25
Debs, M.B., 136; failed to focus on audience, 135
deductive reasoning, 93, 94
Department of Health and Human Services, 10
dependent variables, dependent measures: *see* experimental research
Devault, Marjorie: on interviewing, 171
Devitt, A.J.: analysis of intertextual relationships, 50; use of genre system, 53
Dewey, John, 218; diversity enhances rationality, 223; results of community experiences, 217;
Dillman, D.A., 107
discourse: analysis, viii, 34, 48, 49, 50, 52, 53, 57, 58; community, 26, 140; conventions, 33; coding, 53; professional, 234
dissertations: narrow focus of, 85
diversity, 166, 223
Doak, J., 194, 201–202; on technical communicator as author, 196, 197–98
documentary films, 76
documentary reality, 51–54
Doheny-Farina, Stephen, xi, 25, 26, 146; audience selection and ethics, 134; on audiences, 38, 39; on audiences classification, 138–39, 140, 141, 142, 146; on citing field notes, 31; lists audiences, 137; non-academicians attitudes toward research, 134; on "observer effect," 29; and practical validity of research, 32; on recording interviews, 34; role-based audience classification, 132; on roles of ethnographers, 28–29; and use of ethnography, 8
Dooley, D.: on sampling, 98
Dragga, Samuel: on women wages, 174
DuGay, P.: and linkages, 190
Duin, A.H., 25

Ede, Lisa: and gender preference, 170
Educational Review, 84

About the Contributors

Jo Allen is the Assistant Vice Provost for Undergraduate Affairs and Associate Professor of English at North Carolina State University, where she oversees seven programs and offices, including Undergraduate Assessment, Honors, Cooperative Education, Tutorial Services, the Transition Program, New Student Orientation, and the Virtual Advising Center. In addition, she oversees planning, budgeting, and proposal writing in promotion of collaborative relationships and special curricular initiatives regarding undergraduate education throughout the university. With a Ph.D. in English/Technical and Professional Communication, she has published books and papers and presented on higher education and communication issues in over 100 scholarly venues, has served on four editorial boards, and is a former member-at-large, current vice president, and rising President for the Association of Teachers of Technical Writing. She has consulted extensively on issues regarding technical and administrative communication.

Carol A. Berkenkotter is Professor in the Department of Rhetoric at University of Minnesota where she teaches genre theory, critical ethnography, editing and style in technical communication, and a variety of undergraduate courses. She is currently at work on a book on the epistemic function of narrative case histories in psychiatry titled *Psychiatrist as Author: Case Histories and the Constitution of Patient Identities.*

Nancy Blyler is Professor Emeritus in the rhetoric and professional communication program at Iowa State University. Her research interests include cultural and social aspects of professional communication and narrative and professional communication. She has published in such journals as the *Journal of Business and Technical Communication* (*JBTC*), the *Journal of Business Communication*, and *Technical Communication Quarterly*. With Charlotte Thralls, she co-founded *JBTC*, and together they co-edited a collection, *Professional Communication: The Social Perspective*, which won an NCTE award. She also won NCTE awards for two of her articles.

Lee-Ann Kastman Breuch is Assistant Professor in the Department of Rhetoric, Scientific and Technical Communication Program, at the University of Minnesota in St. Paul, Minnesota. She earned her Ph.D. in Rhetoric and Professional Communication from Iowa State University. She teaches courses in technical communication, research methods, teacher training, and usability testing. Her research addresses writing theory and pedagogy in technical disciplines, composition, and online environments; she is especially interested in issues of evaluation of online instruction. She currently directs the Online Writing Center, an online tutorial service at the University of Minnesota, and is a board member of the University of Minnesota Usability Services Laboratory.

Davida Charney has been Professor in the Division of Rhetoric and Composition at the University of Texas at Austin since 1997. Her work appears in such journals as *Written Communication*, *College Composition and Communication*, *Journal of Business and Technical Communication*, *Technical Communication Quarterly*, *Human-Computer Interaction*, *Information Design Journal*, and *Research in the Teaching of English*. She investigates the nature and structure of texts and the processes that people use to read, write, and learn from them. Her goal is to identify factors that make a text effective by looking at a text in context, as it is read by members of the intended audience. She has conducted research on resumes, forms, computer manuals, and scientific journal articles. On the practical side, this research contributes to strategies for teaching writing and critical reading. Most recently, she has written about the methodology debates (or "science wars") in composition and technical writing. She questions ideologically based characterizations of scientists and their epistemologies. She also critiques claims that only "humanistic" methodologies have social and ethical value.

Andrea Breemer Frantz is Assistant Professor of Communication Studies at Wilkes University in Wilkes-Barre, Pennsylvania, where she teaches journalism and serves as advisor for the weekly student newspaper. She is also responsible for teaching the senior capstone class for all Communication Studies majors, a qualitative research methods course. She received her M.A. degree from Iowa State University in Rhetoric and Professional

Communication and will defend her doctoral dissertation there this fall. She is now engaged in a collaborative oral history project with a colleague in the School of Pharmacy at Wilkes University.

Roger A. Grice is Clinical Associate Professor of Technical Communication and Information Technology at Rensselaer Polytechnic Institute in Troy, NY. He holds a B.S. in Electrical Engineering from Polytechnic University, an M.S. in Computer Science from Union College, and a Ph.D. in Communication and Rhetoric from Rensselaer. He is a Fellow of the Society for Technical Communication (STC) and Assistant to the President for Outreach. He is Senior Member of IEEE and past-president of IEEE's Professional Communication Society. He is also a member of ACM, including SIGDOC and SIGCHI. He received STC's Jay R. Gould Award for Excellence in Teaching Technical Communication and IEEE Professional Communication Society's Alfred N. Goldsmith Award for Contributions to Engineering Communication. Retired from IBM Corporation, he now teaches on-campus and distance-education courses on human-computer interaction, communication design for the web, information usability, and technical communication.

Laura J. Gurak is Professor and Department Head of the Rhetoric Department, Scientific and Technical Communication Program, at the University of Minnesota. Gurak received her Ph.D. from Rensselaer Polytechnic Institute in 1994. Her specialties include rhetoric of technology, intellectual property, and Internet studies. She is author of *Cyberliteracy: Navigating the Internet with Awareness* (2001) and *Persuasion and Privacy in Cyberspace: The Online Protests over Lotus MarketPlace and the Clipper Chip* (1997). She has also authored two textbooks and numerous book chapters and articles and has been a co-principal investigator in several federal grants using the Internet to study social and health issues. She is a sometimes commentator on "Future Tense: A Journal of the Digital Age" from Minnesota Public Radio.

Susan M. Katz is Associate Professor of English and Director of the Professional Writing Program at North Carolina State University, where she teaches graduate and undergraduate courses in business and technical writing. Her book, *The Dynamics of Writing Review*, has been excerpted in an anthology on professional writing and rhetoric. She has also published articles in journals such as the *IEEE Transactions on Professional Communication* (for which she won the 1999 Outstanding Paper Award), the *Journal of Business Communication*, the *Journal of Engineering Education*, and the *NSEE (National Society for Experiential Education) Quarterly*. She is the co-author (with Lee Odell) of a textbook, *Word and Image: Writing in a*

Visual Culture, to be released by in 2003. Her research interests include the role of review in workplace writing, organizational socialization processes, and the integration of verbal and visual rhetorics.

Teresa Kynell is Professor of English at Northern Michigan University and holds a Ph.D. in Rhetoric and Composition from Michigan Technological University. She is currently Chair of the NCTE Committee on Technical and Scientific Communication and Book Review Editor for *Technical Communication Quarterly*. Her articles have appeared in a variety of journals, including the *Journal of Technical Writing and Communication, Reader*, the *Writing Instructor*, and *Technical Communication Quarterly*. She is the author of *Writing in a Milieu of Utility: The Move to Technical Communication in American Engineering Programs, 1850–1950*, and (with Wendy Stone) *Scenarios for Technical Communication: Critical Thinking and Writing*. She edited, with Michael Moran, *Three Keys to the Past: The History of Technical Communication*. Forthcoming are two volumes which she edited with Gerald Savage—Volume I (*Power and Legitimacy in Technical Communication: The Historical and Contemporary Struggle for Professional Status*) and Volume II (*Power and Legitimacy in Technical Communication: Strategies for Professional Status*).

Mary M. Lay is a Professor in the Department of Rhetoric at the University of Minnesota and a fellow and former president of the Association of Teachers of Technical Writing. In 2002 she was awarded the Ronald S. Blicq Award to recognize distinguished contributions to technical communication education by the Professional Communication Society of the Institute of Electrical and Electronics Engineers. She has directed the Center for Advanced Feminist Studies at Minnesota and is former chair of the department of Technical Communications at Clarkson University. She is author of *The Rhetoric of Midwifery* (2000), which won the 2001 NCTE Award for Excellence in Technical and Scientific Writing, Best Book. She is co-editor of *Body Talk: Rhetoric, Technology, Reproduction* (2000) and *Technical Communication*. From Fall 1997 to Spring 2001 she directed the M.A. and Ph.D. programs in Rhetoric and Scientific and Technical Communication at the University of Minnesota.

John Monberg is Assistant Professor in the Department of Communication Studies at the University of Kansas. He holds a Ph.D. in science and technology studies. His research explores the models of democracy and rationality designed into Internet-mediated social spaces. His work on aspects of technology, public policy, and civil society has been published in a variety of journals and book chapters; his forthcoming book is titled *Technology as Social Ecology*.

Daniel J. Murphy is Vice President for Resource Development and CEO of the College Foundation at the State University of New York (SUNY) Institute of Technology at Utica Rome, where he is also Associate Professor of Technical Communication. He has collaborated in communication survey research projects involving the Association for Aeronautics and Astronautics (AIAA), NASA, and the Indiana University Center for Survey Research to investigate media use in aerospace knowledge diffusion among U.S. aerospace engineers and scientists. His research was funded in part by a grant from the Society for Technical Communication (STC); the research findings were published in *Knowledge Diffusion in the U.S. Aerospace Industry: Managing Knowledge for Competitive Advantage* by Ablex Press in 1998. He holds a Ph.D. in Communication and Rhetoric from Rensselaer Polytechnic Institute.

Andrea M. Olson is Assistant Professor of psychology at the College of St. Catherine in St. Paul, Minnesota. She earned her Ph.D. in industrial/organizational psychology from the University of Minnesota in 2000 and her B.A. in psychology from Luther College in 1992. She teaches general psychology, statistics, and industrial/organizational psychology. She is a member of the college's Institutional Review Board committee and she serves as program evaluator for two projects: one designed to broaden young women's knowledge and opportunities in information technology and one on virtual mentoring for math teachers. Her primary research interests are individual team member performance and the gender gap in information technology occupations.

Bruce Seely has been a historian of technology at Michigan Technological University for 16 years and is now serving as Chair of the Department of Social Sciences. He earned his Ph.D. at the University of Delaware and taught at Texas A&M University from 1981–1986. His research interests focus on the history of engineering education and research, the history of American highways and transportation, and the iron and steel industry. He has authored several prize-winning publications, including his book on the Bureau of Public Roads, *Building the American Highway System: Engineers as Policy Makers* (1987). He also served as Secretary of the Society for the History of Technology (1990–1995) and as Program Director for Science and Technology Studies at the National Science Foundation in Washington (2000–2002).

Christine M. Silker has an M.S. in Scientific and Technical Communication and an M.S. in Forest Recreation. She works as a systems analyst for a regional telecommunications provider. She currently lives in Minneapolis, Minnesota.

Sherry Southard administers the Professional and Technical Communication program at ECU, including both post-baccalaureate online programs (Certificate and M.A.). She has also been active in developing web-based courses for those programs. Before joining the ECU faculty, she taught at Oklahoma State University where she first met Jo Allen. Her TPC publications include book chapters, proceeding articles for international and national conferences, and articles in journals such as *Technical Communication, Technical Communication Quarterly, JBTC*, and *IEEE Transactions on Professional Communication*. A Fellow of the Society for Technical Communication, she has served in numerous chapter- and Society-level offices. She was one of the first to receive STC's Jay Gould Award for Excellence in Teaching Technical Communication. Her other professional memberships include ATTW and CPTSC.

Charlotte Thralls is Associate Professor and teaches in the undergraduate and graduate professional communication programs at Utah State University. Her research and teaching specialization is rhetorical/cultural theories of communication. With Nancy Blyler, she co-founded the *Journal of Business and Technical Communication (JBTC)* and co-edited *Professional Communication: The Social Perspective*. Thralls has been the recipient of several teaching and research awards in professional communication, including the Louis Thompson Distinguished Undergraduate Teaching Award at Iowa State University and a National Council of Teachers of English Research Award in Scientific and Technical Communication. She was named the Researcher of the Year in 2001 by the Association for Business Communication.